A Tale of Ritual Murder in the Age of Louis XIV

STANFORD STUDIES IN JEWISH HISTORY AND CULTURE

EDITED BY *Aron Rodrigue and Steven J. Zipperstein*

A Tale of Ritual Murder in the Age of Louis XIV

The Trial of Raphaël Lévy, 1669

Pierre Birnbaum

TRANSLATED BY ARTHUR GOLDHAMMER

STANFORD UNIVERSITY PRESS

STANFORD, CALIFORNIA

Stanford University Press
Stanford, California

A Tale of Ritual Murder in the Age of Louis XIV was originally published in French under the title *Un récit de "meurtre rituel" au Grand Siècle. L'Affaire Raphaël Lévy, Metz, 1669*. © Librairie Arthème Fayard, 2008.

This book has been published with the assistance of Université Paris I—Panthéon Sorbonne.

Printed in the United States of America on acid-free, archival-quality paper

Library of Congress Cataloging-in-Publication Data

Birnbaum, Pierre, author.
[Récit de "meurtre rituel" au Grand Siècle. English]
A tale of ritual murder in the age of Louis XIV : the trial of Raphaël Lévy, 1669 / Pierre Birnbaum ; translated by Arthur Goldhammer.
pages cm
"Originally published in French under the title Un récit de "meurtre rituel" au Grand Siècle."
Includes bibliographical references.
ISBN 978-0-8047-7404-8 (cloth : alk. paper)
1. Blood accusation—France—Metz—History—17th century. 2. Lévy, Raphaël, 1613-1670—Trials, litigation, etc. 3. Trials (Murder)—France—Metz—History—17th century. 4. Jews—Persecutions—France—Metz—History—17th century. 5. Antisemitism—France—History—17th century. I. Goldhammer, Arthur, translator. II. Title.
BM585.2.B5613 2008
944'.033—dc23

2011040720

Typeset by Bruce Lundquist in 10.5/14 Galliard

To my parents,
Jacob and Ruth Birnbaum

Contents

A Tale of Ritual Murder in the Age of Louis XIV

Introduction

A Strange Encounter at Montigny-lès-Metz, February 2001

The scene unfolded in Montigny-lès-Metz, in a quiet retirement home called "La Sainte Famille" (The Holy Family). On February 13, 2001, in a peaceful, spacious library filled with books, three men and a woman sat in comfortable armchairs facing one another. An image of Christ dominated the entrance to the room. Emotion ran high and tears flowed as the conversation brought a forgotten past back to life.

In 1669, Didier Le Moyne, a four-year-old boy, vanished and later turned up dead in the forest of Glatigny. A Jew, Raphaël Lévy, was unjustly accused of kidnapping and murdering the boy and sentenced to burn at the stake. Now, 332 years later, Bernadette Lemoine, age ninety, the last descendant (ninth generation) of Didier's brother Jean Le Moyne, met for the first time Pierre-André Meyer, a historian of Lorraine and sole surviving member of the eleventh generation of the family of Raphaël Lévy. By the strangest of chances, these kin of the parties that had clashed so bitterly in this extraordinary affair of alleged ritual murder found themselves engaged in a dialogue based on a shared belief: that Raphaël Lévy was innocent.

Bernadette Lemoine led the discussion with characteristic verve.[1] Elegantly dressed and still in possession of all her faculties, Mme. Lemoine went straight to the point. In her family, she said, many were convinced of Raphaël Lévy's guilt. The memory remained intact. But Lemoine, a former teacher of piano and organ who had once played in churches and made no secret of her devout Catholic faith, had set out to get to the bottom of the allegations.[2] Late in life, she had transformed herself into an amateur historian, explored the Lévy file in the departmental archives of the Moselle,[3] and managed to get her hands on the few extant documents that dealt with the case.

Before long she had made up her mind: contrary to the firm conviction of her entire family, including her father, she decided that Raphaël Lévy was innocent. She saw him as the victim of a "conspiracy," "a settling of scores among rival businessmen." As she saw it, "the child had indeed been murdered, possibly by a butcher hoping to rid himself of a cleverer competitor, Raphaël Lévy."[4] To prove her point, Lemoine produced a text of thirteen pages, written in her careful, almost calligraphic hand, reminiscent of the handwriting of another era.

It was published a short while later in a Metz newsletter. In the meantime, she had corrected her manuscript: Joseph Reinach, for instance, was no longer described as "an obscure but thoroughly trustworthy historian" but simply as "a thoroughly trustworthy historian." She now placed the tragedy not on the eve of Rosh Hashanah but on the very day of the holiday marking the beginning of the Jewish New Year. The most important change, though, came at the end of the text, where she added these sentences concerning her father, "who remained convinced of the legend's veracity": "But without hatred or bitterness. In his eyes, the author of the crime was a madman not responsible for his actions." She thus minimized the anti-Semitic implications of her father's beliefs.[5]

Lemoine wrote, "The first in my family to recognize the innocence and sanctity of Raphaël Lévy, I felt that it was my simple duty to correct the record," adding that "my ancestors in all good faith committed a monumental error and glaring injustice and perpetuated it for three centuries." The centenary of the Dreyfus Affair having been celebrated a short while earlier, Lemoine hoped to draw attention to this other tragedy and discredit the results of another "hasty and clearly biased trial."[6] Courageously contradicting her family's memories, she wrote: "My ancestor unwittingly caused an enormous injustice to be committed, but he was under heavy pressure from prominent local citizens when he accused the unfortunate Lévy of the crime. It is more difficult for me to understand his attitude later on."[7] In a private letter, she made this moving comment on the case: "My ancestor was used as an instrument by criminals who will remain forever unknown. How can we judge the behavior, three centuries ago, of an illiterate peasant traumatized by the tragic loss of his child?"[8]

*

Yet a careful reading of the documents from the trial as well as of various narratives recounting the circumstances of the case fails to support this allegation against "criminals who will remain forever unknown" and who supposedly used Gilles Le Moyne as their "instrument." This reading amounts to an exculpation of the man who hounded Lévy to his death. Nor is there any evidence of a crime committed by a person or persons unknown—perhaps, as Lemoine apparently believed, by one of the butchers who "could no longer stand competition from Jews" and "sought to have the king expel all Jews from the region."[9] When she asks if "the criminals had set their sights on the Le Moyne child, or was the kidnapping a chance occurrence, abetted by circumstances?" she assumes the existence of a veritable conspiracy, a kidnapping that ended tragically in a murder. Again, there is no evidence for this hypothesis, which overlooks the more likely possibility that the boy had simply lost his way in the forest and been torn apart by wild animals. In short, we still know nothing about the actual circumstances of little Didier's death, but there is no evidence of a crime and no proof of a conspiracy of butchers to rid themselves of troublesome competitors "too clever at business," as Lemoine put it. The affair cannot be put down to ordinary commercial rivalry, and a tragedy that awakened ancestral fears cannot be explained without saying something about the beliefs of the people involved.

*

Although Bernadette Lemoine said nothing about the Catholic faith of her ancestors, she exhorted today's Jews to remain faithful to their values, the values for which Raphaël Lévy unhesitatingly gave his life. For instance, on February 24, 2002, she wrote to Schumann, the man who arranged the memorable meeting with Meyer: "Thanks for your kind wishes. Please accept my very sincere wishes for a good and happy new year for yourself and your family. But for you the year begins in September. I hope that you continue to keep faith with your age-old traditions as much as possible. It must not be very easy!"[10] Thus she explicitly evoked the tragic Rosh Hashanah of the past, suggesting the importance of continuing to celebrate it as a symbol of perseverance in a faith that the Le Moynes and many of their neighbors had sought to eradicate.

In another letter, this one addressed to Meyer, she wrote, "Please accept my sincere best wishes for 2002. But for you the year begins in

September. I hope that you continue to keep faith with your beautiful age-old traditions as much as possible. Roughly forty centuries stand between us and Abraham, our common Father. It's enough to make you dizzy, but what a miracle! . . . Life is short: a fleeting episode, a time of preparation for the perfect Joy that will reunite us in our one and transcendent God."[11]

With these touching letters, which insisted on the need for Judaism to survive, Lemoine sought to close the book on the tragic affair that had involved her Catholic ancestors in a wicked miscarriage of justice against Lévy, a Jew who in their eyes was the very incarnation of evil—a perverse child killer with a demonic thirst for the blood of young Christians. Memory of this tragedy, which instantly revived traditional accusations of ritual murder that had been all but forgotten in France, remains virtually intact among the Jews of Lorraine, so much so that even today some of them are reluctant to wander at night in the accursed forest of Glatigny.[12]

Like a brave soldier, Lemoine launched a frontal assault on a legend without having the slightest idea how it had influenced her fellow Christians in the past or what they might make of it today. Behind this lurid fantasy lay a bottomless demonology and a culture permeated with magical thinking. It originated in the night of time, and no one woman—even one of the Just like the courageous and obscure Bernadette Lemoine—can put it to rest.

This legend was born in the Catholic West. Between the twelfth and thirteenth centuries, Christian anti-Judaism was built around three closely related myths: (1) that Jews crucified young Christian males in order to reenact and mock the crucifixion of Christ, (2) that they kidnapped and killed Christian boys to obtain blood for their rituals, and (3) that they sought to profane hosts that through transubstantiation had become the body of Christ, in order to kill him again.

These three myths formed the basis of medieval anti-Judaism, even if it was often difficult to distinguish them with such analytic clarity.[13] For Gavin Langmuir, these fantasies, which can be related to beliefs about cannibalism, are not so much irrational as nonrational. Going beyond anti-Judaism, he argues, they established a true ideology of anti-Semitism, a product of medieval Christianity.[14] During centuries of crusades and intense faith, Christians consciously or unconsciously associated the crucifixion of Christ at Easter with Passover, the "Jewish Easter," which marks the exodus from Egypt and calls for preparation of *matzoh*, or unleavened bread, in commemoration of what the Hebrews ate during their flight across the desert.[15]

The myth of ritual murder was based on the preposterous idea that Jews cannot make matzoh without Christian blood. Despite abundant evidence that Jews do not eat food contaminated with blood and do not eat meat unless all the blood has been drained out of it, and despite all the indications of the constant vigilance that this atavism, so deeply embedded in their beliefs and customs, obliged them to maintain, the idea that Jews thirsty for the blood of Christian children kidnapped them and collected their blood in special receptacles became the central theme of countless sermons, legends, and plays as well as paintings by the greatest masters, which decorated any number of churches.

*

In view of the significant contact between different cultures and religions in this period, contemporary historians such as Israel Jacob Yuval have proposed the provocative and controversial thesis that accusations of ritual murder appeared in the wake of the crusades (in 1096), and indeed that they were almost a consequence of the crusades. To prevent conversion of their children, it is argued, Jews did not shrink from sacrificing them. Horrified at the sight of Jews taking the lives of their own children, their accusers supposedly concluded that if they were prepared to commit such atrocities to hasten the redemption of their own offspring, they would not hesitate to do the same or worse to Christian children. This led to the first tales of ritual murder, which were then repeated again and again in one place after another.[16] In this sense, the *Kiddush Ha-Shem*, sanctification of the name of God, might unwittingly have been responsible for the legends of ritual murder that were so widespread throughout Christendom at the time.[17]

*

Traditionally, the first appearance of this superstition is said to date from the death of little William in Norwich, England, on the eve of Easter 1144. His mutilated body was found in a forest, and it was alleged that he had been murdered during Pesach (Passover) in the home of the

Jew Eleazar, who, with the help of confederates, had stabbed him repeatedly with a knife in order to collect his blood before crucifying him. Threatened with burning by the local authorities for offenses against Christianity, the accused Jews took refuge in a royal castle after the king took them under his protection.[18]

The best-known accusations of ritual murder of Christian children by Jews come from England and France: Lincoln (1255), Blois (1171),[19] Bray-sur-Seine (1191), and Le Puy (1320).[20] In Spain the best-known example remains that of La Guardia, which took place in 1488. Between the twelfth and sixteenth centuries, there were many cases of this type, the majority of them in German-speaking countries (forty-three, compared with only seven in France, and none after the fourteenth century, because the Jews had been expelled from both France and England).[21] As Hillel Kieval has observed, France was a nation-state and therefore less prone to accusations of this type, which were more common in regions of uncertain political status, especially in German-speaking areas and in the Russian Empire.[22]

⁂

In the Rhineland, one of the most celebrated cases occurred in Würzburg in 1147.[23] In 1470, in the town of Endingen (not far from the French border), three Jewish brothers were accused of committing a ritual murder during Passover. Under torture, they confessed to the crime in lurid detail, denounced other Jews who had allegedly taken part in the ceremonies, and described how they had drained the little boy's blood into a glass receptacle. Every time they were tortured, they added new details to the story, hoping to satisfy their judges and thus put an end to their suffering. Strappado was the method generally used: the victim's hands were tied behind his back, and he was then lifted by a rope attached to his wrists, while heavier and heavier weights were attached to his feet. Ultimately, his arms were broken. He was then burned at the stake as a sorcerer or servant of the devil. The execution, carried out before a cheering crowd, symbolized the victory of Christianity over the evil incarnate in the Jew.

The burghers of Endingen were also asserting their political autonomy vis-à-vis the emperor, who had offered his protection to the Jews. The trial "represented nothing less than the victory of one Christian civic community over the Jews and, by implication, over their noble protector as well."[24] In other words, the accusation of ritual murder figured in an ongoing confrontation between local and central powers. Myths deeply rooted in popular Christian beliefs, which drew analogies between ritual murder and the crucifixion of Christ and desecration of the host, were mobilized in this battle. In Regensburg in 1470, Jews were also accused of ritual murder and desecration of the host. Under torture, six of them, including a rabbi, invented fantastic tales that reflected Christian beliefs in their magical powers. The intervention of Emperor Frederick III proved decisive in thwarting citizens whose thirst for vengeance was encouraged by clerics preaching violent retribution against the Jews.

*

Five years later, in 1475, a similar accusation was made in Trent. The unusual dimensions of this affair ensured that it would remain engraved in memory for centuries as the most celebrated case of ritual murder, and one that would go on being cited repeatedly until quite recently. Two centuries before the Metz tragedy, a young boy named Simon disappeared. Somehow the idea that he had been murdered for his blood by Jews during Passover took hold. Rumor had it that the boy's body was discovered in a ritual bath in the cellar of a prominent Jew named Samuel on Easter Sunday, and that the corpse was seen to bleed when Jews were present.

Inevitably, Simon's death was linked to that of Christ, and in the eyes of municipal authorities this constituted irrefutable proof that Jews were responsible for the crime. Magic was involved, and the Jews were compared to sorcerers acting on behalf of the devil. Their alleged crime was likened to cannibalism. Fantasies of this type are common when accusers and accused mingle socially and are involved in relations of economic dependence. A midwife, married to a man named Le Suisse, had recently assisted in delivering the child of a prominent Jew named Samuel. A dispute over wages led to the midwife's dismissal, and Le Suisse accused Samuel of ritual murder.

Six Jews were immediately arrested and subjected to horrible tortures, including strappado. When they could bear it no longer, they invented out of whole cloth a "theater of death," constructed around details of the murder of which they stood accused. Their judges were satisfied;

"Tell me what I have to say," one of the defendants implored, "and I will say it." The accused concocted a series of horrors, each more improbable than the next, and declared themselves guilty of the most perfidious crimes in order to put an end to their torment. Solidarity among the defendants was destroyed by the same methods, and in their extreme suffering they denounced one another, though nearly all of them tried desperately to save at least the women among them, who were also subjected to appalling tortures. The extreme cruelty and large number of Jews accused in Trent ensured that this case would leave an indelible impression.

Despite the fanatical climate, some Christian neighbors of the accused did not hesitate to come to their assistance. Once again, outside political and religious authorities also intervened on behalf of the Jews. For instance, the doge of Venice expressed incredulity about such myths, and Pope Sixtus IV was convinced of the innocence of the accused. But none of this made any difference; fourteen Jews were executed after extended torture. Sixtus IV was no more able to stop the spread of anti-Semitic violence than Innocent IV had been in 1247, and the incendiary preaching of the Franciscans only added to it.[25] In Trent, a veritable cult of Simon developed, with paintings, statues, and processions celebrating the death of the innocent child. This cult was not abolished until 1967, and traces of it remain today.[26]

The Trent trial haunts the centuries: the story of ritual murder, confession, and torture has spawned a long list of publications and been cited repeatedly by anti-Semitic authors, in nineteenth-century France for example, as an archetypal instance of Jewish culpability.[27] Elevated to the status of a model, the example of Trent also attests to the limits of imperial power in dealing with events on the periphery of the empire. Successive emperors did not cease to protest, however, against such extreme forms of intolerance, which flew in the face of imperial law. A century later, in 1544, Charles V also extended his protection to the Jews and ended the prosecution of several Jews accused of ritual murder. He also ordered that no such case be prosecuted in the future without his consent. Other emperors followed suit: Ferdinand II (1562), Maximilian II (1566), and Rudolph II (1577). These imperial interventions contributed to the rapid decline of the practice in the Holy Roman Empire in the sixteenth century.

Although the theme of ritual murder remained common in ballad and legend in the sixteenth century, and although it figured in conversation and fed rumors that lent force to anti-Semitism, no Jew was executed on such a charge in a German-speaking country after the sixteenth century.[28] But the slack was taken up, however briefly, by France, as the extraordinary case of Raphaël Lévy attests.

*

The Lévy affair was also linked to another myth, related to that of ritual murder but different from it in a number of respects. In roughly the same period, Jews were also accused of desecrating the sacred host. With knives, daggers, and swords they would allegedly attack a host that they somehow obtained, usually by bribing a Christian woman with promises of cash or cancellation of a debt. The host thus became a form of currency, and this legend later culminated in the image of the Jew as a rich capitalist manipulating the poor innocent Christians. Once they got hold of the host, the Jews went wild, heaping insult after insult upon it, beating it, and slashing it with violent blows. Then, the legend has it, a miracle would occur, as blood flowed from the host, striking fear into the Jews, who often begged to be converted, having been convinced of the truth of transubstantiation, of the mystery of the Eucharist. These desecrations generally occurred around the time of Easter. The basis of the myth was of course the story of the Last Supper. According to Matthew, "And as they were eating, Jesus took bread, and blessed *it*, and brake *it*, and gave *it* to the disciples, and said, Take, eat; this is my body." The blood of Jesus Christ was thus supposed to replace the "blood of the covenant" with which Moses had anointed his people. And in Paul's 1 Corinthians 11, we read: "This cup is the new testament in my blood: this do ye, as oft as ye drink it, in remembrance of me. For as often as ye eat this bread, and drink this cup, ye do shew the Lord's death till he come. Wherefore whosoever shall eat this bread, and drink this cup of the Lord, unworthily, shall be guilty of the body and blood of the Lord."[29]

Many legends accused the Jews of "indecent" treatment of the host, which, once consecrated, became the body of Jesus Christ. By devious means involving the use of money, Jews were said to obtain Christ's body in order to crucify him anew. For them, only the cruelest punishment would do. This other accusation against the Jews also appeared at the beginning of the thirteenth century in the Rhineland, Spain, and Paris, among other places. Linked to the allegation of ritual murder, it shows that, owing to the influence of Thomas Aquinas, the Jews were now held to have crucified Jesus deliberately in full knowledge of who he was. In Saint Augustine's earlier interpretation, the Jews were supposed to have been unaware that Jesus was the Messiah. But Aquinas and other Paris theologians, Franciscan as well as Dominican, insisted that the Jews had acted deliberately. When they attacked the sanctified host, therefore, they were simply persisting in their criminal behavior, because "the body of Christ is the symbol of both spiritual things and Christ on the cross."[30] In this respect, the accusation of desecration of the sanctified host is of a piece with the older accusation of ritual murder.[31] "Internal enemies" living on the fringes of Christian society,[32] the bloodthirsty Jews were thus portrayed as veritable monsters.[33]

*

Desecration of the sanctified host, which was also said to occur around Easter, received its ultimate symbolic consecration in an altarpiece that Paolo Uccello executed between 1467 and 1469. The miracle of Les Billettes, one of the "gentiles' tales,"[34] occurred in 1290 in what is today the rue des Archives. It inspired Uccello's predella, which can be seen today in the ducal palace in Urbino and which depicts the symbolic murder of the host: "The Christian child is replaced by the sacramental body of Christ; the battered and boiled host will again produce the theophanic effect by transforming the body of Christ into the eucharistic child."[35] The story that Uccello tells in his six panels presents the desecration of the host in a perfectly convincing manner. In the first panel, a woman displays a round host to a Jewish merchant in Florentine dress standing behind a counter. He can be identified by insignia visible on the mantle of the fireplace. In the second panel, two children, one crying, can be seen between a man and a woman clad in red. As a red liquid flows from a pot on the fire, soldiers force their way into the room. The other panels recount how the host is saved from the machinations of the Jewish merchant and how the man, his wife, and his two children are tied to a stake and burned. Meanwhile, an angel has prevented the hanging of the woman who had tried to sell the host.[36]

The miracle of Les Billettes, with its dramatic ending, spread across Europe between the thirteenth and sixteenth centuries.[37] In every instance, the cruelty of the Jew was recounted in lavish detail. The host was always obtained in exchange for cash or other goods. Countless paintings and plays substituted this story of desecration for the tale of ritual murder. Jérôme Séguier's version, which was published in 1604, sixty-five years before the Raphaël Lévy affair, is worth citing at length:

> This cruel and barbaric Jew, having obtained the sanctified Host, was blinded by the dark beliefs to which he clung tenaciously and refused to believe that this piece of bread contained the true flesh of Our Savior [...] He began to talk to himself in the following terms: "Now I will know, and with this blow I will find out whether there is any truth in what these mad Christians say." With that he took a dagger or small knife [...] and began to pierce in several places the living host of the holy Body of Jesus Christ, which he had placed on a chest. No sooner had he done this than he saw a large quantity of precious blood flow out of it [...] He once again took the same Host and with a nail pierced it through with several blows from a hammer, and again abundant quantities of blood began to flow from it [...] With a heart as hard as Pharaoh's, he again took the Host from his foul hands and threw it into a large brazier. But it immediately jumped out and began dancing about, to the great astonishment of the infidels. The impious Jew now took a large kitchen knife and tried to cut it and carve it to pieces to complete its punishment. The wretch went to a great deal of trouble, but all in vain, because the Body of Jesus Christ remained intact and perfect. So as not to forget any of the torments and tortures to which Our Lord was subjected in his first Passion, the cruel Jew nailed the Host to a filthy and foul-smelling place and with all his strength hurled a lance at it, unleashing a torrent of Blood from the wound, as before. Not yet satisfied by all this cruel punishment, this henchman and minister of Satan plunged the Host into a boiling cauldron, the last of his damnable inventions. Immediately the boiling water turned blood red, and the holy Host by dint of its own Majesty raised itself up from the bubbling liquid and displayed itself to the infidel in the form of a crucifix.[38]

The end of the story is easily guessed: the Jew persists in his error, while his wife and children convert. Condemned to the stake, he asks for his Talmud. After it is brought to him, "he is tied up and attached to a criminal in the cart, and when wood that has been laid around the stake is set ablaze, the Jew along with his Book is consumed by the flames as easily as he stubbornly refused to convert." This description of the cruelty of the Jew is chilling. Given its wide circulation in the early seventeenth century, it is easy to imagine the influence it had in that period of militant Counterreformation.

*

What is lacking in these stories, however, is another miracle that gives a more explicit indication of their meaning: the resurrection of the body of Christ in the host in the form of a young child, symbolizing innocence. This miracle occurred in a celebrated case in which a host was stolen in Passau (Bavaria) in 1477. According to the legend:

> On the Friday before Saint Michael, when the abbey gate was open for the Feast of Our Lady, the tabernacle was broken into, and Christopher Greisshammer made off with four pieces of the venerable sacrament, touched them with his sinful hands, wrapped them in a handkerchief, and kept them about his person from Friday to Sunday morning. He then turned them over to the Jews, a dishonest race, in exchange for Rhenish florins. A host earned him thirty pfennigs, to the great shame of the Holy Christian Church. The Jews and their God kept them. Gripped by doubt, they took the body of Christ in their sinful hands and carried it into their synagogue. With greedy zeal they touched the crucified body in order to protect themselves from the Christian faith. A Jew took a sharp knife and pierced the body of Christ on the altar of their synagogue, so that blood flowed from it. The face of a child appeared, which greatly frightened the Jews.[39]

Before Lent in the year 1477 the malefactor and the Jews were arrested, and after Easter all were executed. For centuries, the culture believed in "the transubstantiated host as the real Christ and in one of his suffering personas as a sacrificed . . . bleeding child."[40]

*

In Metz in 1513 twenty-five actors performed a play in several acts, "The Mystery of the Sacred Host." Violently hostile to the Jews, this drama left its mark on the inhabitants of the city. It also took its place in a long tradition of local infanticides that were mostly blamed on natives of

Germany. This is mentioned in any number of later Metz chronicles. It was so popular that several editions were published in the sixteenth century.[41]

> *The Jew*: We will now find out whether this God, in whom the Christians believe and in whose name they despise us, has any virtue, strength, or power. Gather round this chest and contemplate the foolishness of these Christians, who believe in this piece of bread and say that it contains life and blood, that it is God Himself [...] I will now test it with this dagger.
>
> *The Jew's Wife*: Oh! Oh! It bleeds! [...] What sacrilege! Oh! By Mohammed! It is alive.
>
> *The Daughter, on her knees*: Oh! Good papa, I beg you, do not hit it.
>
> *The Son, in tears*: Alas! It bleeds! Alas! Alas! Father, for God's sake, stop! Oh! It is so beautiful, so gentle. Give it to me. I will keep it.
>
> *The Jew*: I will look in back for the big knife I use to cut meat. I will cut it into a thousand pieces. One, two, three, four, five. By God Almighty! After each blow it seems to put itself back together. It remains intact, as it was before. But thou shalt suffer even worse, if possible. [...] I will kill it. [...] *He takes the host and nails it to a column. Blood runs down to the ground.* [...] I will burn it in my fireplace. *He throws the host on the fire. . . . He takes his lance and pierces the host on the brazier.* [...] *He then takes a kitchen knife and hacks it to pieces all over the house. . . .*
>
> *The Son, in tears*: Oh! Good papa, please stop. Would you kill this beautiful child? Look how its blood is flowing. No sadder sight has ever been seen. [...] *A crucifix appears in the cauldron next to the fireplace.* O crucifix, divine and pure, I beg thy pardon. I will leave this place, which thy grandeur abhors. Accursed be the man who engendered me and the woman who brought thee here to suffer such misfortunes.[42]

Once again, Jacob Mousse, the Jew, asks for his Talmud to protect him, and then, as the provost noted, "this sorcerer was burned along with his book."[43] In a rather unusual departure for these theatrical performances—which shaped history itself—the Jew is here identified as a sorcerer and thus associated with the witches who were also mercilessly put to the stake in sixteenth-century Lorraine. What is more, the host was explicitly transformed into "a small child." In a contemporary chronicle of these events, Philippe de Vigneulles wrote: "As if it were a pissing baby."[44] Thus we have here another rare example of the link that was often drawn between ritual murder and desecration of the host. In the Christian imagination, host desecration, here located in Metz, replaced ritual murder as another way Jews could obtain the blood they needed to prepare matzoh for Passover, the holiday celebrating their own redemption via exodus from Egypt. Host desecrations were thus identified with accusations of ritual murder because "the logic of the principle of transubstantiation implies that the Jew did not require a flesh-and-blood Christian; all he needed to do was to stab the host or dip it in boiling water."[45] In fact, by drawing blood from the host, the Jews presumably proved the truth of the Eucharist, which some Christians doubted. Thus the accusation served a second purpose: it relieved Christians of their own doubts.[46]

Still, it was in Metz, in this play, that the assimilation of the desecrated host to the body of Christ resurrected in the form of an innocent child brought the two types of accusation together. But it was not just in Metz that the innocent child appeared, its radiant features serving to highlight the cruelty of the Jew and to reveal the truth of transubstantiation. A similar apparition occurred in 1725, in the miracle of Les Abeilles, which is depicted in a tapestry in the château de Langeais. Like the tale of the miracle of Brussels in 1370, the definitive version of which would not be published until 1720, all of these stories survived the sixteenth and seventeenth centuries and remained alive in the eighteenth.[47] Clearly, the seventeenth-century public would have been well aware of these famous stories of host desecration, so that in the atmosphere surrounding the trial of Raphaël Lévy for ritual murder it was only natural for such tales to be revived in Metz and figure in the local discussion of the event. As we shall see, they would become an overlooked but crucial element in the Lévy affair, which substantially transformed their meaning.[48]

One "Metz Covers the State"
The Royal Order, Witches, and Jews

The 1660s, which ended with the Raphaël Lévy affair, marked a crucial turning point for French society: with peace restored, Louis XIV triumphed, and his reign ushered in the absolutist state.[1] Although the king still faced considerable opposition, still depended on powerful nobles, and still moved cautiously with respect to various clients and *parlements*—in other words, although compromise was still the order of the day—this moment stands out as a "great caesura,"[2] a time of transition to the society of the "classical era" that presaged the Enlightenment. In the Kingdom of the Lilies, during those few years of glory, art, culture, festivals, and a host of other things all contributed to the celebration of the king's power, brilliance, and splendor. Paris was transformed, as were Versailles and Fontainebleau. Wit, civilization, and learning gathered in France. The Louvre and the Tuileries were refurbished, followed by the château of Saint-Germain, where the court took up residence. In 1669, Le Brun completed a baroque masterpiece, a study in homage to Apollo in the king's private apartment.[3]

The great work attesting to the symbolic importance of this decade was of course the vast construction project in Versailles. The preparation of the gardens was in full swing as work began on the Grand Canal (1667), Le Nôtre created the central perspective, the parterres were transformed, the Labyrinth was completed (1666), and statues of Apollo sprouted everywhere. Work also began on the Trianon. The court gathered around the king, whose glory outshone that of all other sovereigns. A rigid ceremonial protocol was established to honor the monarch, and everyone abided by the new rules. Festival followed festival, one more sumptuous than the next.

In this respect, the year 1668 was especially noteworthy. The king himself took part in the celebrations. As late as 1670, it pleased him to show off his talent as a dancer. On February 4 of that year, he played the role of Apollo, vanquisher of the Python, but on the fourteenth, the eve of Raphaël Lévy's execution, he had someone else take his place; he had decided to dance no more.[4] Soon thereafter, at carnival time, an exceptionally sumptuous event was staged in the Theater of Apollo in the presence of the king and queen: "There, a gallant rural comedy was performed, with the love of a shepherd and shepherdess as its subject. The court turned from business to pleasure, but the king neither fell asleep nor slumped in his chair. Soon, however, he returned to the serious business of government."[5]

Following the example set by the king himself, aristocrats did not trouble to hide their dissolute morals and libertine ways. In 1667, in Avesnes, Louis XIV took a new mistress, Mme. de Montespan, who in early 1670 bore him a child, the future duc de Maine. Meanwhile, his previous mistress, Louise de La Vallière, languished in boredom while awaiting another child, the future comte de Vermandois, who was born after the king returned from Avesnes in October. A year later, the king visited Flanders and appeared in public with the queen and two mistresses: the "three queens."[6] As the fate of the unfortunate Raphaël Lévy was being decided, the king was gallivanting from bed to bed. Mme. de Maintenon, whom the king would secretly marry in 1683, made her entrance at court in 1669.

*

Pleasure and culture seemed to go together. The decade was remarkably fertile in every respect. To take the year 1669 alone, La Fontaine published *Les Amours de Psyché et de Cupidon*, Madeleine de Scudéry *La Promenade de Versailles,* and Pascal his *Pensées*, while Racine put on *Britannicus* and Molière again performed *Tartuffe*. In 1670, Racine staged *Bérénice*, Corneille *Tite et Bérénice*, and Mme. de Lafayette *Zaïde*, while Boileau published his first *Épître*. While preparations were made to inaugurate the first Paris opera, dozens of mathematicians, physicists, and chemists gathered to organize the Académie des Sciences, which pledged "to carefully examine all books of mathematics and physics and perform all important experiments related to them." Thus, science as well as art flourished in this period. As of 1665, the *Journal des savants* began publishing the most advanced scientific debates. In 1667, the Observatory of Paris was established as a center of scientific research. An age of experimentation, methodical doubt, critical spirit, and reason—in short, an age of science—had begun.

Yet this decade blessed by the gods of arts and sciences was also a decade of militant, intransigent Catholicism, which harshly attacked Protestants, chipping away at the benefits conferred by the Edict of Nantes. Between 1661 and 1665, decrees prohibited Protestants from singing psalms in the street and staging funeral processions during hours of daylight, while allowing Catholic priests to minister to dying Huguenots. Protestant places of worship were razed, and everything possible was done to marginalize them. Meanwhile, Catholicism flourished: the number of convents increased, many new seminaries were established (fifty-six between 1661 and 1682), new catechisms were published, and officials reported that nearly everyone seemed to be attending mass and taking communion at Easter. New temples were erected in honor of the Virgin Mary.[7] The triumph of Counterreformation Catholicism coincided with the rise of science, public celebrations, and the frenetic search for pleasures of all kinds.

*

The Age of Louis XIV was thus shot through with contradictions, but this did not prevent the construction of an absolutist state, which sought to rationalize its administration of people and territory. In that sense, "the state was indeed the king,"[8] for it was the king who was the instigator of administrative institutionalization. He attacked courts and parlements that attempted to limit his powers. "Gentlemen," he said in 1655, "everyone is aware of the woes for which Parlement is responsible. I warn them to end all hearings on the edicts that I have submitted, which I want to see executed."[9] The king also imposed his own much-reformed system of justice and promised in August 1665 to "see that justice reigns, and that through justice I reign, over the state." He increased the power of the *intendants*, who represented him in the provinces. Although their position remained delicate, their role was to assert control over the general administration and to exclude the parlements, whose members retained power in the cities where they were located.[10]

The king also relied on governors, who ranked above the intendants. He ordered a major reform of the police and proposed a number of reforms of the justice system. In April 1667, the Code Louis established uniformity in civil procedures, limited the autonomy of the courts, and reduced certain punishments, particularly in regard to the seizure of peasant property. The criminal ordinance of 1670 established an appellate procedure that limited the prerogatives of local courts, protected prisoners from their guards, established rules for questioning suspects and organizing trials, defined the role of the investigating magistrate in seeking legal evidence of guilt rather than being guided by his own "intimate conviction," and limited the use of torture, which was now regulated but not abolished, despite hopes that it might be. All of this attested to an interventionist idea of the state. The death penalty remained common; some six hundred death sentences were handed down in the seventeenth century.[11]

The Age of Louis XIV was also a time of acute crises of mortality. In the 1660s, death descended on France. Between 1663 and 1670, poor harvests, famine, and epidemics of the plague and other diseases struck, first in Saint-Malo, then Toulon, and finally northern France. Winters were so harsh that people died of the cold, and brigands roamed the countryside, while rampaging soldiers pillaged and raped. Fear and violence were everywhere. The king waged war constantly to assert his power and glory, and although there were resplendent victories, there were also defeats, corteges of victims, provinces occupied, ransoms to be paid, and soldiers billeted on the population.

Some of these wars directly affected Metz, an eastern city that "covers the state," as Vauban would put it later, as well as Lorraine, which was caught between the Hapsburg Empire and the Kingdom of France. Lorraine was a peripheral region yet central to the royal strategy of taking the fight to Strasbourg and the Hapsburgs. It had long been a fragmented territory, coveted by all, a no-man's-land where the imagination could run wild. It was a heterogeneous region of uncertain status, marked by successive occupations and fragile intervals of independence, which left its battered inhabitants in a state of constant uncertainty. The State of Lorraine consisted of the Duchy of Lorraine, east of the Meuse, which was under the protection of the Holy Roman Empire, along with the Duchy of Bar to the west, whose duke paid homage to the French king. It was therefore a region of contradictions, coveted by rival powers that aimed to annex it, while the duke of Lorraine maneuvered warily to maintain his independence.

Since 1552, moreover, the French monarchy had seized control of a number of places in this disputed region: the famous Trois-Évêchés (that is, the bishoprics of Verdun, Toul, and Metz, the latter nothing less than an urban republic, since it enjoyed independent status as an "imperial city" and therefore did not have to pay formal obeisance to the king). The duke, in keeping with his strategy of independence, nevertheless favored the emperor over the king. Louis XIII had seized the Duchy of Bar, laid siege to Nancy, and taken control of the Duchy of Lorraine, where it set up a parlement in Metz in 1633. Violence knew no limits; in 1635, for instance, imperial troops camped outside Metz and used force indiscriminately. According to one contemporary observer, the Croats were particularly brutal: "They made martyrs of every man, woman, and child they encountered, cut out their tongues, and cut off their arms and genitals. Others they strung up in fireplaces or made them drink three or four buckets of cow urine and then killed them by jumping on their stomachs. Attila was never crueler than those Croat tyrants."[12]

This occupation had no legal basis, since the Treaty of Westphalia (1648) had confirmed that the Trois-Évêchés belonged to the king, but not the Duchy of Lorraine. In 1652–53, Lorraine was a battlefield in the civil war between the armies of the prince de Condé and Cardinal Mazarin. As always, bands of mercenaries and pillagers laid waste to the countryside, seizing livestock and grain. Villages were emptied, houses fell into ruin, and the population collapsed. In November 1659, the Treaty of the Pyrenees was signed with Spain, granting the Duchy of Lorraine to Duke Charles IV, while the region north of the Meuse and Moselle, including Thionville, fell under French sovereignty. In 1661, following further negotiations with the royal government, the Treaty of Vincennes awarded the Duchies of Lorraine and Bar to Charles IV, while several strips of territory went to the French. A connection between Champagne and Alsace was thus reestablished, a sign of French progress in asserting control over the region. On April 14, 1661, royal troops quit the duchies after an occupation of twenty-eight years. They would not return until 1670, after the tragic demise of Raphaël Lévy, whose fate was thus determined in part by the conflicting laws of rival powers.

In August 1670, royal troops occupied Lorraine without firing a shot. The king's goal was to seize this territory in preparation for war on Holland. (Eventually, in September 1683, Lorraine would be annexed to France.[13]) In 1669–70, Metz once again found itself in the midst of violent conflict, with soldiers constantly in the area. It was beleaguered by Spanish, German, and English troops, and by the clashing armies of the king and the duc de Lorraine. Violence and uncertainty were the common lot, and "sad evidence of the people's poverty" was apparent everywhere.[14]

*

The city of Metz, in which the trial of Raphaël Lévy would unfold, was at the epicenter of a number of devastating conflicts. The city had been ruined by the depredations of the "king's men," who contrived to chip away at local liberties and at the independence of this "urban republic." A French enclave in foreign territory, Metz was crucial to Louis XIV's strategy. Its fate was shaped by constant rivalry between the king's men and local notables. The parlement proved to be "a docile and devoted servant."[15] Under the leadership of Colbert de Croissy, the brother of the great Colbert, whom the king appointed to head the important *généralité* of Metz, the monarchy sought to strengthen its position in the city, whose income was threatened by war. The ultimate goal was to integrate Metz into the kingdom. The city was the key to controlling the region and pursuing other military objectives, so the Bourbon monarchy kept a careful eye on it. The goal was to hasten its "*francization*": the king's men—the governor, the intendant, the bailiffs, the treasurers general and tax collectors, the judges of parlement, and many others, who came from Burgundy, Normandy, Dauphiné, and Paris—did battle day after day with the municipal authorities, including the Council of Master Aldermen, whose members were chosen by the people of the city, and the Council of Thirteen, which was stripped of all but its police powers and ordered to enforce the laws of France. In the battle for influence, the municipal authorities nevertheless managed to defend their prerogatives vis-à-vis the intendants, who agreed, for instance, to retain the aldermen.[16] Local officials were able to pass their offices on to their children, and they thus formed a homogeneous group of notables able to substantially limit the authority of the king's men. Little by little, "a power inherently hostile to the direct influence of the king's men was established."[17] This resistance of the notables of Metz, many of whom were adepts of the Catholic Counterreformation and had deep local roots, would weigh heavily on the fate of Raphaël Lévy.

*

The parlement of Metz was slow to assert its power. Created by Louis XIII in January 1633 to the great satisfaction of the Jews, who "looked upon it as the protector and guardian of their privileges,"[18] it was formally installed at the cathedral in accordance with firm instructions from Richelieu and despite the petitions of local authorities, who feared that it would mark the end of their influence. Jews expected the parlement to afford them royal protection, probably underestimating the commitment of its members to the most orthodox brand of Catholicism. Richelieu had "boldly placed [the Metz parlement] in the midst of a province antipathetic to French sovereignty." It sought to impose royal order by destroying the power of the master aldermen and petty seigneurial courts. The power of the latter was also threatened by the creation of a royal court of first instance, the *bailliage* (bailiff's court), in 1634. The magistrates invested with royal authority were nevertheless slow to overcome the opposition, despite the abolition of the Council of Thirteen, which resisted in vain. As Emmanuel Michel has shown, "the lower courts did not always bow to the authority of parlement as they were supposed to." In 1660, the mayor and master aldermen were able to hold on to their power to allocate municipal funds and scored victories over parlement in certain other areas. The "royal government was incapable" of bringing the aldermen to heel, and they continued to do as they pleased, resisting their main enemy, the bailiffs, with all their strength, even though the bailiffs were invested with absolute authority in criminal and civil cases.[19] In the 1660s, the king's men were at last able to assert their power, reducing the influence of local magistrates and notables jealous of their influence and hostile to the centralization of power effected by the absolute monarchy.[20]

*

The Raphaël Lévy affair erupted in this highly disputed territory—a Lorraine ravaged by war and epidemics such as the plague, which reduced the population of Metz from 19,000 in 1636 to 3,000 in 1643. Death was constantly on the prowl.[21] Calamity and insecurity may have made the population more susceptible than people elsewhere to belief in black magic and witchcraft. To be sure, witches were frequently prosecuted in other parts of Europe during this period. Scholars have found that in all of France roughly 100,000 witchcraft trials took place between 1450 and 1750, resulting in at least 40,000 death sentences. Of these cases, 20–25 percent involved men, and the vast majority of the trials took place before 1640.[22] The witches were seen as internal enemies, marginal individuals versed in black magic, rebels against Christian society who engaged in blasphemous practices and rituals associated with cannibalism; indeed, people believed that witches and sorcerers killed and ate children during their nocturnal flights.

Witches and sorcerers were not imagined to come from outside the society that accused them, however. Folkloric images notwithstanding, migrant beggars and seasonal laborers rarely numbered among them. On the contrary, the practitioners of black magic and cannibalistic rites were nearly always neighbors of their accusers. This social proximity of accusers and accused seems a fundamental point if we want to understand the sudden eruption of ineffable hatred that almost always led to the stake. Close and apparently unthreatened social relationships dissolved overnight, as if people were seized by a sudden overwhelming desire to cast out those who had previously been accepted as similar. Many cases involved settling of scores, rumors, conflicts of interest, jealousy, and seduction. Among the many things that could generate fantasies leading to the exclusion of neighbors we find allegations of casting spells, transmitting infectious diseases, destroying harvests, abducting children, and desecrating the host or holy water.

The list of demoniac crimes was endless. Local disputes, gossip, fears, and grievances nursed by people of low social status could degenerate into witch hunts, whose function was to regenerate the social group, thought to be threatened by a spell cast by an insider who was actually an agent of the devil. Witches were of course persecuted for numerous reasons. Many historians reject psychiatric explanations involving hallucinations, madness, or the superstitions of a prescientific age. Instead, they seek a functionalist explanation of why charges were brought at a particular point in time and why allegations of heresy and black magic focused on certain individuals. One hypothesis is that witch hunts were triggered by efforts to impose Christian orthodoxy through suppression of popular beliefs. Another is that they were responses to social controls imposed by the nascent state. A third is that the upper strata of the peasantry sought to distinguish themselves from the culture and beliefs of the poor by attacking not only their superstitions but also their nocturnal amusements, demonizing the female body in the process.[23] In any case, it is important to note that local disputes due to any number of causes were frequently at the bottom of these persecutions.[24]

*

Local disputes stemming from various beliefs and prejudices could swell to considerable proportions, especially in small territories such as duchies or principalities headed by a bishop, squeezed between rival states, and often fought over and occupied, with attendant atrocities and rumors. In such places, the political order was likely to be unstable. For example, in the corridor between Switzerland and the Netherlands, or in Franche-Comté and Lorraine, in small and scattered possessions of the Holy Roman Empire, such accusations, backed by local notables and amateur judges, were far more common than in states that had already established their authority.[25] In this respect, witch hunts can be compared with accusations of ritual murder against Jews, which were also more common in these types of places. Things scarcely improved when France occupied the region, because it also turned over judicial responsibility to local authorities, despite their lack of legal competence and record of erratic judgment. To make matters worse, justice was rendered at the time by wealthy notables, who passed their offices on to their heirs. Thus in "weak and marginal" states such as Scotland and Lorraine, one can "test the hypothesis that there is a link between witch hunting and the process of state building,"[26] because the dukes of Lorraine relied on local administrators susceptible to popular pressure. By contrast, the stronger the state, the fewer the trials for witchcraft.

"Bewitched" Lorraine[27] experienced an intense bout of witch hunting just before the Lévy affair broke out in the same political context. In the overall geography of witchcraft, this region occupies a prominent place: between 1580 and 1630, roughly 3,000 people were accused of witchcraft.[28] The ceremonies allegedly took place in woods, forests, heaths, and other unoccupied land. Witches were believed to consume human flesh during their feasts, preferably the flesh of unbaptized newborns. Acts of cannibalism were commonly alleged, and witches' sabbaths in Lorraine were said to involve a sort of porridge made from the body of a child.[29] The charges against witches always reflected their weakness, marginality, and broken ties to the surrounding community, which participated in the trial. Complaints came from close neighbors of the accused, and they were often responsible for involving rival local authorities in the investigation, given the confused political status of the region. The investigation was based entirely on the testimony of witnesses, thus leaving the accused no chance of exonerating themselves. They were cut off from the community and left to fend for themselves, assaulted by questions intended to destabilize them. Questioning proceeded for days on end, and the accused had to remember their previous answers to the same questions, which were tirelessly repeated day after day.

*

To obtain confessions from the accused, extreme torture seems to have been used in Lorraine more frequently than in France. In 1616, for example, Jacquotte Tixerand was subjected to torture by thumbscrew, stretching on the rack, crushing in a vise, and strappado. This finally overcame his astonishing resistance, and he confessed to acts of black magic and traffic with the devil.[30] In Lorraine, accusations of witchcraft were especially common in small villages and towns in which rumors spread rapidly during religious ceremonies and public holidays. Murmured gossip could ruin the reputation of certain members of the community. The rumors were often related to socioeconomic questions: a person who lent money might be denounced as an instrument of the devil. Disputes over wages, theft of fruit, injuries to livestock, and questions surrounding the sale of livestock—all of these things could arouse resentment leading to charges and prosecution that might end in the wiping away of a debt.

*

The region seems to have been especially fearful of child murders. There were so many cases that up to the 1660s even pigs were frequently hanged on rumors that they had killed and eaten young children.[31]

Infanticide by mothers was also common,[32] and children were abducted, with the blame sometimes falling on witches. For instance, in 1553 Fat Alison confessed to killing a small child and burying it, to be eaten at her next sabbath.[33] Midwives were often seen as witches: for instance, in 1609, in the small town of Raon, a midwife named Jennon Petit admitted under torture that her master, the devil, had ordered her to kill all the children she could, reduce them to powder, and bring them to him at her next sabbath.[34] All these women were subjected to horrible torture, and they were obliged to invent ever more appalling details to satisfy their tormenters. As we have seen, the same was done to Jews in Trent and elsewhere; the "theater of death" was ruled by the fantastic expectations of the torturers, and Jews, like witches, were expected to play their assigned role. The fate of nearly all witches was sealed in advance. In this period, only 5–10 percent escaped the stake in France and Lorraine. It took superhuman strength to resist the most extreme torture, to remonstrate with one's judges, even to mock them and accuse them of "having lost the fear of God" and of behaving like "smug and hard-hearted Christians."[35] At the time, torture was seen as an infallible test, a veritable ordeal designed to reveal the truth, so that for the very small minority who could hold out against it, it was possible to prove that they were not Satan's henchmen. For the salvation of their souls, nothing could be worse than perjury, than a false confession of sorcery, which would earn them eternal damnation. But most gave in at the mere idea of torture and were quick to denounce supposed accomplices.

*

After accelerating for a time, the persecution of witches in Lorraine fell off sharply around 1640. The region had been devastated for some time by terrible wars, which profoundly disrupted society and exacerbated antagonisms, as some grew rich while others were plunged into poverty. Between 1560 and 1660, warfare caused extensive damage and claimed an exceptionally large number of victims; revolts against the Netherlands, the Thirty Years' War, the Wars of Religion, and conflict between France and Spain followed one another in quick succession. Lorraine suffered incalculable devastation, and its population decreased by nearly 60 percent within a short period of time. As Robin Briggs observes, the causes of these misfortunes were obvious, so witch hunting ceased.[36] Although there were new outbreaks of persecution in Normandy and southwestern France in the 1670s, an overall decline was apparent by then, in large part thanks to Colbert's firm interventions.[37] Fantasies, superstitions, and rumors vanished in the face of a reality that surpassed fiction and silenced the imagination.

Thus the misfortunes of the period reduced beliefs in black magic to less cosmic proportions. In Lorraine, the year 1663, a short while before the Lévy affair, marked a clear turning point: accusations of witchcraft all but vanished from court dockets. As late as August 1652, Anne Couppechausse, who lived in the high valley of La Meurthe, was executed for witchcraft, and in 1661 there was another execution in Saint-Dié. But in July 1673, the sovereign court of Lorraine, sitting in Pont-à-Mousson, quashed a decision by the prosecutor of Saint-Dié, who had unjustly convicted Mougeon Vaudechamp of witchcraft and sentenced her "to be chastised with rods," tortured, and ultimately burned.[38] Witchcraft in Lorraine was finished. Administrative centralization put an end to local justice, and, on appeal, the sovereign court in Nancy commuted most death sentences for witchcraft.

⁂

Social relations were henceforth more firmly regulated by the Church with the backing of the state.[39] For the scholar Michel de Certeau, witchcraft, which was classed as a heresy along with mysticism, was supplanted by instances of possession, which occurred more often in cities than in the countryside and in relatively well-off segments of society, where devout believers were especially numerous. The devil thus made a renewed appearance in 1632 in Loudun, where the local priest, Urbain Grandier, was convicted of being a "sorcerer" and practicing "black magic." He was sentenced to death and burned after torture.[40]

Can we assert, however, that the end of witches and the growing unwillingness of the Church to allow them to be used as scapegoats encouraged a return to the persecution of Jews—another deviant group that the Church had always combated? And if so, was this especially true in places like Lorraine, devastated by war, liable to political uncertainty, and not yet governed by "raison d'état?" Furthermore, did the demise of witchcraft allegations favor the reemergence of the largely forgotten charge of ritual murder, especially in Lorraine, where an intransigent

Catholic social hierarchy was harsh on heretics in general, as we saw in Loudun, and in particular on Jews? Did the "decline of magic"[41] that we see in the West in this period open the way to the persecution of a group that insisted on maintaining its identity despite the threat posed to the cultural homogeneity of the kingdom? And did this persecution lead to the revival of a dramatic accusation—the charge of ritual murder—that had been heard before in German-speaking regions?

Although the fundamental antagonism toward Protestants remained, ultimately resulting in separation, Jews now became the sole target of allegations of magic, despite the fact that belief in magic, with its potions and superstitions, had been a European obsession since the Middle Ages. The "disenchantment of the world" that went along with the explosion of science and rationalism in this period put an end to the belief in witchcraft but did not eliminate accusations of ritual murder against Jews. If "it was the abandonment of belief in magic that allowed the flourishing of technology, and not the reverse,"[42] note that strong prejudices against Jews persisted in late–seventeenth-century France alongside powerful currents of science and rationalism. With the disappearance of witches, Jews, depicted as the most implacable enemies of Christianity, took their place as the main target of attacks on devil-inspired magic. The ritual murders that Jews had long been accused of committing stood as proof of this.[43] Although Jews were rarely accused of participating in witches' sabbaths and were not charged with witchcraft, Christians from the Middle Ages to the seventeenth century often associated them with witches, whose diabolical secrets they were believed to share. In this respect, Jews and witches were "two alikes that were not the same."[44] Analogies were drawn: as Carlo Ginzburg has observed, "from a relatively limited group (lepers), one moved to a larger group identified religiously and ethnically (Jews), and ultimately to a still broader set (sorcerers and witches). Like lepers and Jews, sorcerers and witches were supposed to live on the fringes of the community. Their conspiratorial attitude was, as always, inspired by the ultimate external enemy, the devil."[45]

*

Indeed, if Jews were often likened to witches because of the magical powers they were supposed to wield, they also found themselves bewitched by the very witches they were said to resemble. In 1608, for example, Marion Flandrey confessed that she had used her powers only to kill "wicked people, traitors and Jews."[46] Once witches vanished from the popular imagination, traditional fears and fantasies involving Jews came once again to the fore, crystallizing anxieties stirred up by daily violence in a period of incomprehensible devastation. Under the leadership of Bossuet, who in 1655 became canon of the cathedral of Metz and began delivering violent sermons against Jews,[47] the Counter-reformation[48] focused its hostility on Jewish heretics almost exclusively, before turning attention back to Protestants somewhat later. In 1668, the Jesuits founded a monastery for the Propagation of the Faith, which, along with a convent for women, sought to convert Protestants and Jews. Throughout the kingdom, the close alliance of church and state and the theory of divine right justified violent repression of all who failed to respect sacred values, including blasphemers. In September 1666, Louis XIV declared in Fontainebleau that "nothing can attract the blessings of heaven to our person and our State more than respecting and obliging others to respect the holy commands of God, and punishing those who blaspheme, swear, and detest His holy name." The harshest of punishments were envisioned, from mutilation to the stake.[49] A severe Catholic orthodoxy extended its hold over the city of Metz, whose small ghetto was encircled by churches and convents. Benedictine and Franciscan monasteries were flooded with new recruits. The ardor of the Jesuits to conquer the consciences of the inhabitants of Metz achieved impressive results; for instance, the confraternity of artisans grew from 250 members in 1658 to 800 in 1669, the year of the Lévy affair. Construction of new religious edifices attested to Catholicism's success: in 1665, the Jesuits began work on the church of Notre-Dame, and in the same year the Saint-Arnould cloister was rebuilt. In 1668, a year before Raphaël Lévy's arrest, construction work began on the chapel of the Visitandines. In 1670, work began on the church of the Carmes Déchaux.

Clearly, then, the "Catholic offensive" scored significant victories in Metz,[50] molding the values of residents and making Protestants and Jews feel increasingly suspect and in many ways rejected. The ubiquitous clergy lured the vast majority of the population into the churches, and no Christian avoided Easter communion; the saints were the object of superstitious devotion.[51] In this "frontier diocese,"[52] ultramontanism triumphed in the name of the Most Christian King, predisposing inhabitants to despise those who stubbornly sought to preserve a different faith. These developments preceded by a few years the revocation of the Edict of Nantes and the increasingly violent repression of Protestants, particularly in this part of eastern France. The court frolicked and danced in Versailles, and Parisian scholars strove to defend science by extolling rigorous empirical observation in ignorance of the drama that was soon to play out; but in defiance of all rational norms, in this showcase city of absolutist France, the Counterreformation was establishing a firm foothold in Metz, setting the scene for a new "theater of death," which replaced the witchcraft trials of old. It was on this stage that the Raphaël Lévy affair would unfold, sealing the fate of Lévy and a number of his co-religionists.

Two Neighborhood and Prejudices

After the Jews were expelled from France in 1306, some settled in the county of Bar. The duke of Lorraine was accused of accepting too many, so in 1350 they were driven out of the Barrois and the Duchy of Lorraine. In 1422, the Jews of Metz were granted rare privileges, but at the end of the century they too were expelled and did not begin to trickle back until 1562, as France gained a foothold in the region. Although Jews had lived in Metz legally or illegally since time immemorial, only four were authorized to return when the city came under French control. Known as "the king's Jews," they were granted free residence and allowed to lend money at interest against collateral.

When a move was made to expel them in 1567, they turned to the king's lieutenant general in Metz, Marshal de Vieilleville, who authorized them to stay in return for payment of a special tax. They were expelled again in 1574, but Henri III restored their privileges shortly thereafter, and in 1595 a group of twenty-five families, comprising roughly 120 individuals, formed an official Jewish community: "The Jews, placed under the king's direct protection, lived in Metz in full security from that point on [...] The Jewish community of Metz was reconstituted and would never again dissolve."[1]

In 1605, Henri IV expressed his gratitude to the Jews of Metz and took them under his protection as well. Benefiting from this royal protection and a stable situation, the Jewish population grew significantly in the years before the Lévy affair. In 1621, there were 400 Jews in Metz. Their number had increased to 665 by 1678 and to 950 by 1698.[2] The families elected syndics, who enjoyed absolute power thanks to support from the royal governor. The syndics were well-to-do notables who enforced rules of dress, morality, and modesty so as to avoid offending their Christian neighbors. They kept order in the Jewish quarter and issued edicts that had the force of law within the Jewish community. The chief rabbis, nearly all eminent Talmudists, were elected and together presided over the rabbinical court, which enforced respect for Jewish ritual and tradition.

The Jews of Metz often encountered hostility from their Christian neighbors. Although the Catholic clergy and populace frequently called for their expulsion, they continued to enjoy the king's protection.[3] As frequent suppliers to the military, they were on the best of terms with the king's lieutenant. By contrast, relations were tense with the city's tradesmen (drapers, butchers, bakers, mercers, tanners, etc.), who envied them and filed numerous complaints against them. For instance, "in 1656, 1657, and 1695, . . . the intendant received numerous briefs from guilds complaining about the commercial activity of the Jews."[4] But thanks to their substantial contribution to royal state-building efforts, they usually managed to retain the support of the king's local representative, the intendant.

In 1619, the city's first synagogue was inaugurated. Louis XIII visited it in 1661 and shortly thereafter confirmed the privileges granted to the Jews. In 1634, the Metz parlement defied the local clergy and bourgeois and issued a decision in favor of maintaining these royal privileges. Thus "the dual protection of king and parlement reassured the Jewish colony in Metz that it had nothing more to worry about."[5] Prestigious rabbis encouraged religious studies, and Metz became "the city of the Torah."[6] As Abraham Cahen notes, "By 1650 the community was well organized and firmly established. It enjoyed an excellent reputation and was considered one of the finest and most important [Jewish] communities. [...] Its members were generally respected and had easy access to the highest authorities and most influential people in the region."[7] Among European Jews, Metz was regarded as a model Jewish community.[8] In 1657, the governor of the city, the duke de Lavalette, fixed the number of Jewish families at ninety-six, each consisting of four or five individuals living in the Saint-Ferroy quarter, in which they had recently been granted the right to buy property.

*

When Louis XIV came to Metz in 1657, he visited the synagogue on the first day of Succoth. As the rabbi recalled:

> On the day after Yom Kippur in the year 418 (5418), the sovereign of the country, Louis, king of France and Navarre, came to the city with his queen, his mother, and his brother, the Duke d'Anjou. The following Saturday, the first day of Succoth, the king came to the synagogue in pomp and circumstance, accompanied by his brother and a great many dukes and nobles. [...] The next day, the secretary of the Count de Brienne, a great knight, came to the synagogue and said in all sincerity to the Israelites: "The king has expressed satisfaction with the Jews and has ordered the chancellor to prepare letters confirming their privileges."

After the king signed these letters patent, the guilds again protested and tried to block their registration by parlement and to limit the economic activity of the Jews.[9] In 1667, the king permitted the rabbi and seven members of the council to wear black hats in town (while authorizing everyone to wear black hats in the country).[10] The parlement, more susceptible to popular pressure, sought to reduce the privileges that the king had granted to the Jews and to defend the interests of the corporations.[11] Furthermore, "in a peasant society attached to its customs, rites, and faith, the Jew was seen as an intolerable intruder, protected by another group of foreigners, the French military and administrators."[12] Subject to the active hostility of the corporations, frequently hated by the population, and rejected by the Counterreformation, the Jews of Metz had only the king's protection to rely on for their security. Is it correct to argue, however, that "the benevolence of Louis XIV toward the Jews never faltered during that monarch's long reign"?[13]

⁂

In fact, despite the quite exceptional privileges that the Jews of Metz enjoyed, "the march of time and ideas did not bring about significant changes in the situation of a group of individuals who were seen as foreigners constituting a separate political body within the city, a distinct sect."[14] Not only in the city, where they enjoyed the king's favor, but also in the rest of Lorraine, which at the time was not occupied by French troops and where the duke made the law, the Jews stood apart. They were viewed as foreigners and were often objects of the opprobrium of the Christians among whom they lived. According to a report of the intendant Turgot, they were "like a kind of republic, and a kind of neutral nation for trade among different states." The Lévy affair thus occurred in a context where Jews were the target of permanent, generalized suspicion. Living in Boulay, not far from Metz, Raphaël Lévy belonged to one of the oldest Jewish communities in the region. Since the beginning of the sixteenth century, Boulay had been under the authority of the duke of Lorraine and at the heart of clashes between him and the republic of Metz, and later the king of France.[15] It was thus caught up in a series of conflicts, wars, rivalries, and sieges, which often ended in arson, pillage, and theft. The Jews residing in the city were frequently targets of these attacks.

The town also suffered other misfortunes. During the winter of 1635–36, for example, more than two hundred of its nine hundred residents died of the plague.[16] In Boulay as in the rest of Lorraine, people therefore lived in constant fear of calamity and tragedy. A worried population was prey to superstition and fear.

*

In 1660, the presence of thirteen Jewish families provoked the wrath and hostility of the population. In 1664, after the duke of Lorraine approved the provisional return of the Jews, other residents of the town demanded their expulsion, but the duke was unable to act on this request until French troops returned in 1670. Throughout this period, the Jews of Boulay, like others throughout the Moselle, were forbidden to own land or buildings for rent and were excluded from membership in the various corporations. They therefore made do by selling basic necessities, and many became livestock dealers, butchers, or short-term moneylenders.[17] Hence their position in the small town in which Raphaël Lévy lived was a fragile one, given the resentment they aroused in the local population.

Shortly before the accusation of ritual murder against Lévy, the people of Boulay were openly calling for the expulsion of the Jews—a community of only some fifty individuals yet still too large in the eyes of the town's other residents, who felt that the Jews threatened their economic interests because they circumvented the local market and dealt directly with people in Metz.

The number of churches and chapels in the small town of Boulay suggests a high level of Christian devotion. On January 16, 1664, the sovereign court of Nancy ordered the Jews of Boulay to abjure their faith and convert. By contrast, in 1670, the year of the drama that concerns us here, a new synagogue was inaugurated, to the furor of Boulay's non-Jewish population, which was outraged by the sight of Jews wearing *talittot* (prayer shawls) in public on their way to services. The number of complaints increased dramatically in the second half of the seventeenth century, and many expressed the view that Catholics could no longer tolerate a Jewish presence in their midst. As late as 1701, Boulay's Jews were sentenced to pay a heavy fine, the proceeds of which were to be used for decorating the church, for "having held an open synagogue and public assembly, and in derision of the Catholic religion, they donned masks and ran through the streets of Boulay on Holy Thursday and Friday last."[18] Indeed, threats, tensions, and temporary expulsions never really ended in Boulay, because even after the French Revolution "children, following Holy Week services, created a disturbance in the rue des Juifs, forcing the Jews to barricade the entrance to the synagogue during that time."[19]

⁂

Raphaël Lévy, the son of Isaac Lévy, was born in 1613 in the tiny village of Chelaincourt, where a small number of Jews had lived since 1577. His father was mentioned in the account books of the seigneurie of Ennery, a nearby village to which Jews came for religious services. Raphaël Lévy lived in Chelaincourt probably until 1636, a year in which villages in the region were pillaged in connection with the Thirty Years' War. Like many other Jews in vulnerable villages, Raphaël took refuge for a time in Metz before settling temporarily in Grimont and then marrying in Boulay, where he set up shop as a small-scale livestock dealer. A Metz notary recorded one of his transactions in 1654. A document dated 1665 refers to him as living in Boulay, and the signature, in Hebrew, confirms that this was the same person who lived in Grimont in 1639–40. When he was arrested in 1669, he seems to have been a member of the Boulay Jewish community who was well known to Jews in Metz because of his frequent business travels to that city. He is mentioned in a few contracts showing that he made small loans and dealt in grain and livestock. A document dated October 22, 1665, shows that he owned several flocks of sheep (the exact number of head is not mentioned) and was not impoverished but relatively well off, yet still of modest means compared to the prominent Metz Jews with whom he did business. In it we read:

> Before the undersigned *amans* [word unclear in original document, perhaps "witnesses"] of Metz appeared in person Pierre Daigu, shepherd, residing in this city, who contracted with Raphaël Lévy, a Jew residing in Boulay, to keep, tend, and feed a flock of white animals belonging to said Raphaël for a period of one full year from the day and month of the present document and to return the flock to said Raphaël at the end of one year in the best possible condition, said Daigu promising to that end to do all that a good and faithful shepherd is obliged to do, in return for which said Raphaël promised to pay him and deliver the sum of three hundred Metz francs, half in six months and the other half at the end of the year, plus a pair of shoes; in addition he will be allowed to select from the flock half a dozen lambs to profit from them as he sees fit, said lambs to be claimed at the end of the year. In recognition of which the parties respectively pledge their movable and immovable possessions present and to come. Done and concluded in Metz this twenty-second day of October one thousand six hundred sixty-five, before noon, and said Daigu declared that he could not write or sign this document, whereas Raphaël signed in Hebrew characters. [illegible] to provide said Daigu with room and board during said period.
>
> [Daigu's mark]
>
> Rafael bar Yitzhak ha-Levi z'l[20]

In January 1670, Raphaël Lévy died at the stake, leaving a wife and three children. The children's fates are mentioned in the Metz *Memorbuch*, which, oddly, does not recount Raphaël's tragic end:[21]

> —Righteous and cherished Jacob, son of the martyr, the *haver* Raphaël Lévi, who lived in righteousness and traded fairly. [...] His wife and sons made a gift in his behalf to the hospital. Deceased and buried on Tuesday 23 Lyyar 5447 [May 6, 1687]
>
> —Cherished Reizele, daughter of the martyr, the *haver* Raphaël Lévi, may God avenge his blood, who lived in righteousness. [...] Her husband made a gift to the hospital in her behalf. Deceased and buried on Friday, 26 Tichri 5451 [September 29, 1690]

—The righteous and worthy Juda Leib, son of the martyr, the *haver* Raphaël Lévi. May God avenge his blood, who traded fairly and served in the hospital. [...] He went to the royal court several times to petition on behalf of the community. [...] His sons made a gift to the hospital in his behalf. Deceased Sunday and buried Monday 11 Ab 5481 [August 4, 1721].[22]

As a resident of the close-knit Jewish communities that sprang up in many small villages around the city of Metz, Raphaël Lévy embodied a certain social and cultural osmosis among groups that interacted and mingled in ways that fostered relationships of trust and facilitated trade and even solidarity. Although the Lévy affair would put an end to some of these social relationships, others survived. Many witnesses acknowledge that they recognized Raphaël Lévy as "an acquaintance and neighbor" or admitted that they "had seen each other in Boulay and knew their families because they lived in the same place."

Many witnesses lived in Glatigny, Les Étangs, and Boulay and thus had frequent occasion to run into Raphaël Lévy. One such witness was Frémin Moireau, who "knew the accused from having seen him on the road several times." Like other Jewish and non-Jewish men and women who "talked freely" or even gossiped endlessly "on the same stone bench," Raphaël thought he could count on these close relations with neighbors who knew him well to prove his innocence. So when the prosecutor tried to trip him up by accusing him of wearing a coat of a certain color during the alleged abduction of the Le Moyne boy, he confidently responded that his "neighbors can testify that they never saw him wearing a coat of that color."[23] He was sadly mistaken: his neighbors were for the most part of no help to him, except for the young serving girl who lived in Boulay and trusted him to the end, and who agreed without hesitation to carry messages that he tossed from the window of his prison.

*

Although the residents of Boulay lived in detached houses, the streets of the town were really narrow alleyways, so everyone lived cheek by jowl and had rather intimate knowledge of one another's affairs. They kept a close eye on what went on in the village, especially on anything new or unusual. This was also true in other nearby villages. Thus, Jean Poulain, who was a "neighbor of the Jew from Helz, saw and heard a number of Jews arguing all night in the home of said Gédéon [Lévy, an acquaintance of Raphaël's who lived in Helz]," while Jean Jaquet, whose "house was close to Gédéon's," "several times heard other Jews" who came to visit, and Paul Jul observed that "Jews from Metz and Boulay came at all hours and even during the night to home of the Jew from Helz named Gédéon Lévy." In these tiny villages, it was impossible to escape one's neighbors. Such close observation at times heightened suspicions of unusual activity. As we will see, Gédéon Lévy's neighbors hastened to attack him on the basis of their observations of his behavior, which they interpreted as signs of guilt. Familiarity proved incapable of overcoming prejudice; for instance, Marie Royer, the wife of Paul Jul, stated during the trial "that she would not want to be the friend of her Jewish neighbor," Gédéon's wife, with whom she gossiped frequently.

Also worth noting is the intense hostility that a number of women felt toward Raphaël. They played a key role in the prosecution, as if they were even more sensitive than their husbands to the strangeness of the Jews, so "oriental" in their appearance. Some of these women proved to be crucial and unusually vehement witnesses, on whom the prosecution relied for much of the evidence of Raphaël's guilt. They did not hesitate to stir up hatred or repeat their hostile and prejudiced statements ad nauseam. Their aggressiveness helped to drive the trial forward, and when confronted with their own contradictions they stumbled for a moment but then blithely ignored their mistakes and picked up without embarrassment where they had left off.

A case in point is Idote Charpentier, a butcher woman and key witness, who claimed that she had seen Raphaël enter Metz with a child slung over the back of his horse, although she had just given birth and could not see passersby from her window. Another was Marie Royer, who was far more aggressive than her husband. And Marguerite Close and Clémence Paquin literally invented the Schwabe affair out of whole cloth, as we will see later on. Indeed, nine women—whom Raphaël had frequently encountered in everyday life—played a particularly aggressive part in his prosecution.

It was these women, moreover, whose accusations were most explicitly shaped by racial prejudice. For example, Idote Charpentier testified that the little boy she claimed to have seen on the back of Raphaël's horse had blond hair, while the Jew had black hair: "He was a beautiful child, not at all like a child of Jews." In Raphaël's presence she repeated her statement but rather strangely added, without backing off her charge in any way, that she "could not say whether it was the accused who was carrying the aforementioned child; remembers only that said Jew had black hair, as she stated in her deposition." Marguerite Gassin also described the child as blond. On December 2, 1669, she exclaimed, "Alas! A Jew passed by with a very beautiful child," and this struck her as a strange contrast since the Jew was "a big man with black hair." With great assurance she went even further on December 23, when she stated that she "did not get a clear view of the features" of the accused but "only remembered that he had curly black hair quite similar to that of the accused." Of course it was taken for granted that Jews can only have curly black hair, an indelible sign of their alien nature. "Orientalism" magnified this alienness, underscoring the fundamental physical difference between Jews and non-Jews, while "innocent Catholic children" were invariably wreathed in halos of golden blond hair. These orientalist fantasies confused some witnesses; one of them, Oulry Coureur, testified that Abraham Spire had allegedly told her that the child had "been taken by Gypsies." Just imagine Spire, one of the most assimilated Jewish notables in Metz, confiding such a thing to this woman.

So the Jews' Catholic neighbors imagined that they were infallibly set apart by their curly black hair. Their customs and habits also separated them from the community. Furthermore, little Didier's father charged that they cast "spells" and engaged in black magic. Although this was a period in which belief in magic was on the wane, questions were raised throughout the trial about Jewish consultations with practitioners of the black arts. For instance, a servant girl reported that Raphaël had told her that "his son had gone looking for a sorcerer or magician to find the child." Raphaël himself seemed to confirm the presence of a seer while disclaiming knowledge of whether or not Jews had ever consulted him. He testified that "he does not know whether Jews have been to the seer, there having been one in Boulay in the past, but who was now dead." Many witnesses attested to similar contacts. Marie Royer said that "the wife of the accused spoke to her about the seer, she said that it was the accused who had been to see him, and the seer told him that a bit of cloth had been found," alluding to one of the pieces of little Didier's clothing that had been retrieved. Despite Raphaël's denials, this allegation dogged him to the end. As late as January 16, 1670, he was repeatedly asked under torture whether he had consulted the seer who had supposedly glimpsed the shred of Didier's clothing:

> Asked why someone wrote to him to put a small bit of straw under his tongue when he went to the criminal chamber and to say certain words that were left blank in the French translation, whether these were not characters and charms,
>
> Said that it is true that someone sent him the aforementioned piece of straw, but he threw it away and never used it; and as for the words, they were not charms but a prayer that might help to alleviate the torture,
>
> Asked whether the Jews who took charge of his defense had consulted the seer to find out where the child was, what that meant, and whether there were seers among them,
>
> Said that he did not know whether Jews had consulted the seer, there having been one in Boulay in the past, but who was now dead.

Raphaël was thus accused of using "charms," especially since he admitted having received the piece of straw, although he claimed not to have used it. When the prosecutor asked him to explain the meaning of a statement he had written in Hebrew—"Jew me, live Jew, Jew live, dead Jew, Jew dead"—Raphaël assured him that it was not a "charm" but simply a prayer: the words were "not charms but a prayer that might help to alleviate the torture." That same day, Gédéon Lévy was also asked repeatedly under torture whether he had consulted the seer for help in finding little Didier's clothing. This was a crucial question in view of the fact that Gédéon was in prison because he had been seen in the forest of Glatigny shortly before certain items of Didier's clothing were found, and he was suspected of having brought them there to help in Raphaël's defense. Under torture, Gédéon invoked the name of God and adamantly denied having consulted the seer. Jews were thus suspected by their neighbors of using sorcery and charms. This association with worrisome magical practices made them outcasts, as witches had been in the past, despite everyday social relations with people outside their group.

Despite this spatial and even social proximity and familiarity, everything in fact separated the Jews of Boulay, Helz, and Metz from their non-Jewish neighbors. They belonged to separate and rival social universes and to starkly contrasting cultural milieus. In seventeenth-century France, the Jews still formed a separate, homogeneous, endogamous group. Some actors in the drama were joined by family ties: Lazare Wilstath was Mayer Schwabe's nephew, and Marc Wittlich was his son-in-law. Since Jews were barred from most professions, they stood out from their Christian neighbors by their high degree of specialization in activities related to commerce and finance. The individuals who figure at every stage of the case all exercised similar professions. Mayer Birier, who lived in Metz, was a horse trader, as were Raphaël Lévy, one Lambert (first name unknown), Abraham Morhange, Lazare Wilstath, and Abraham Spire, who also sold fodder to the army. Gédéon Lévy was a butcher in Helz, and Mayer Schwabe, a merchant, lived there as well; Aaron Halphen, also a merchant, lived in Metz. Several of these men were well-to-do notables and played the role of *parnas*, or syndics representing the Jewish population to the authorities; among them were Schwabe, Wilstath, Spire, and Aaron Halphen, who was the son of Goudchaux Halphen, one of Metz's wealthy syndics, who held that post for more than thirty years. Thus a number of the Jews in the case were, thanks to their professions, relatively well off compared to their non-Jewish neighbors, who were engaged in quite different lines of work.

Those who accused Raphaël Lévy and Mayer Schwabe were, in contrast, the embodiment of *la France profonde*, hardworking, inventive, and tough but unfamiliar with the laws of exchange, interest, and the market. Jean Poulain was a blacksmith in the village of Helz, while Didier Tixerand did the same kind of work in the hamlet of Les Étangs. Sébastien Moreau and Jean Humbert were both masons in Glatigny. Among the accusers were also two weavers, Nicolas Boêmey and Humbert Brouillard; and three woodcutters, Frédéric Moreau and Claudin Massat, who lived near Les Étangs, and Nicaize, who lived in Helz. Martin Cuny was a cobbler (as were two witnesses for the defense, Jean Mouseler and Jean Cordonnier). Mathieu Demange was a farmer, as were Jaquemin Noz and Le Polot. Jean Christophe, also known as Daffrl, was a tavernkeeper who lived in Les Étangs. Three anonymous charcoal burners also figured on the list of accusers. The presence of minor justice officials is also noteworthy: Jean Jaquet, a sergeant of police, and Nicolas Gergone, a bailiff, both lived in Helz.

On the other hand, some of the accusers belonged to almost the same social milieu as their victim: Jean Maréchal was a butcher in Les Étangs and Jacques Moitrier a bourgeois merchant in Metz. Jean Bachelay and Antoine Clausquin were both master tailors in Metz; and finally, Oulry Coureur was a horse trader. Only this latter group, few in number, could be construed as rivals of Raphaël Lévy who might have felt threatened by Jewish competition. Most of the accusers were situated at the bottom of the social hierarchy and engaged in manual labor, so such considerations would not have concerned them.

Still, differences of economic or professional status may exacerbate ties of dependency between neighbors who are in frequent contact but debtors or creditors of one another. Such actors may be close yet preserve distinctive identities and belong to distinctly different cultural universes. In this society, which had only recently emerged from the Middle Ages, there existed a surprising diversity of socioeconomic ties, which gradually emerged as the trial proceeded. These ties created many thinly disguised grudges, or even deep hatreds, sometimes stemming from very old conflicts, which suddenly resurfaced in the testimony of the witnesses. As an example, on January 18, 1670, Mayer Schwabe refuted the testimony of the peasant Mathieu Demange by saying that "said witness is his mortal enemy because said Lambert, Jew, brother-in-law of the accused, sold horses roughly nine years ago to said witness against his promise to pay, and as said witness did not pay the price of said horses contained in said promise, the accused was forced to put the furniture of said witness up for sale, since which time said witness has always wished him ill."

The same day, Gérard Mangeot, one of Mayer Schwabe's most vehement accusers, was described by Schwabe as "his mortal enemy for having refused to lend money against collateral, in particular on an item of gray clothing, and that because of this refusal said witness had even threatened the accused several times with a beating." During the same confrontation, Schwabe contended that the cobbler Martin Cuny was "an insignificant person who for five *sols* would swear a hundred false oaths and once even threatened the accused and his wife because they refused to give him a thirty-*sol* coin." Clearly, among the witnesses who testified that a macabre ceremony had taken place at the home of Mayer Schwabe—testimony that proved essential in the Lévy affair in that it introduced the question of desecration of the host—many were in his debt. Their repeated accusations were therefore tainted by the economic dependency of these cobblers, gardeners, and farmers on the man they accused, Mayer Schwabe, a particularly well-to-do syndic and privileged notable who no longer wore the notoriously degrading yellow hat and who was on his way to integration into the local community.

The tailor Antoine Clausquin occupied a central place in these networks of exchange, from which, as we have seen, deep frustrations arose. A careful reading of the trial record reveals two independent stories that come together by way of Clausquin: the alleged murder of the Le Moyne child and the session of black magic alleged to have taken place earlier in the home of Mayer Schwabe, during which a number of Jews had supposedly attacked a human form. In fact, Clausquin served as an indispensable intermediary between Jews and non-Jews. He was at the heart of the network of buyers and sellers of horses that included both the accused and their accusers. Aaron Halphen testified that Clausquin "was much given to wine and sometimes bought horses from him," while Clausquin accused Halphen of taking him into a house to bandage his wounds after he was injured by Schwabe. Meanwhile, Clausquin's wife denounced Mayer Birier, another horse trader, for "several times wiping Clausquin's blood with his handkerchief." Furthermore, Jaquemin Noz, known as Le Polot, purchased horses on credit from Abraham Morhange by way of Clausquin, while the Metz merchant Jacques Moitrier asked Clausquin to go see Lambert, Schwabe's brother-in-law, who was also a horse trader, to find out if he would accept the price he had "bargained" for a horse. All of these actors were thus engaged in an intense network of exchanges revolving around the purchase and sale of horses, prominent members of which included a number of Jewish merchants, and in which the central figure was Clausquin, the hero of the Schwabe affair, which occurred on Good Friday and greatly contributed to accrediting the idea of a ritual murder allegedly committed by Raphaël Lévy.

Others who participated in this same network of exchanges contributed equally to merging the two affairs. For instance, Martin Cuny alleged that Mayer Birier had attempted to treat Clausquin's wounds. Cuny also accused Schwabe of holding black masses in his home. Furthermore, Birier had "several times sold horses" to Raphaël Lévy, who stated that he had not paid for them and was "the most brutal fellow in the world." Gérard Mangeot and Mathieu Demange also attacked both Raphaël Lévy and Mayer Schwabe in similar terms. Although the two cases were widely separated in time and seemingly unrelated, making the insistent evocation of the Schwabe affair during the Lévy trial seem incongruous, we see that in fact the two were related via individuals who purchased horses sold by Lévy and Schwabe. What is more, it was Jaquemin Noz, also in debt from having purchased horses, who was the first to point out that the Schwabe affair occurred on the Day of Trumpets (the Jewish Rosh Hashanah, or New Year), thus establishing a link between the two dramas because the same "trumpets" (*shofars*) were the reason for Raphaël Lévy's trip to Metz. Thus the Jewish religious symbolism in the background of these two unrelated affairs helped to establish a link between them: both were seen as attacks on the Catholic order—the vital symbolic order in the good city of Metz, which was home to a particularly muscular version of Counterreformation Christianity.

Money was thus central to imaginary representations of relations between Jews and non-Jews—money and also credit (debts, repayments, interest). These inegalitarian relationships underpinned both affairs and gave Catholic debtors an incentive to demonize their Jewish creditors, perhaps in the hope of seeing their debts wiped out along with their creditors. Social relationships, intimacy, face-to-face dealings, and mutual knowledge in no way hindered the spread of prejudice, hatred, and lies in this deeply Catholic and politically uncertain region where, in the absence of a normal state, everything could change overnight. The belief that money in the hands of Jews was all-powerful provided a favorable ground for the wildest rumors, which were tirelessly propagated by witnesses quick to expose the alleged maneuvers of Jewish notables, who, they claimed, offered to bribe them or buy their silence in order to help Lévy and Schwabe. To be sure, Raphaël admitted having given money to the servant, but in gratitude for carrying messages, not to suborn perjury. Gédéon Lévy also admitted that the Jews of Metz had promised a hundred silver *écus* to anyone who found the child's body, but this was to prove Raphaël Lévy's innocence and not to bribe witnesses. Yet this confession confirmed that money had been used for what was portrayed as a corrupt purpose.

Rumors of corruption continued to spread, though based on hearsay without the slightest tangible proof. Impressed by the power of money, some witnesses nevertheless firmly believed in what they heard. Some of these stories drew on ancestral prejudices deeply rooted in collective memory. These emerged from the depths intact, as when Raphaël was accused of winking in a certain way or making a certain sign with his fingers—gestures that had long been linked to Jews and their money, signaling transactions from which they would profit. Here we enter the realm of myth, belief, and unsubstantiated assertion. For instance, according to Jean Bachelay, as the investigation proceeded in November 1669, "the rumor was that the Jews had given money to one of the cavalrymen so that he would not testify against" Lévy. Anne Gadelet "heard from cavalrymen that the Jews promised money to Pillard, a cavalryman, so that he wouldn't say anything." Similarly, Anne Willebert "heard that Raphaël's son offered the cavalryman favors." Later, Jean Poulain also "heard from Mangeotte, Georges Mangin's wife, that Gédéon Lévy and the Jews of Metz had offered them thirty *pistoles* to look for the child." Nicolas Gergone "heard from Jean Gondrecourt that the Jew from Helz named Gédéon Lévy had offered said Gondrecourt a sum of money to look for the child." Or again, Jean Bachelay "heard from Benedict Auchembourg, Jew, that he had gone with Marc Wittlich to offer peasants some money to look for the child." Gondrecourt testified on December 2, 1669, that "in the middle of the village of Luc he met a Jew from Helz, whose name he did not know but whom he recognized because he had seen him often," who asked him "to search for shreds of the child's clothing or remains, and that he would give him satisfaction for his trouble, to which he responded that he didn't want anything. . . . heard that the son of said Raphaël told the cavalryman that everything in their house was at his disposal." Marguerite Jeanne, the wife of vintner George Aubertin, maintained that "two Jews from Metz, on horseback, whose names she did not know and whom she would have difficulty recognizing, told her that if her husband could find something, they would give him twenty gold *louis*." It will be clear that within this small world of neighborly relations and close cohabitation, Jews were still anonymous; their neighbors met them repeatedly without learning their names.

In the many depositions related to the Lévy case, we also find rumors involving actors who did not belong to these narrow neighborhood communities. On November 19, 1669, Pierre Menue, known as Larie, a cavalryman, "heard from Sainte-Marie, cavalryman, speaking to his comrade Payer, also a cavalryman in the same company, who allegedly told him that the Jew prisoner, in speaking to his comrade, had told him that if he kept quiet he would want for nothing." This farrago of approximations and suppositions was treated as evidence. Rumors were bandied about and passed on without the slightest proof. Anonymous gossip was accepted by the judges as if it came from the most reliable sources. On January 29, 1660, the prosecutor expressed his belief that the Jews "want to corrupt or prevent depositions," adding that they were even "selling what they have at low prices in order to turn everything into money and deceive the Christians from whom they have received collateral or cash"—an assertion subsequently repeated by the parlement itself.

The highest local authorities thus joined in denouncing the power of money, which enabled the Jews to "deceive the Christians," to corrupt them by buying their souls. Ultimately, according to this logic, money even served as an equivalent for the blood spilled by the Jews, which was purchased for cold, hard cash: Martin Cuny in fact claimed that the Jews had offered money to Clausquin but that he had responded by saying "he would never sell his blood." Clausquin, at the heart of all these intrigues, gave clear voice to the link that obsessed many Catholics and ultimately led to the Jews' being sentenced to damnation. Clearly, neighborly relations changed nothing. Mutual knowledge, commercial relationships, and the trust that these implied proved almost worthless; once the charge of ritual murder reappeared, prejudices deeply rooted in collective memory returned to the surface, irrevocably consigning the Jewish neighbor to his doom.

Three The Social and Mental Universe of the Jews

The Jews of Metz, according to the intendant Turgot (writing in 1698), "are very religious and scrupulously respectful of their ceremonies, observing the Sabbath from Friday night until the same time on Saturday, during which time, ignoring pressing needs, even for the service, they do not do any work; indeed, they abstain from all transactions, while observing all other holidays, fasts, and ceremonies." The Jewish community met with the hostility of its neighbors. It obeyed its own laws and traditions and tolerated no neglect of its rules. The Jews of Metz, like those of Boulay, with whom they were closely associated, adhered strictly to their rites. They inhabited the small, insalubrious quarter of Saint-Ferroy, and on certain days, such as Sundays and important Catholic holidays, they were not allowed to leave the ghetto, even to practice their professions, because the sight of them on such occasions was deemed an offense to Catholic eyes. Religion lay at the heart of their values; strict respect for daily prayers and observance of dietary restrictions and religious holidays governed their existence.

This attachment to ancestral customs durably shaped the life of the community. Almost thirty years after the Lévy affair, in 1699, Gluckel Hameln, a very orthodox Jew, left Hamburg to marry in Metz, a city that she admired for its "fine pious community [...] all the *parnassim* [elected leaders of the community] were men worthy of the greatest respect. It never occurred to anyone to wear a wig, and no lawsuit between Jews was ever taken to a non-Jewish court."[1] In her memoirs, Hameln describes the religious atmosphere that prevailed in Metz, where the Jewish community gathered around "erudite" rabbis from Vienna and Prague and sent its children to be educated at the Talmudic school. She moved to Metz in order to marry a wealthy syndic. Although he eventually went bankrupt, her marriage made her a member of the closed circle of Jewish notables, especially after her daughter Esther married Moïse Schwabe, the grandson of Mayer Schwabe, who had been imprisoned in connection with the Lévy affair after being accused of organizing a macabre Good Friday ceremony intended to mock the crucifixion of Christ.[2]

Hence Hameln soon became familiar with the history of the Jewish community of Metz, which was still haunted by memories of the Lévy affair almost thirty years later. Her enthusiastic descriptions of her wealthy circle of peers do not accurately capture the reality of the Jewish community, many of whose members lived close to the poverty line. Nevertheless, her memoirs give us "a puritanical portrait of Jewish life" that accurately reflects the mores of the endogamous circle of orthodox Jews, who apparently did form a "pious" and "holy" community.[3] Somewhat later, moreover, Abbé Grégoire referred to Metz as a place where "they [the Jews] were allowed to retain most of their customs, because in their case religion influenced all aspects of the law, down to the most minute details of public order." He also had the Jews of Metz in mind when he said that "where there are no syndics . . . there is no Jewish community." He predicted, moreover, that "the Jews will be obliged to learn the national language. . . . The use of the vulgar tongue for religious rites does not contradict their principles."[4] From these comments it is clear that the Jews of Metz were able to preserve their orthodox community well into the eighteenth century.

The Jews of Metz were a community apart, governed by beliefs and mores that left them largely untouched by the changing culture around them, and in particular by the French and German Enlightenment, which would later lead to a radical transformation of European Judaism. Although *Haskala* (the Jewish Enlightenment) was slow to make inroads in Metz, in 1666, three years before the arrest of Raphaël Lévy, the Jews of the city "did not escape the wave of messianic fervor that washed over all the Jewish communities of Europe in the wake of the false messiah Sabbatai Zevi."[5] Piety, regular religious study, extremely strict sexual morals, a sense of solidarity with the group and its history, honesty in commercial relations—all of these things shaped the mental universe of the Jews. There was no separation between the religious and civil spheres. Teaching remained strictly religious. At the basic level it meant learning the rudiments of Hebrew, the Bible, and the Talmud, but it was not until 1690 that young men were required to attend the *heder* (Hebrew school). The Jews of Metz and Boulay expressed themselves in Yiddish transcribed into Hebrew characters, which tended to limit communication with non-Jewish neighbors.[6] Basic problems of translation would emerge during the trial, and they had an important influence on the outcome, as we will see in due course.

The trial itself would reveal a good deal about the daily life and values of the Jews of Metz and Boulay. The statements of the witnesses disclosed habits of mind and action that tell us a lot about the limits that tradition imposed on the humblest individuals. As we have seen, Raphaël Lévy was a pious Jew who respected the Torah, a *khover* (an honorific connoting a high level of Jewish learning), though he was not himself a scholar. Although he was given the title "rabbi," as someone who inspires respect, it was simply because of his wisdom and strict discipline, his involvement in the life of the small Jewish community, his concern for others, and his heroism. He was a simple livestock merchant. He had certainly been a pupil in a *heder*, like many other young Jewish boys in this period.

From the testimony recorded by court scribes during the trial, we can form a better idea of his personality. He signed all of his statements in Hebrew letters as "Rafael bar Yitzhak Ha-levi." Mayer Schwabe also signed in Hebrew: "By me, Meir, son of the *haver* Abraham Schwabe of blessed memory." It was also in Hebrew, using the same formula, which he signed in place of the witness Clémence Paquin, the wife of Antoine Clausquin, the most zealous of the accusers, who was unable to write her own name: "Said accused signed and not said witness, who cannot write." All the Jews who testified, such as Aaron Halphen and Mayer Birier, signed in Hebrew, the latter in a more orthodox manner as "Meir bar Yakov Yimiha z'l Birier of blessed memory." Gédéon Lévy, who appeared in the anonymous journal under the conventional name Juda Loeb, also signed in Hebrew, "Yuda Levi," and when faced with torture he "promised and swore by the God of Abraham, Isaac, and Jacob that he worshiped the truth." In each case, the clerk was careful to note that the interrogated witness "swore an oath in the usual manner of the Jews," or again, "in the usual manner of people of his nation." Jewish women followed the example of their husbands; Sybille Zay, the wife of Mayer Schwabe, swore "in the way that Jews customarily swear."

We do not know, however, if any of these Jews really knew Hebrew, used it among themselves, or could read, understand, and comment on Hebrew texts. Modest and aware of the limits of his knowledge, Raphaël Lévy acknowledged his inability to cite Hebrew texts to prove that Jews do not abduct children for ritual purposes. To understand the true source of this myth, he testified on December 18, 1669, "one must ask other Jews more learned than he." He admitted that his knowledge of Hebrew was quite rudimentary; he "said that he knows how to read [the characters] but could not explain them." On another occasion, however, when asked to explain a note in which he had written the enigmatic phrase "Jew me, live Jew, Jew live, dead Jew, Jew dead," he stated that he did know how to read and write Hebrew. He also ended his last wishes with the statement "I am Jewish and wish to die Jewish." More commonly, he wrote his notes in Judeo-German using Hebrew characters and occasional Hebrew words. Did he speak fluent French? To be sure, the servant girl, who was favorably disposed toward him, heard him speak to his son in French. But in his plea to parlement, he claimed that "he does not understand French perfectly." The use of Judeo-German seems more natural, and according to the clerk of the court, under torture Gédéon Lévy "invoked God in the German tongue." Obviously, it is not easy to say more on this question or to delve more deeply into the linguistic universe of Raphaël and others like him. What were the respective roles of Judeo-German, French, and the Hebrew that they used systematically to sign their statements?[7]

From his first interrogation, on October 14, 1669, Raphaël Lévy tried to prove his innocence by insisting that he was scrupulous in his observance of the Jewish holidays. After giving his name and place of residence, he immediately stated that if he had gone to Metz, "it was to obtain a trumpet [i.e., a *shofar*, or ram's horn] for the celebration of the [Jewish] Day of Trumpets [Rosh Hashanah, the Jewish New Year] in said village of Boulay, which holiday fell on the next day and began on said day of Wednesday at five o'clock in the evening." His time was meticulously organized around the celebration of Rosh Hashanah, and he was aware of the precise beginning and ending of the holiday. He believed that he could prove his innocence by insisting on his scrupulous respect for the religious timetable. He could not have been where he was accused of being at the time he was said to be there because, as a Jew deeply immersed in Jewish tradition, his schedule was rigorously determined by the preparations for the holiday. He clung to this defense to the very end, refuting the allegations of witnesses who accused him of being in various places at various times for the purpose of kidnapping and killing the Le Moyne child. From the beginning to the end of the trial, his entire defense rested on his repeated insistence that he respected the Jewish holidays. So, for instance, when he was asked during the same interrogation how he knew that he had arrived in Boulay before four o'clock, he said that "their Rosh Hashanah began that day at five o'clock; he would not have dared to be out in the countryside at that hour."[8]

From the beginning of his interrogation, then, Raphaël Lévy gave precise answers to justify his brief journey to Metz. He went there to buy a *shofar* for the holiday service, which would begin at five o'clock in the evening at the Boulay synagogue. He also intended to return to Boulay with some fish and casks of wine. He noted that both the miller's horse and his son's horse were laden with ten to twelve casks each. His own horse carried only two, which explains why he left later than they did, so he would be sure of catching up with them en route. Thus his religious devotion and attachment to ritual—signified not only by his purchase of the *shofar* but also by his transport of a large quantity of wine needed for the communal banquets that would sanctify the new year—stood in his eyes as irrefutable proof that would save him from the fantastic allegation of ritual murder.

A few days later, on October 24, during his second interrogation, Lévy repeated the same story in even greater detail. When asked why he had gone to Metz, he answered "that he had gone there to obtain two casks of wine and a *shofar* for the holiday." He added that he had put the *shofar* "in his pocket, from which it protruded roughly three-quarters of a foot under his tunic." And when asked if he didn't have a cloak to cover it—a crucial detail, because he was suspected of having hidden the child beneath his cloak—he "said no, and that the *shofars* they use in their ceremonies are at most only an aune de Metz [three-quarters of a yard] in length and made of a ram's horn or buck's horn."[9]

Lévy displayed a good deal of knowledge of the *shofar*, whose sound punctuates the very solemn service marking the beginning of the Jewish year. He was perfectly comfortable describing the instrument in detail, believing as he did that its presence in his pocket would serve as proof that he had not committed the murder of which he was suspected. To further bolster his defense, he observed that "the Jews were all supposed to be in the city, in which the respondent would have stayed had he not been obliged to hold services on said day." Under the most extreme torture, on January 16, 1670, shortly before his execution, he repeated this statement: "If it were true that he returned to this city, he would have remained there because of Rosh Hashanah, which began that day at five o'clock in the evening, and he would not have wished to be in the countryside at that hour for any reason whatsoever." He did not understand that his interrogators wanted to cast doubt on everything he said, and he repeated that "it is the truth that he did not descend from his horse and that he had no time to lose because of their holiday, which began at five o'clock in the evening," and that therefore he could not have abducted the child because his feet had not touched ground owing to his haste to return to Boulay, where the Jews of the village were waiting for him. His profound faith and firm position within the orthodox community were offered as proof of his innocence.

Lévy believed that he was well integrated into his community and thought he could count on its support in his dramatic ordeal. He had full confidence in the Jewish notables who were "in charge of their community." He counted on his "friends," whom he named explicitly, such as Mayer Schwabe and Salomon (the Metz cantor), whose support and assistance he expected. He also maintained close ties to the Jews of Trêves, who "come to buy livestock" from him, and with the Jews of Metz, whom he saw regularly. When in Metz, he stayed with Salomon, a central figure in the orthodox community. Lévy thus hoped to escape the nightmare that had befallen him; after all, as a Lorraine subject he could have refused the subpoena of the court, stayed away from Metz, and remained in safety in Boulay, which lay outside the jurisdiction of the Metz courts. But he did not hesitate to return to Metz, because he felt it was his duty to his community. Certain of easily proving his innocence, he wanted to make sure that no shame would attach to his people. As a member of the community, he counted on the solidarity of his co-religionists. In the event, he was deeply disappointed by their cowardice, but he knew nothing of the efforts of those Jews who had gone to Frankfurt to urge the emperor to intervene,[10] or of those who had gone several times to see the prosecutor and chief judge in seeking a quick end to the trial. Nor did he know at that point that several of his friends had tried in vain to locate the body of the child in the hope of proving his innocence.[11]

Raphaël Lévy felt unjustly abandoned at the conclusion of the trial, which he was now certain would end in his condemnation. In his tenth note, he remarked in a tone of helplessness that "I put myself in this wretched situation for the sake of the community." The same comment appears in the dramatic letter that he sent to the prison warden on January 7, 1670, which ends as follows:

> I ask for help in extricating myself from this wretched situation, and I was surprised that I could not speak with my dear wife and child. Since I want to ensure that [...] my dear good wife and my children will have a bit of bread to eat, I will suffer death like a son of Israel and sanctify the name of God. I ask only that my daughter Blimelé, who is engaged, be married. I put myself in this wretched situation for the sake of the community. The great God of Israel will help me, and I desire a Jewish burial, or else I will pardon no one.

On the last day, the notable Seligman and a rabbi, Zanville, came to visit Raphaël Lévy in prison. We do not know the tenor of their discussion, but it is easy to imagine Lévy's bitterness at the extent of his solitude, given his unhesitating sacrifice for his community. The dialogue seems to have ended rapidly, because his pusillanimous co-religionists were afraid for their own safety. We do not know whether Rabbi Yon Fraenkel, a great Talmudist responsible at the time for the Metz community, intervened with the authorities on Lévy's behalf. There is no evidence that would permit such an assertion. From the journal kept by an anonymous Metz Jew, we know only that Raphaël "cried, prayed, and put on phylacteries." On the other hand, there is evidence that the Jews of Metz and the region tried to find the child's remains in order to prove Lévy's innocence. They acted as a unified "community" concerned with the fate of one of their own. Gédéon Lévy readily admitted that Marc Wittlich and Benedict Auchembourg, Jews of Metz whom he identified by their first names only, "told him that they promised one hundred *écus* to anyone who found [the body] and that [the money] would be provided by the Jews of Metz." He admitted that he had offered one hundred silver *écus* or thirty *pistoles* to Nicaize, the woodcutter, and Georges Mangin of Helz, and he did not deny having offered to pay Jean Gondrecourt to find the child while advising him "to say nothing."

Furthermore, during the trial, Oulry Coureur stated he had been told that "the community would assist him and his family" if he helped find the Le Moyne child. And the wife of Gédéon Lévy did not deny that someone had given a silver *écu* to the seer, "all expenses borne by the Jewish community." This testimony contradicts the suggestion that the Jews were passive. Indeed, they tried to find the child in order to refute the charge of ritual murder and prove Raphaël Lévy's innocence. Many of them took part in the search and offered to pay for the help of people who knew every nook and cranny of the forest. To be sure, their efforts risked being turned against Raphaël, because the Jews were accused in the trial of attempting to destroy evidence and pay witnesses for their silence. Still, Gédéon Lévy, Wittlich, and Auchembourg, among other Jews, seem to have done everything they could to help Raphaël Lévy, even at the risk of being charged themselves with obstruction of justice and destruction of evidence. Lévy, languishing in his cell, apparently knew nothing of these efforts. He felt helpless and abandoned. It is easy to understand his reluctance to forgive. He would never learn of the statement by the Jews of Metz, recorded on April 18, 1670, by the Council of State, according to which

> said supplicants, who have no intention of defending the cause of a foreign Jew, would have remained silent, despite the harm to themselves due to this sentence, had their enemies not seized upon it to oppress and ruin them as witnesses against Raphaël Lévy. [...] He was placed in a dungeon, where he languished for more than three months, although there was no sufficient proof against him. [...] The principal supplicants, some of whom were imprisoned without being told the cause of their detention, and the others are in flight to avoid similar treatment, in view of the fact that in Metz today it is enough to be a Jew charged with a crime to be convicted.

"Said supplicants," including Mayer Schwabe among others, had therefore taken risks to help Raphaël Lévy. They were hardly passive, indifferent, or cowardly. Yet such solidarity could not be taken for granted when it came to a "foreign Jew," even if business dealings brought him into close contact with the Metz community. To them, Raphaël Lévy remained a "foreign Jew," and according to the statement they would have preferred to "remain silent" about his case, "despite the harm to themselves" due to his conviction. Attacks by enemies out to "ruin" them compelled them to speak out and openly assert Raphaël's innocence. Unfortunately, Raphaël himself would never learn of this.

In the condemned man's ultimate message to the warden, he openly avowed the intensity of his faith and his devotion to strict orthodoxy and to the Jewish community. He said that he intended to die in a manner worthy of "a son of Israel" and asked for "a Jewish burial" as the price of his forgiveness. At the end of Raphaël's ninth note, carried from the prison by the serving girl, he wrote the enigmatic sentence quoted earlier, which illustrates his quasi-mystical engagement and passion: "Jew me, live Jew, Jew live, dead Jew, Jew dead." When he was asked on December 18, 1669, to explain what those words meant, and whether they might not be a "charm or characters to stop the pain of torture," he "said no, that it was a prayer." To bear up under repeated torture, Raphaël prayed. When his legs were broken in the course of "ordinary" torture, he "said, crying out and invoking the name of God, that he had told the truth." When the torturer continued on to "extraordinary" torture, by attaching heavier weights to his feet before once again raising his body off the ground and then dropping him quickly "lest he die from his torments," Raphaël "said that he did not want to damn his soul, that he wanted to go to heaven, and that he had told the truth."

In this tragic situation, Lévy's faith in Judaism enabled him to face the charges against him. On January 7, 1670, he flew into a rage against the prosecutor, to whom he referred as "Homan." Later that day, he said that by this he meant "man." But was he perhaps referring to Haman, who threatened the Jewish people in the Book of Esther and was the archetype of the wicked official in Jewish tradition? This might imply a link between Haman and Christ, since the hanging of Haman corresponds to the Catholic Easter and not to the Jewish holiday of Purim. This parallel would reverse the chronology; the murder is supposed to have occurred on the eve of Rosh Hashanah, but its full meaning emerges only when we recognize the significance in the trial of the strange ceremony presumed to have taken place at Mayer Schwabe's home on Good Friday, which I described earlier.

This ceremony came to assume such importance in Raphaël's trial that the prosecutor asked him at several points to explain its meaning, implicitly suggesting a link among Good Friday, Purim, and Yom Kippur. Accordingly, it was reasonable for Raphaël to see the pitiless prosecutor as a latter-day Haman, bent on his execution. In a remarkable short article, Cecil Roth called attention to the coincidence between the dates of Purim and Good Friday that occurs in certain years: "In consequence, it happens with relative frequency that the traditional Jewish carnival season—the sole occasion for a certain degree of licensed libertinism in the Jewish calendar—can coincide approximately with the most solemn period of the Christian year."[12] Christians might be tempted to believe that Purim festivities were in fact a blasphemous parody of the Crucifixion, allegedly signifying a Jewish predilection for ritual murder. And this might be the origin of the belief that Haman, the butt of so much mockery, was a symbol of Christ, since the day on which Jews celebrate the death of Haman is also (in some years) the same day on which Christians remember the crucifixion of Christ.[13]

Drawing upon the deepest recesses of the culture in which he lived, Raphaël Lévy somehow guessed what the trial would reveal, namely, that confusion existed between distinct moments in the calendar, and in particular between the Christian holidays of Good Friday and Easter, when ritual murders were supposed to take place, and the Jewish holidays of Pesach (Passover) and Purim, and therefore saw his persecutor as another Haman.

To the end, Raphaël proclaimed his attachment to Israel and vehemently refused to convert, as the priest who accompanied him to the stake proposed. In his final moments, and in the presence of the royal prosecutor, on January 17, 1670, Raphaël Lévy screamed:

> "O! Your Excellency, I am finished." Whereupon I replied that he should convert and think of saving his soul by following the advice of Father Daras, the priest of this city, and of the guardian of the Capuchin fathers

> and his companion, who were there to exhort him, and he answered me in a tone of voice indicating anger and swearing in the holy name of God, saying that he had not wanted to say under torture everything that he knew for fear of embarrassing many people, concluding, "Never mind, I am a Jew, I want to die a Jew."

We will never know what Raphaël Lévy meant by the strange confession that there were many people whom he did not want to embarrass. We can only reiterate the solidity of his convictions, the firmness of his faith, which impelled him to express his wish in "anger" to die a Jew and to do so in the presence of both his persecutors and his co-religionists; failing this, he refused to pardon anyone. His indignant refusal to convert manifested itself more than once; when Louis Anne, the translator of Lévy's notes (a Jew who had converted to Christianity and was previously known, curiously enough, as Raphaël Lévy), translated certain passages in such a way as to prove his guilt, Raphaël rejected his testimony on the grounds that he was "suspect because he had been of the Jewish faith" and abandoned it by converting. He thus became a potential enemy, and his translation inevitably reflected his ill will.[14]

In this close-knit milieu, in which Jews rubbed elbows with converts like the two translators who were assigned to make Raphaël's words comprehensible and who knowingly distorted what he had written in order to conform to the prosecution's theory of the case, Lévy's angry refusal to convert indicates his attachment to his people. His loyalty to his wife and children, which he mentioned several times, gave him the strength to resist. According to Jewish tradition, the family was foremost among all social ties, and Lévy showed concern to the very end for his wife's fate and for the future of his daughter Blimelé, who was engaged to be married. He wanted to be sure her marriage would take place in order to ensure that the tradition would be passed on from one generation to the next. The word *kalle* (or *kalla*) was the word he instinctively chose to refer to his engaged daughter—proof that he had at least some knowledge of Hebrew. As he himself put it, "*kalle* means wife, which he brought up because of his daughter, who is engaged." From the Metz *Memorbuch*, moreover, we know that Blimelé did marry, that she had children, and that in keeping with Jewish tradition one of those children was also named Blimelé, the name of her grandmother,

Raphaël's wife, who in her distress was able to ensure transmission of the name across the generations.

The anonymous Jew's journal emphasized the religious implications of Raphaël's behavior during the trial. He tells us that during torture, "when he came close to losing his soul on account of his great suffering, they tried to make him drink wine to fortify himself, but he refused because it wasn't *kosher*" (pure). As the executioner prepared to set fire to the wood piled around the stake to which Raphaël had walked in dignity, he removed the victim's phylacteries,[15] which the "pious man" wanted to have with him as he faced death. "And so it was," the anonymous Jew continued in his invaluable journal, "that his soul was extinguished in sanctity and purity with the help of God on Saturday *Parachat Vayerah*. [...] His soul went to rejoin the Lord, who accepted it as a holy sacrifice." The death of "the pious man," as the journal writer refers to him repeatedly, stirred the heavens themselves, symbolizing the wrath of God:

> I have heard several people worthy of belief say that a great windstorm descended on Metz that day. God of Israel, be jealous of Thy Holy Name and let us not succumb to false accusations. We allow ourselves to be slaughtered, burned, and roasted for the sake of Thy Holy Name, as it is written. May his righteousness serve the cause of Israel, and may it please God to deliver us from similar accusations and deliver us soon from exile. [...] It was clear that the soul of the holy man was pleasing to God. [...] For that reason his name was changed and he was given the *khover* and commemorated along with the other holy sons of Israel.[16]

Raphaël Lévy, who is described throughout the anonymous journal as "the pious man," now became a saint (*kadosch*) in the eyes of his co-religionists and was granted the honorific "rabbi" after his martyrdom. The journal—which must have been written at the time of the affair, given its detailed knowledge of events (despite the author's obvious lack of knowledge of the trial documents and interrogation reports themselves)—is an invaluable document for understanding the religiosity of the Jews of Metz and the surrounding region. Written in Judeo-German but in Hebrew characters, it begins thus:

> The man Raphaël of Boulay was burned in the city of Metz to sanctify the holy name of God, wrongly accused, because of a Catholic village child who was lost between Glatigny and Metz, and it was alleged that

> Raphaël had taken the child to Metz. Because of this indictment, the [Jewish] community of Metz found itself in great danger. But the great miracles that God, praised be His name, performed by His grace are indescribable, and we were miraculously saved. [...] The reader will discover as he proceeds that everything had a reason or produced a good. We wrote in German so that every man, woman, boy, and girl might read of the many miracles of God, praised be His name, and how he saved us from the enemies of Israel. Let each person therefore take this case as an example of how to serve God, praised be His name, in fear and with all his soul, until the coming of the Messiah. Amen.[17]

Written in Judeo-German rather than Hebrew, the latter a language that relatively uneducated men and women generally did not speak at the time, the journal is suffused with faith, veneration of God, and anticipation of the Messiah, despite the catastrophic episode of Sabbatai Zevi, which apparently left a lasting impression on the people of the region. The various phases of the affair are arrayed in the journal according to a religious chronology. Just as Raphaël, in his defense, reckoned time in terms of the days and hours of the Jewish new year, the author of the journal meticulously retraced the episodes of the story not only in terms of the Jewish calendar, which he knew intimately, but also in relation to successive Torah readings. In his very first sentence, he puts down the time of Raphaël Lévy's departure from Boulay for Metz as "the eve of Rosh Hashanah [New Year's Day], 430, according to the little calendar," that is, Wednesday, September 25, 1669. He wrote that it was "on Wednesday, 7 Tishri," that is, October 2, that a rumor about the abduction of the son of a "Catholic peasant" began to spread, and "on Thursday, 8 Tishri," October 3, that this peasant went to Metz along with his wife. "On Sunday, the day after Yom Kippur," October 6, the intendant summoned Raphaël to Metz, and when Raphaël answered that he could not come immediately, the intendant informed him "that he did not have to appear until Thursday, the first day of Succoth." And so it was that "after leaving the synagogue on Thursday, the first day of Succoth," Raphaël answered the intendant's summons. The narrative proceeds in this way throughout, with dates given in terms of Torah portions and Jewish holidays. After Raphaël returned to Boulay with the permission of the intendant, the lieutenant of police "notified him that he must appear without fail, since the holiday and Sabbath were now over. [...] Raphaël resolved to sanctify the holy name [that is, to offer himself in sacrifice] in order to save the house of Israel. In any case, he believed that he ran no risk because he was innocent. He therefore went, on the second day of the lesser holidays of Succoth, to see the lieutenant of police."

Clearly, the anonymous Jew's narrative of the case rests entirely on a religious chronology. The child's remains are discovered on Tuesday, 3 Kislev. On 9 Kislev the brain, bones, and clothing are brought to Raphaël in his cell. On 18 Tebeth the child's father files a complaint. On Friday, 25 Tebeth, Raphaël is taken to the torture chamber and then to the stake. On Saturday, Parachat Vayerah, Mayer Schwabe is interrogated. On Wednesday, Rosh Rodesh Schevat, the parlement meets to hear his case. The last imprisoned Jews are finally released after the king intervenes. The account ends with this invocation: "May God help his people Israel in the future, may he preserve them from all wicked indictments, and may he send the Messiah soon, in our time. Amen."[18]

Thus the journal ends as it began, with an invocation of the Messiah, whose imminent coming was the writer's expressed hope. The trial documents and the journal kept by an unknown Metz Jew thus afford us a glimpse of the mental universe of pious Jews such as Raphaël Lévy.

Four The Myth of Ritual Murder

In an area beset, as we have seen, by much fear and uncertainty, early on Wednesday afternoon, September 25, 1669, Mangeotte Villemin, the wife of Gilles Le Moyne, a wheelwright in the small village of Glatigny, on the road from Boulay to Metz, went to the fountain some two hundred meters outside the village to do her washing. On her way there, she noticed that her son Didier, age three, whom she had allowed to follow along behind her at his own pace, had disappeared. She ran from one place to another and enlisted the help of her husband and neighbors in the search for the child, but in vain. Witnesses, including a cavalryman on his way from Metz and a resident of that city who lived near the gate known as the Porte des Allemands, claimed to have seen Raphaël Lévy on horseback with a small child. Before long, the traditional charge was raised once more: the Jews had kidnapped a small Christian child.

This legend, which had emerged from the depths of the Middle Ages but which had somewhat faded from view since the Trent affair, was suddenly revived. The context was somewhat unusual, however. Most accusations of ritual murder (as in Norwich, Würzburg, Blois, and Trent) coincided with the crucifixion of Christ at the Christian Easter and explicitly referred to that event, whereas this latest charge was made in September, on Rosh Hashanah, the day marking the start of the Jewish New Year. Furthermore, previous allegations (in Würzburg, Gloucester, and Blois) had been associated with a river or stream,[1] while the events in Lorraine, despite the minor role of the fountain, occurred mainly within a rather treacherous forest through which many of the actors in the drama traveled regularly. The Lévy affair began in a dark wood, which still exists. Little Didier suddenly vanished from a clearing in this vast expanse of woodland. The village of Glatigny sits in a draw, and from the town fountain, whose location can still be dimly made out, a trail leads up to the Boulay road, where the forest begins.

The myth of ritual murder had long haunted the German-speaking regions of the Holy Roman Empire, along with Poland; but in France, where it had been forgotten for centuries, it now suddenly reemerged. It did so, moreover, precisely in this no-man's-land, between French- and German-speaking territories, and was directed against Jews who spoke Judeo-German, a language incomprehensible to most of the local population—a tongue that was mysterious, troubling, and alien, like the Jews themselves, who lived their daily lives in keeping with the dictates of orthodoxy.

The time has come to consider the narrative in detail.[2] On Wednesday, September 25, Raphaël Lévy left the small town of Boulay with his son Lion and a miller. The three set out for Metz to buy wine, supplies, and a *shofar* for the Jewish New Year celebration. At ten in the morning, Raphaël and his companions reached the city, which they entered at the same time as a Lorraine cavalryman. Their intention was to return home after lunch. Lévy sent his son to look for the miller, who was waiting for them at the inn, in order to suggest that they should leave immediately for Boulay. The pair's horses were heavily laden, while Raphaël's was not, so that he could easily catch up with them. He left the city shortly after one in the afternoon and caught up with the other two travelers in the woods between Glatigny and Les Étangs, where at around three in the afternoon they encountered two cobblers from Boulay headed toward Metz. In Les Étangs, Raphaël visited the blacksmith, to whom he owed money, and then the three men hastened to Boulay, where they arrived around four o'clock. Rosh Hashanah services began an hour later.

It was not until the following Wednesday, October 2, that a rumor began to circulate: a peasant from Glatigny had lost his son. Apparently, he and his wife were accusing Raphaël Lévy of kidnapping the boy. The next day, October 3, Gilles Le Moyne and his wife, the parents of the vanished child, went to Metz to file charges against Raphaël. They based their accusation on the word of a cavalryman, who claimed to have seen Raphaël with a child on the withers of his horse on his way to Metz. Shortly thereafter, Raphaël was summoned to Metz by the intendant, who had been assigned to lead the investigation on behalf of the king. He went to the city and told the intendant that he had witnesses who could prove his innocence. The intendant asked him to return on October 9, at which time he could face his accusers, the parents and the cavalryman. When Raphaël appeared for that hearing, the police lieutenant, a local notable, took charge of the investigation and ordered the intendant to prevent the Jew from leaving Metz. The intendant agreed to leave the case to the courts, even though he was the king's official representative, but he did allow Raphaël to return to Boulay on the grounds that the village was not part of his jurisdiction. Raphaël had therefore come to Metz voluntarily, and the intendant decided that he had no right to keep him against his will. The police lieutenant summoned a number of witnesses, including the cavalryman and a wood turner who lived near the Porte des Allemands, both of whom testified against the Jew. On October 12, the police lieutenant ordered Lévy to come to Metz. Knowing that he was innocent, Raphaël complied, thinking that he was sacrificing himself to save the Jewish community. He was immediately imprisoned.

The interrogation of witnesses resumed. Their stories were contradictory: some denied recognizing Lévy, while others were no longer certain that he was the man they had seen. The miller and the two cobblers testified in his favor. The tide seemed to be turning. But then the butcher's daughter-in-law, whom an anonymous Jew (mentioned in the preceding chapter) characterized in his journal as a "wicked woman," claimed that she had seen Raphaël, whom she knew personally, entering the city with the child on his horse. Little Didier was wearing a red cap over his blond hair. Other witnesses also testified against Raphaël. It was pointed out, however, that the butcher woman had just given birth. Since she was bedridden, she could not possibly have seen the Jew. Others stated that Raphaël never rode any horse but his own and that its saddle cloth was not the same color as the one seen on the horse that the kidnapper was supposed to have ridden. Still others pointed out that at three in the afternoon the child had been seen, still alive, in Glatigny, so that it was impossible for Raphaël to have taken the boy to Metz and returned to Boulay by four, as several witnesses maintained.

Once again, Raphaël began to breathe easy, but now the case took another turn that would have very serious consequences: the court of the *bailliage* criticized the police lieutenant for allowing witnesses favorable to the defendant to testify and relieved him of sole charge of the case. At this point, the anonymous journal writer remarks on an event to which no other commentator seems to have paid attention: a notable from Metz went to Frankfurt on Sunday, October 27, and returned the following Friday with an order from the emperor, who retained certain prerogatives in Lorraine, certifying that the Jews never engaged in this type of crime and that accusations of ritual murder against them had always proved false. Given this background, the emperor insisted on his right to review the trial.[3] But his request was ignored, because he had no power over the courts in Metz. By acting as he did, the emperor was simply according the traditional protection that sovereigns had always accorded to the Jews. Yet this whole episode is not mentioned anywhere other than in the anonymous journal.

On Monday, November 25, the pace of the investigation picked up, as peasants tending hogs in the Glatigny woods found the child's skull and skeleton. Apparently, the boy's father asked them to say that they had also found his clothing in order to bolster the case against Lévy and undermine the most likely hypothesis, that the child had gotten lost in the forest and was eaten by animals. The testimony that the boy's shirt had been found dangling from a bush, still white and immaculate, was supposed to prove that he had not been attacked by animals. The witnesses also claimed to have found two tunics, one of which was untied and showed no evidence of having been ripped from the child's body and no sign of blood, and this was presented as irrefutable evidence of a ritual murder. One of the peasants testified that he did not believe the boy had been devoured by animals because animals usually attack the head, and the boy's skull had been found intact. Surgeons were consulted, and on November 29 they turned in a report stating that although certain parts of the body seemed to have been devoured by animals, the condition of the skull suggested that it had remained exposed in the woods for forty days, that is, since October 20, one week after Raphaël surrendered to the authorities in Metz. This was taken as further evidence of a ritual murder, since it was supposed to prove that the child remained alive from the time of his abduction until the sacrifice at some later date. It was at this point that the peasants claimed to have met Gédéon Lévy in the woods. They assumed he had come to deposit the boy's skull and bones along with clothing not stained by blood in order to exculpate Raphaël Lévy—a hypothesis that contradicted the previous interpretation. Gédéon Lévy was then imprisoned as well and, like Raphaël, subjected to both ordinary and extraordinary torture despite his protestations of innocence to the end.

The witnesses were heard again, and their accusations continued to contradict one another. Their stories varied and became increasingly vague. There were differences regarding the times and places where Raphaël had supposedly been seen, the nature of his comings and goings, the color of the saddle cloth on the horse ridden by the person said to be carrying the little boy, the shape of the horse's ears, and the clothing worn by the Jew (was it a tunic, as he claimed, or a cloak with which he might have hidden the child from view?). It would be impossible to list all the contradictions; for instance, the butcher's wife said that she had seen Raphaël enter Metz via the Porte des Allemands with the child at around noon, whereas the boy's father admitted that Didier had not gone missing until three in the afternoon! Some witnesses accused others of having accepted money from Jews to testify in favor of Raphaël Lévy, while still others claimed that prominent Jews had offered them money to look for the boy's remains and clothing in order to destroy evidence against the defendant. In their defense, the Jews confirmed that they had made such offers but said their purpose was to find evidence of Raphaël's innocence, not to obstruct justice.

At this point, a number of witnesses came forward to tell the judges about an incident that had occurred several years earlier. Antoine Clausquin, they said, had entered the home of Mayer Schwabe without warning on Good Friday. There he allegedly saw a number of Jews sitting around a table, armed, and mocking the passion of Christ. He tried to flee but was caught and in the confusion wounded in the hand. He claimed that he was offered money in exchange for his silence. Several days of the Lévy trial were now devoted to this picaresque tale, with witnesses testifying they had heard it discussed. Another myth—the mockery of the Crucifixion—was thus woven together with the principal myth of ritual murder, further exacerbating the emotional climate. For the first time, these two obsessions of the Catholic imagination were merged into one.

Meanwhile, Raphaël, worried about this latest turn of events, tried to contact his friends and family. He enlisted the help of a young woman who worked in the prison as a servant, a girl from Boulay whom he knew well from having met her frequently in the village. Through her, he sent ten notes asking for information about the progress of the investigation and the roles played by the various witnesses. He also asked for help for his wife and daughter and requested a Jewish burial, failing which he would refuse to "pardon" anyone. The prison steward got wind of what he was doing, confiscated a note, and then collected all the others, which he took to the deputy prosecutor, who ordered a translation. On December 20, 1669, the first translator, a converted Jew, called attention to what he regarded as a crucial passage: Raphaël, he said, had written that the child was garroted or tied up (*gebunden*), when in fact he had asked whether "the child had been found" (*gefunden*). When questioned, the serving girl denied that Raphaël had told her that the child was "tied up." A significant portion of the trial was taken up with this deliberately or accidentally mistranslated word, which Raphaël's enemies seized upon to prove that he knew that the child had been tied up or strangled and therefore that he was guilty. This proved to be a turning point in the case: the confusion of two verbs weighed heavily in the judges' decision to sentence the defendant to death despite his insistence that the translation was faulty. Many hours of the interrogation were devoted to the difference between *gebunden* and *gefunden*. On December 28, a second expert, also a Jewish convert, was called to testify, and he confirmed the original translation: in his opinion, the word was *gebunden*, not *gefunden*. Raphaël's protestations to the contrary fell on deaf ears.

On Thursday, January 16, 1670, the parlement of Metz, sitting as a court of justice, pronounced its guilty verdict at three in the afternoon. Raphaël Lévy was to be subjected to both ordinary and extraordinary torture. Several other Jews, including Mayer Schwabe, were also imprisoned, and their property was quickly seized. Finally, the parlement ordered the expulsion of Jews who had allowed their co-religionists to settle in the region; they were accused of driving the king's subjects into ruin. These various anti-Jewish measures were conveyed to the king. As "the rabble" throughout the region threatened to attack the Jews, who depended on the king's soldiers for their safety, Raphaël was subjected to ordinary and extraordinary torture, which he withstood courageously, insisting on his innocence to the very end, despite his suffering. On January 17, the sentence was read, and he was again taken to the torture chamber. As he lay in agony, two prominent Jews paid him a visit, and he asked them to look after his wife and daughter. Then he prayed and put on his phylacteries. At two in the afternoon, he walked to the stake after refusing to carry a candle. This was the end; apparently, the executioner strangled him just before throwing him into the fire. On January 19, the Jews dispatched two representatives to Paris. They contacted the marquis de Berny, the son of the comte de Lionne and secretary of the Commandements du roi (a bureau of the royal administration). "What do you want?" M. de Berny reportedly asked. "Your Jew is dead. Why didn't you come to me sooner?"

Meanwhile, on January 17, 1670, Mayer Schwabe was questioned, and several witnesses corroborated Clausquin's story. This "trial within a trial" would last several months, with the master alderman presiding and despite protests from the royal intendant. On February 5, the parlement of Metz authorized the deputy prosecutor to issue a new call for witnesses, to be posted in all churches. Many witnesses came forward, each with a story more extraordinary than the last. These had nothing to do with the Lévy affair or even with Clausquin's allegation against Schwabe. One witness testified that "some years earlier" he had come upon a human head while crossing the rue des Juifs one night. A surgeon claimed that a Jew had come to him for a piece of skin, because Jewish women cannot give birth unless they are wearing a belt made of Christian skin. Another witness recalled that after he sold pearls to a Jew in Amsterdam, the Jew immediately "massacred" a string of pearls decorating a cross. Several women testified that they had seen Jews flagellate a statue of Christ in their synagogue on Good Friday.

In April, a new episode began. Wilstadt Liberman was arrested and taken to prison, where he joined Mayer Birier and Aaron Halphen. Abraham Spire, the head of the rabbinical tribunal of Metz, was out of town and escaped arrest. All were accused of attempting to destroy evidence of Raphaël Lévy's guilt, at Raphaël's behest. Finally, on June 26, the long-awaited royal decree arrived, ordering the release of all imprisoned Jews. Parlement attempted to oppose the order. Wild, alarmist rumors of kidnappings again began to spread, and two notables again traveled to Paris to meet with the highest authorities; on October 2 they returned with a new order ending all the prosecutions, including that of Rabbi Spire, who had received a harsh sentence.

In broad outline, this was the Raphaël Lévy affair, which kept Metz and the surrounding region in turmoil for several years, requiring active intervention by the royal government and its local representatives. This regional descent into irrationality was abetted by polemical exchanges in Paris between, for example, the translator and publicist Abraham Nicolas Amelot de La Houssaye (or at any rate a writer who signed his text with La Houssaye's name) and the celebrated exegete Richard Simon. Amelot de La Houssaye, whose work would achieve a certain renown, did not conceal his prejudices (if he was indeed the author of the text). He began by saying that "the Jews have always been given to this sort of crime," citing the kidnapping of children in Norwich and Trent. He dwelled on the victim's agony, alleging that the assembled Jews "struck him all over his body. Each of them took pleasure in striking fresh blows, one after another, at intervals, in order to perpetuate his pain, which they would have extended if possible even beyond the end of his life." Drawing upon his fertile imagination, La Houssaye played on his readers' emotions and fears before describing the ritual murder allegedly committed by Raphaël Lévy. He reiterated the medieval allegation that when the Jews could not lay hands on a Christian child, they "mocked the Son of God...by taking a crucifix and reenacting, rods in hand, the flagellation they inflicted on him."[4] The reader, his appetite thus whetted, could now delight in the colorful account of Raphaël Lévy's wicked crime.

Amelot de La Houssaye wanted his readers to know that such ritual crimes were committed "every day out of hatred and scorn for the Christian religion." For him, there could be no doubt: "Upon finding the child alone by the side of the road, this cruel Jew took him, placed him on his horse in front of him, and carried him off to Metz, where he turned him over to other Jews before returning the same day to Boulay."[5] He charged Raphaël with any number of crimes ("There is evidence that he suborned witnesses"), while Raphaël's alibi—that he had to return to Boulay in time to celebrate Rosh Hashanah—could not withstand scrutiny because "the Jews look upon the kidnapping of Christian children as a religious act much more important than attending services on their holidays."[6] It all fit together. To conclude his narrative, he called for the expulsion of all Jews from France: "Since the king is no less pious than he is just, and since he has always triumphed over his enemies, it is to be hoped that he will also triumph over the enemies of Jesus Christ and the Christian church, of which he is the eldest son, by banishing the Jews from his kingdom, following the example set by his predecessors, in punishment for their many crimes. In this way, His Majesty will deliver our religion from its cruelest and most impious persecutors."[7] Clearly, the work of Amelot de La Houssaye, hastily published, extremely violent, and devoted entirely to the Raphaël Lévy affair, was implicitly an incitement not only to persecute the Jews still imprisoned in Metz (Gédéon Lévy's alleged accomplices) but also to punish all their co-religionists, whom La Houssaye denounced as potential child killers.

In the face of such threats, a number of Jews, among them Rabbi Issachar, a notable by the name of Seligman, and Gompel Wimpen, set out for Paris in search of help. They went to see Jona Salvador, a Jew originally from the Piedmont, who had a tobacco business in Pignerol. Salvador had good connections at court and was deeply interested in science, in addition to which he was a Hebrew scholar who discussed the Bible and Talmud with Simon. That celebrated Oratorian was in regular contact with Salvador, with whom he studied the *Zohar*, commented on the texts of Raschi and Abravanel, and also discussed the new messianism associated with the name of Sabbatai Zevi, which Salvador hoped would lead to the restoration of Jewish Jerusalem.

The Metz Jews therefore went directly to the home of Salvador, one of the few Jews authorized to reside in Paris, and informed him in detail of the suffering of the Jews of Lorraine. Salvador immediately made up his mind to help them and hastened to see his friend Simon, whom he urged to respond quickly to La Houssaye's *Abrégé du procès fait aux Juifs de Metz* (the text in which he rehearsed the charges against Lévy and the other Jews). Simon, who would later engage in a polemic with Bossuet, was passionate about Hebrew studies, a field in which he was without a doubt one of the leading experts.

Heinrich Graetz notes that Simon "was the founder of the scientific exegesis of the Old and New Testaments. . . . Thanks to him, the educated public became more familiar with the rabbinical literature. . . . His close relations with Jewish scholars, essential for the study of Hebrew literature, led him to abandon some of his prejudices against Jews."[8] Those prejudices are obvious to anyone who examines his correspondence, for example. Simon says that the Talmud is full of "daydreams" and refers "to the crude ignorance in which people lived, which made them credulous." He repeatedly makes fun of "the folly of the Cabalists" and repudiates the "lies" of Jewish thinkers.[9] The Jews, he goes on to say, "hate us mortally."[10] Explicitly naming his friend Salvador, from whom he learned the Talmud, Simon pokes fun at him: "It is amusing to watch him read the Bible in the Jewish manner, moving his head and almost his whole body back and forth to animate his reading." He contends that "most Jews nowadays have no religion, although they are outwardly quite observant of their rituals. All their effort tends to be directed toward amassing money."[11] Simon adds that "the Jews are great impostors, and when they deceive a Christian, they think they have done a good deed."[12] "I called him a Jew," he wrote in 1670 to his friend Claude Hardy.[13] Worse still, Simon describes the conditions under which he intervened on behalf of Raphaël Lévy:

> Not long ago, the Jews easily won a case before the King's Council against the parlement of Metz, which had condemned a wretched Jew to the flames. The parlement would also have issued a similar sentence to two other Jews if the council had not taken charge of the case. Salvador, who was in Paris at the time, conveyed some of the trial documents to me. After reading them, I had no compunction about writing a memorandum in favor of the Jews of Metz, which was of considerable help in winning their case before the King's Council. I know that this wretched nation [the Jews] hates us mortally, but we must show them that we treat them as the Gospel intends in commanding us to love our enemies.[14]

Despite these prejudices, many of which were expressed in letters written in 1670 and 1671, Simon set to work at once. Displaying real courage (which may have influenced Voltaire in his defense of Calas in the next century),[15] he drafted his *Factum servant de réponse au livre intitulé: Abrégé du process fait aux Juifs de Metz* (Factum by way of response to the book entitled: Summary of the trial of the Jews of Metz). In the nineteenth century, Graetz had this text in mind when he wrote that Simon "pleaded his case with warm conviction,"[16] while Joseph Reinach included it in his volume of texts dealing with the affair. Both authors praised Simon for his learning and courage, without knowing much about the content of his correspondence.[17] The opening passage of the *Factum* sets the tone: "The author of the defamatory libel against the Jews of Metz gives sufficient evidence of his ill will toward the entire Jewish nation. [...] The evidence that he uses to support the verdict against Raphaël Lévy [...] is so weak that there would be no need to refute it if one did not also wish to demonstrate the falsity of other accusations that have long been made against the Jews."[18]

After showing how various popes defended the Jews and refuted such charges and how a number of kings had also come to their defense, Simon wrote: "The Jews of Metz today hope for the same justice from the Most Christian King and his Council, which will easily discover the many calumnious charges that have previously been leveled against their nation. These calumnies rest on nothing but false reports and made-up stories. The Jews hope that His Majesty, instead of banishing them from Metz, will reaffirm their right to live there, as his royal predecessors did before him."[19]

Simon rejected the accusation of magic, which Judaism condemned, and gave an accurate description of something Christians found very strange, namely, the meaning of *tefillin*, or phylacteries, which contain the Ten Commandments and do not hide anything mysterious. He was ironic: "Christians ought not to be so quick to accuse the Jews of Magic, since they know full well that this was a charge leveled at the first [Christian] martyrs." He emphasized the fact that most contemporary Christians "respect Jewish books, which fill their finest libraries." Returning at the end of his text to Raphaël Lévy, he wrote that he "stands accused of having caused the death of a child. Not only is there no proof, but all presumptions are against it, because this action, which is attributed to religious zeal, is entirely contrary to the principles of religion. He is accused of having kidnapped the child, but that is implausible, since he could not derive any profit or benefit from such an act.... One cannot affirm that there is a single witness who offers proof of his guilt."[20] Having thus refuted Amelot de La Houssaye's venomous accusations, Simon devoted a good deal of space to prayers in which Jews celebrate their kings, which he presented as evidence of their attachment to monarchy and absolute loyalty. Jews, he wrote, "pray every Saturday and on other solemn holidays for the kings and princes of whom they are subjects."[21] These prayers were supposed to persuade the judges of Raphaël's innocence, for he, like his co-religionists, was a pious man who respected the monarchical order and sanctified the law. Simon's *Factum* proved quite helpful to the imprisoned Metz Jews and persuaded the royal authorities to intervene forcefully in order to obtain their release.

Until Reinach rediscovered this story at the end of the nineteenth century, a shroud of silence enveloped it. History seemed to have forgotten Raphaël Lévy's misfortune, which left virtually no trace in the eighteenth century. In 1734, however, François Gayot de Pitaval devoted thirty pages of his *Causes célèbres et intéressantes avec les jugements qui les ont décidées* to the case, under the title "Jews condemned for an enormous crime that revolted humanity." He began thus: "It would take volumes to describe all the impieties, sacrileges, and abominations that Jews commit every day out of hatred and scorn for the Christian religion. The history that I am about to give of the trial that took place in Metz after the kidnapping of a child, of which Raphaël Lévy was convicted, will suffice to give an idea of their execrable and unnatural character."[22] Taking his inspiration largely from Amelot de La Houssaye (whom he did not cite), Pitaval described the various stages of the Lévy affair, embracing as his own some of the wildest allegations, such as the charge that when Jews cannot find a child they instead place a crucifix in the synagogue on Good Friday and take turns whipping it.[23] Pitaval wrote with no distance at all from his subject; he had nothing but scorn for the "abominable Jews," who clung so "stubbornly" to their beliefs.[24]

Fifty years later, in 1787, Abbé Grégoire, in his famous *Essai sur la régénération physique, morale et politique des Juifs*, included this curious passage on profanation of the host:

> Certain Jews in Paris and Cologne are said to have profaned the most sacred objects of our religion. Granted, there are incontrovertible facts of this sort, and the town of Saint-Dié has a record of what appears to be an identical case. Three or four Jews from Trent, Haugenau, Fulde, and Pons are supposed to have immolated Christian children. We might argue with these assertions: What is your authority for them? Christian historians. But if we grant that rage, madness, or desire for vengeance may have led a few fanatics to commit such excesses, does it follow that the nation as a whole is guilty?[25]

In a note, Grégoire remarks, without much evidence of critical scrutiny, that "in Brussels, hosts profaned by Jews have been carefully preserved in the collegiate church of Sainte-Gudule. Others can be found in the convent of Les Billettes in Paris." Concerning the profanation of the host of Saint-Dié, he adds: "I said that this fact *seemed* authentic because I am not yet convinced that this Jew's crime is proven beyond a shadow of a doubt." In the passage quoted above, he seems to accept the veracity of the charges in Trent, the archetypal accusation of ritual murder, which would weigh for centuries on the history of the Jews. Although Grégoire had no intention of accusing Jews as a group, he was nevertheless prepared to consider the hypothesis that a few fanatics might in fact have committed ritual murder.

In the same note, moreover, he turns to the case of Raphaël Lévy, by then forgotten, to refute the interpretations given by the author of the *Abrégé du procès fait aux Juifs de Metz*, who strikes him as "somewhat credulous." He mentions, with apparent approval, Richard Simon's refutation. Himself a native of Lorraine, Grégoire displayed genuine knowledge of the case, which few other people remembered. Yet he ends his discussion with the strange remark, "Whatever may actually have happened."[26] Here and elsewhere in these pages he does not dismiss allegations of ritual murder as preposterous, which is rather surprising for an author noted as a courageous champion of Jewish emancipation and regeneration. Despite this, he finds it plausible to believe that "a few fanatics" might actually have been guilty, even though the Church officially condemned such charges.[27]

We will never know how Abbé Grégoire got wind of the Lévy affair, which had long since faded from view.[28] After Grégoire, there was nothing until the episode suddenly surfaced once again in 1841: Olry Terquem, a reformist and dissident Jew, published in the *Archives israélites* the journal of an unknown Metz Jew who tells the story of the affair.[29] This was an unambiguous brief in favor of Raphaël, a radical attack on the whole fantastic tale. Comparing Raphaël Lévy to the chevalier de La Barre and Calas, Terquem hoped that his publication of the journal would completely rehabilitate the reputation of the unfortunate victim: "Raphaël Lévy—to celebrate your Spartan piety and divine virtue would take the pen of a Chateaubriand. Please accept this tribute of regret, recognition, and admiration from an obscure coreligionist. Your final moments are worthy of an entire lifetime of illustrious deeds. Worthy of the fatherland of Fabert, you rose to the heights of Duvergier, Nicole, and Arnaud, saintly victims who chose suffering, misery, and exile and who, like you, died in obedience to the sacred laws of conscience. This insignificant Jew had a character of steel."[30]

In short, Raphaël Lévy's story remained buried in the far-distant past. Few knew of his exemplary behavior, and he has never enjoyed the recognition of a de La Barre or a Calas. Yet Terquem makes no bones about the importance he attaches to the case; he wants to use it to call attention to the fate of Jews facing yet another charge of ritual murder that most people in France considered justified. This case involved Jews in Damascus in 1840, and for several years it stirred passions across Europe. Terquem was especially interested in this case because French authorities had significant involvement in the imprisonment of the Damascus Jews, who were tortured and unjustly condemned under pressure from Catholics. In this instance, however, the French authorities were overtly and forthrightly challenged by the most prominent French Jew of the day, Adolphe Crémieux, who joined Moses Haim Montefiore in coming to the aid of the accused.[31] The Damascus affair was thus the primary reason for the rediscovery of the Lévy affair, and Terquem's purpose was to celebrate both Lévy's physical courage and his attachment to the Jewish faith. Evidence of this can be seen in the following poem, which Mme. C.-P. Merlieux, née Polack, wrote and Terquem published at the end of his article on the Metz Jew's journal (here I give only an English prose paraphrase of extensive excerpts of the original):

> Ghost of Raphaël, why does your plaintive voice trouble me with its sad accents? You died a hero! And your magnanimous heart fervently blessed the name of the Almighty! In frightened Metz, a rumor emerged out of nowhere and was quickly swelled by lies. It was said that a child succumbed to murderous blows at the edge of a forest. [...] Superstition, always avid for falsehoods, quickly embraced a made-up tale. They said, O blessed God! that our Passover *matzoh* is an abominable mixture of flesh and blood that demands a victim and that we must pierce the heart of an innocent! Your persecutors, cowardly tyrants, spread chaos and panic in the shadows. They accused you, O God! and in the frenzy, they sought to annihilate the faith of Jacob! [...] Fanaticism, burning with impious zeal, tried to offer up to heaven the incense of its furor, pyres, dungeons, irons, humiliation, torture, cries, and livid terror! [...] France, too long in thrall to this rage, saw a decent and virtuous old man perish. Calas followed La Barre, and the reddened earth rose in horror against an odious regime! Raphaël! Your

> sacred cause lacked the noble champion who, jealous of our rights, listens [...] and hears the cries of Damascus in alarm, and dares to devote himself to the salvation of all! His voice would have proclaimed your peaceful innocence. His eloquence would have recounted your humble piety and stayed the sentence of the cruel judges, depriving posterity of its contempt for them. O, why did Louis's tardy justice not extinguish the flames at the stake? Why did he not reach out to you with a protective hand when your dying eyes could no longer look for it! Ah! What am I saying! [...] An invisible and potent hand showed you the Eternal, his throne, his splendor! He stretched out his arm to you! [...] Your radiant soul went up, chaste and pure, to the Creator's bosom![32]

This long poem honors the sacrifice of Raphaël Lévy. Published as a sort of conclusion to the journal of the anonymous Metz Jew who rehabilitated the unfortunate Lévy, it highlighted not only his faith, piety, and confidence in God but also his solitude, the absence of a Voltaire to defend him or even a Crémieux, who took up the cause of the Damascus Jews.

Although the *Archives israélites* devoted many issues to the publication of the journal, which recounted in detail the injustices suffered by Raphaël Lévy, his story remained largely unknown. The impassioned poem did not help; nor did the publication of Simon's courageous defense of Lévy, which ended the series of articles devoted to the case. Only four years later, when Emmanuel Michel published his *Histoire du parlement de Metz* in 1845, prejudices were still such that he knew nothing of the remarkable documents that proved Raphaël's innocence, which the *Archives israélites* had so recently published. He wrote:

> Those who love dramatic emotions will believe uncritically in all the atrocities imputed to the Jews. Others will find it easier to believe in the fanaticism of the court than in the fanaticism of its unfortunate victim, and easier to believe in the perjury of twenty witnesses than in the depravity of one defendant. Impartial men will be more circumspect in forming their opinions. They will remain convinced, first, that in this sad affair, parlement was not driven by persecution and fanaticism. [...] When competent judges have observed legal forms and issued a sentence based on moral certainty, that sentence must be respected.[33]

In fact, the Lévy affair fell largely into oblivion between the Damascus affair and the Dreyfus Affair.[34] Even worse, when it was for once evoked in a more direct way, Raphaël again found himself implicitly condemned. In a work published in Metz in 1861, Justin Worms discussed the trial in much the same way as Emmanuel Michel, ending with these words: "One would like to believe, for the sake of the honor and memory of the parlement of Metz, that the Jew was guilty of the crime of which he was accused and justly expiated his guilt in fiery torment. . . . There is no point in denying or arguing with the presumption that the Jew Raphaël Lévy murdered this unfortunate child in obedience to the secret laws of his faith, the mysterious injunctions of his religion. Whatever actually happened, the parlement may have punished a guilty man, but at the same time it discredited innocent people."[35] Given such an attitude toward the fable of Glatigny, we can understand the indignation of the *Archives israélites*, especially since the journal had twenty years earlier published documents laying out the true facts of the case:

> How can a Jewish writer have so coolly described such revolting facts? How could he have written the words "justly expiated his guilt in fiery torment"? What! Not a word of vehement protest against the iniquity of the procedure? Not a word on behalf of the Spartan heroism of Raphaël Lévy! . . . How is it that M. Worms failed to find words adequate to describe this sublime martyr? How could he fail to quote the ardent protest of the late Terquem or the naïve diary written by a contemporary and translated by the late Hadamard? How could he fail to mention the posthumous declaration of innocence? Is no one in Metz familiar with the authentic documents and magnificent articles published in six issues of the *Archives* about a matter that has a direct bearing on the honor of the Metz community? It is sad to think so.[36]

The complaint was unavailing, as if French Jews were afraid to reopen this case for fear of finding themselves in danger. It took a foreign observer to remind them of the importance of the Lévy affair: Heinrich Graetz, the founder of modern Jewish historiography, published the last volume of his monumental *History of the Jewish People* in 1897, just as the Dreyfus affair was becoming a major public issue. Graetz displayed astonishing familiarity with elements of the case that were not mentioned in the translation of the diary published in the *Archives*. He devoted considerable space to the mischievous role of Du Vallier, the translator of Raphaël's notes. Du Vallier was a very pious former Jew who "introduced false evidence against poor Raphaël. . . . He became a zealous enemy of his former coreligionists." In addition, Graetz was the first to stress the role of Richard Simon in defending Raphaël and other falsely accused Jews.[37]

Despite Graetz's merits, further knowledge of the case would have to await the full flowering of the passions surrounding the Dreyfus affair. Édouard Drumont and his followers knew an astonishing amount about the Lévy case and frequently brandished it as justification for their hostility to Dreyfus. Even more important was the publication of Joseph Reinach's remarkably well-documented work rehabilitating Lévy, as well as the vigorous and substantial article that Henri Prague published in *Archives israélites*.[38]

Within a few years, the tragic fate of Raphaël Lévy was once again a matter of lively controversy, as both proponents and adversaries of Captain Dreyfus began to discuss that affair as a reprise of the Lévy affair.[39] Silence subsequently returned, not only as to the Lévy affair itself but also as to its protagonists, Catholics as well as Jews. To be sure, in 1951 André Spire gave a spirited and rigorous account of the affair, in which his ancestor Abraham Spire had been involved. His very lucid narrative was based on an attentive reading of Reinach's work. He concluded it with these words: "This was the story I told to André Gillois, which he broadcast in the form of a poignant radio play on April 26, 1951, at a time when French fascism, once again on the move, was waging an impudent campaign to free those responsible for delivering the Jews of France over to Nazi torture and extermination: men like Xavier Vallat, Charles Maurras, and Pétain himself."[40] Between Dreyfus and Vichy, the Lévy affair was thus briefly in the news once again.

Yet the countless historians of the Age of Louis XIV, French as well as foreign, rarely mention the case. To be sure, nowadays one finds brief discussion of the circumstances of this extraordinary case in some works on the period. But only an examination of the trial documents, to which neither the anonymous Jewish author of the famous diary nor Olry Terquem nor Heinrich Graetz nor Joseph Reinach had access, can enable us to see the social relations that existed at the time, to guess what sort of disputes and hatreds might have arisen, to learn about the values that motivated the various parties, and to divine the fantasies that haunted the inhabitants of this border region.[41]

Section of "Extension of the French Frontiers, 1601–1766." The dates indicate year of acquisition by France; when enclosed in parentheses they indicate year of loss. *Historical Atlas* by William R. Shepherd, New York, Henry Holt and Company, p. 126, 1926 ed. Courtesy of the University of Texas Libraries, The University of Texas at Austin.

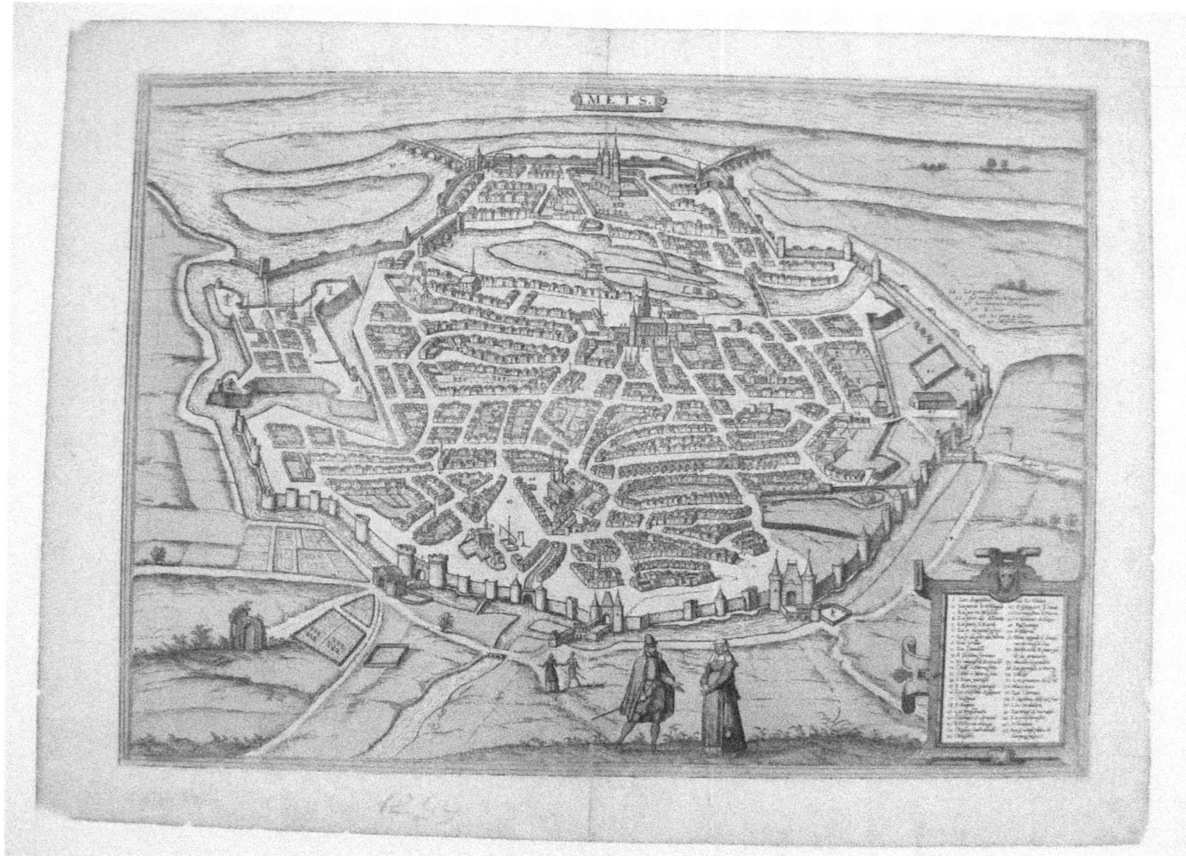

North section of Metz, c. 1575. From Bruin or Braun, *Civitates orbis terrarum* or *Le Grand Theatre des differentes cites du monde, Colonia ou Bruxelles, 1572–1618*. Archives départementales de la Moselle, B 2144.

Metz, c. 1575. German Gate (4). From Bruin or Braun, *Civitates orbis terrarum or Le Grand Theatre des differentes cites du monde, Colonia ou Bruxelles, 1572–1618*. Documents messins, Société d'histoire et d'archéologie, DR.

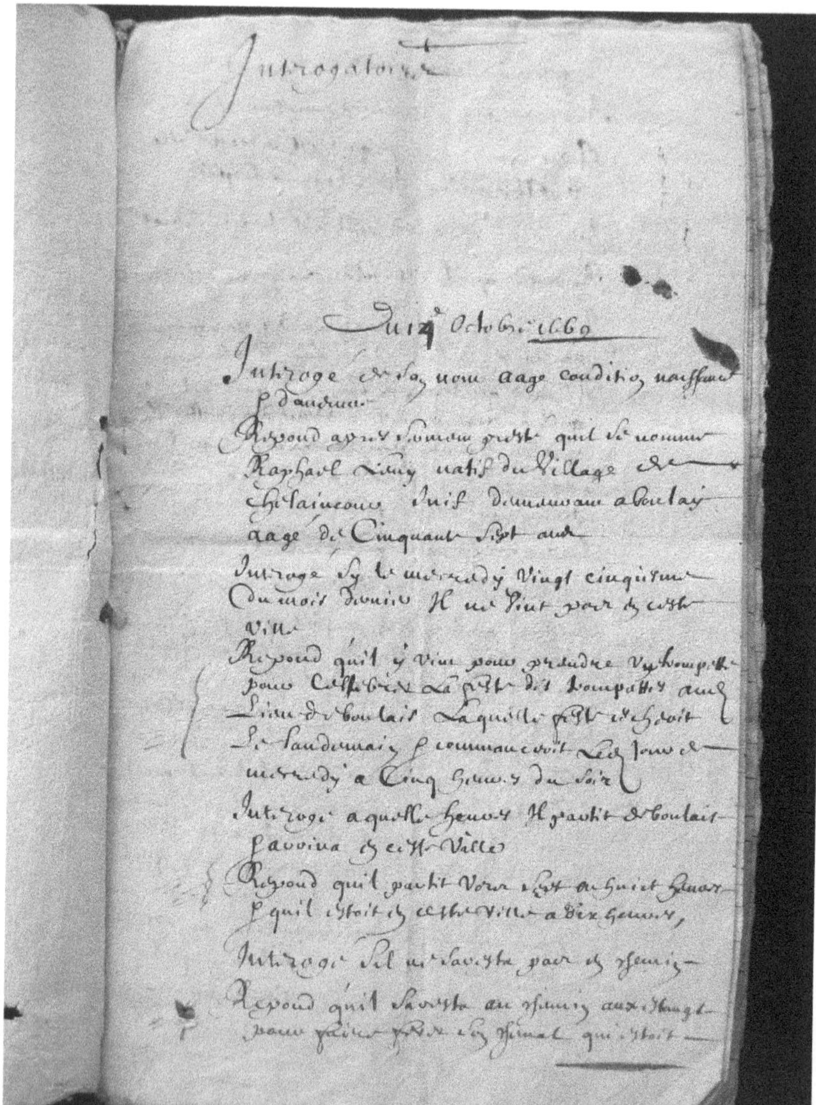

Interrogatoire

Du 14e Octobre 1669

Interrogé de ses nom aage condition naissance et demeure

Respond apres serment presté qu'il se nomme Raphael Levy natif du village de Chelaincourt Juif demeurant a Boulay aagé de cinquante sept ans

Interrogé sy le mercredy vingt cinquiesme du mois dernier il ne vint pas en ceste ville

Respond qu'il y vint pour prendre un trompette pour celebrer la feste des trompettes au lieu de Boulay laquelle feste escheoit le lendemain et commencoit led. jour de mercredy a cinq heures du soir

Interrogé a quelle heure il partit de Boulay arriva en ceste ville

Respond qu'il partit vers les sept ou huict heures et qu'il estoit en ceste ville a dix heures,

Interrogé s'il ne savoit pas le chemin

Respond qu'il savoit le chemin [illegible] pour [illegible] un cheval qui estoit

Interrogation of Raphaël Lévy with his signature in Hebrew (October 14, 1669). Archives départementales de la Moselle, B 2144.

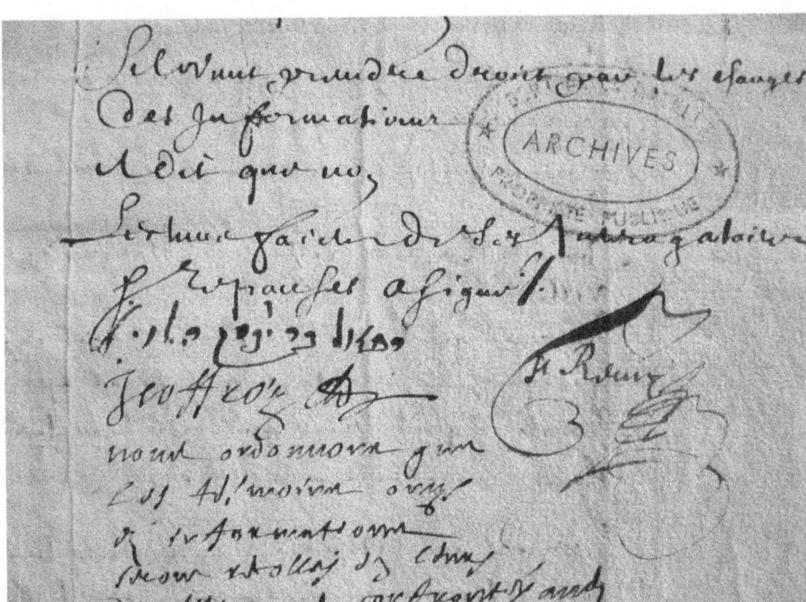
ARCHIVES
PROPRIETE PUBLIQUE

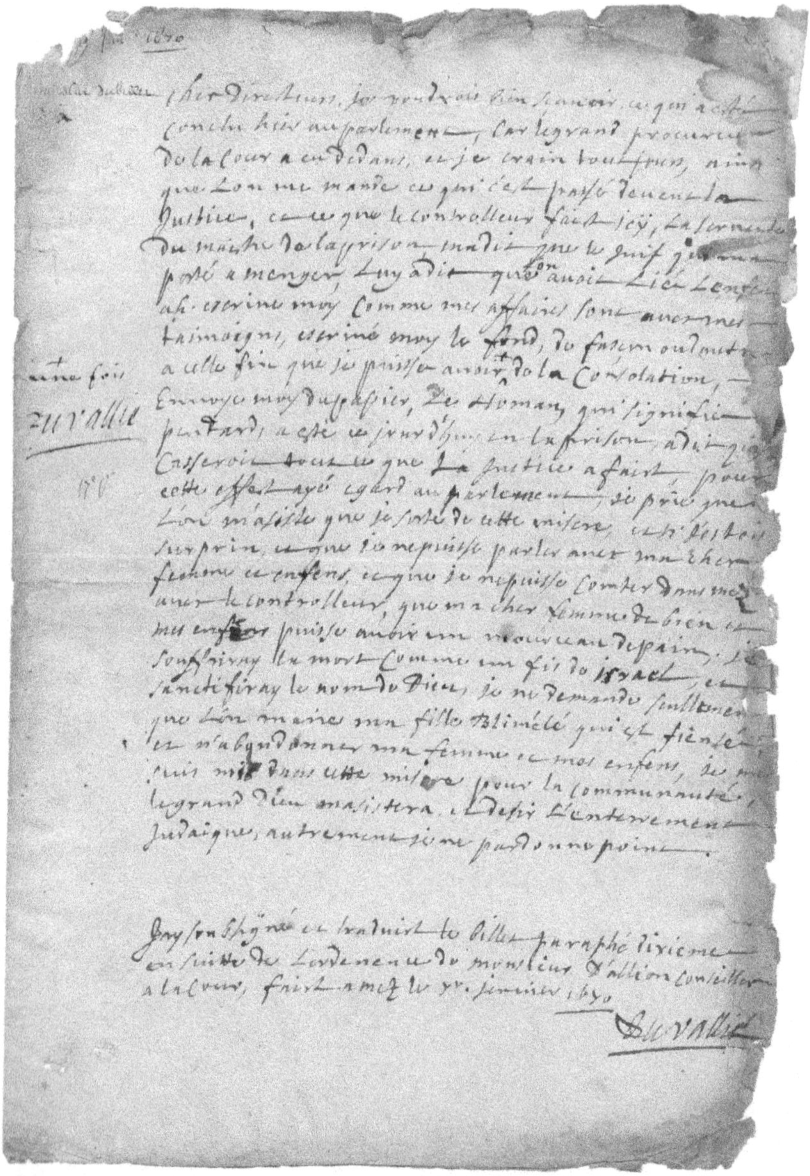

Letter from Raphaël Lévy to the prison warden (January 7, 1670). Archives départementales de la Moselle, B 2144.

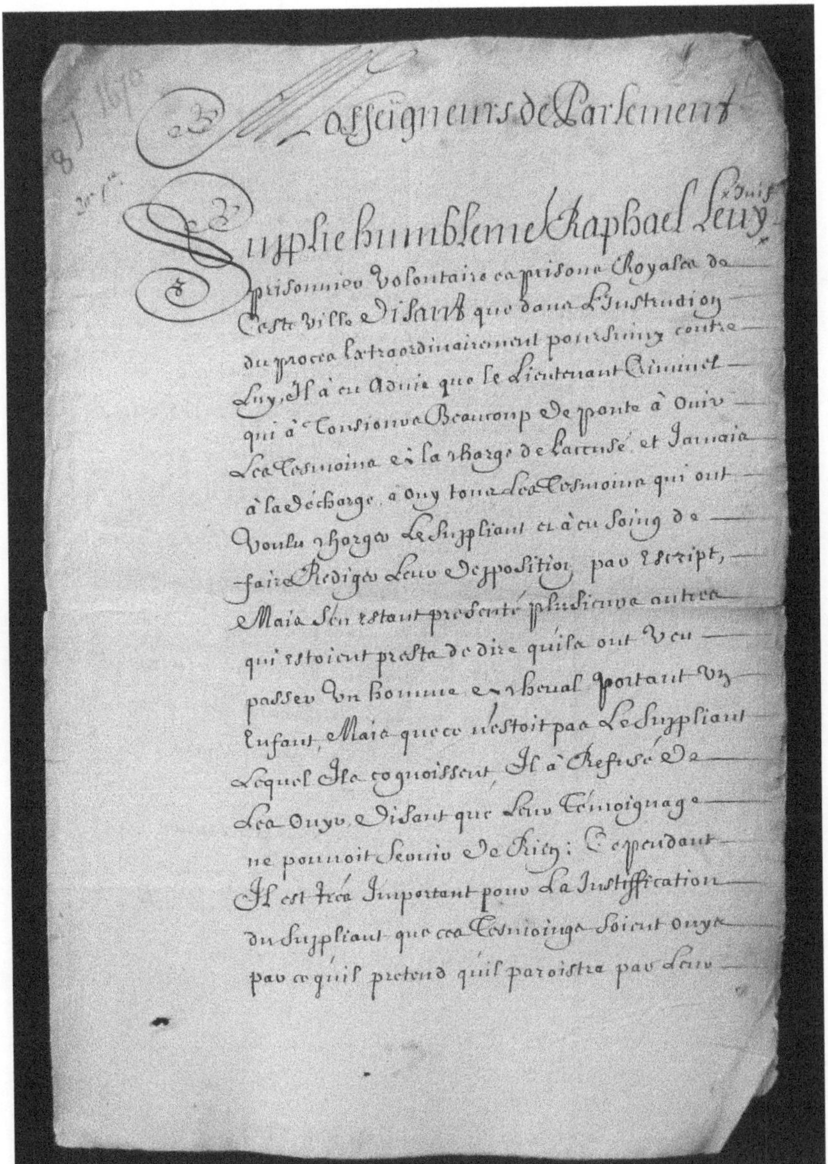

Nosseigneurs de Parlement

Supplie humblement Raphael Levy Juif
prisonnier volontaire es prisons Royales de
Cette Ville disant que dans l'instruction
du procès extraordinairement poursuivy contre
luy, Il a eu advis que le Lieutenant Criminel
qui a [illegible] beaucoup de [illegible] à ouir
les tesmoins à la charge de l'accusé et jamais
à la décharge, a ouy tous les tesmoins qui ont
voulu charger le suppliant et a eu soing de
faire Rediger leur depposition par Escript,
Mais s'en estant présenté plusieurs autres
qui estoient prests de dire qu'ils ont veu
passer un homme a cheval portant un
Enfant, Mais que ce n'estoit pas le suppliant
Lequel Ils cognoissent, Il a Refusé de
les ouyr disant que leur tesmoignage
ne pouvoit servir de Rien; Cependant
Il est très Important pour la Justiffication
du suppliant que ces tesmoings soient ouys
par ce qu'il pretend qu'il paroistra par leur

Petition by Raphaël Lévy to the parlement of Metz (January 8, 1670). Archives départementales de la Moselle, B 2144.

deposition qu'on a veu passer plusieurs
personnes portant un enfant a cheval, &
que ceste consideration peult beaucoup
contribuer a la descharge dudit suppliant.
Il est aussy venu a sa cognoissance que
la Bouchere qui a dit avoir veu passer
le suppliant portant un enfant a cheval
environ trente six heures apres ses
couches, & qui dans la confrontation
luy a soustenu que c'estoit luy, a dit
a diverses personnes, avant et depuis
le jugement du proces au bailliage, que
lors qu'elle vit passer ledit suppliant avec
ung enfant elle n'estoit pas encores accouchée
& cela estant verifié il se trouvera qu'estant
accouchée un jour seulement avant que
l'enfant pretendu enlevé, fust egaré, le
suppliant auroit esté veu entrant dans
la ville avec un enfant plusieurs jours
avant que celuy duquel il est question,
fust perdu, ce qui seroit tres relevant pour
la justification de son innocence.

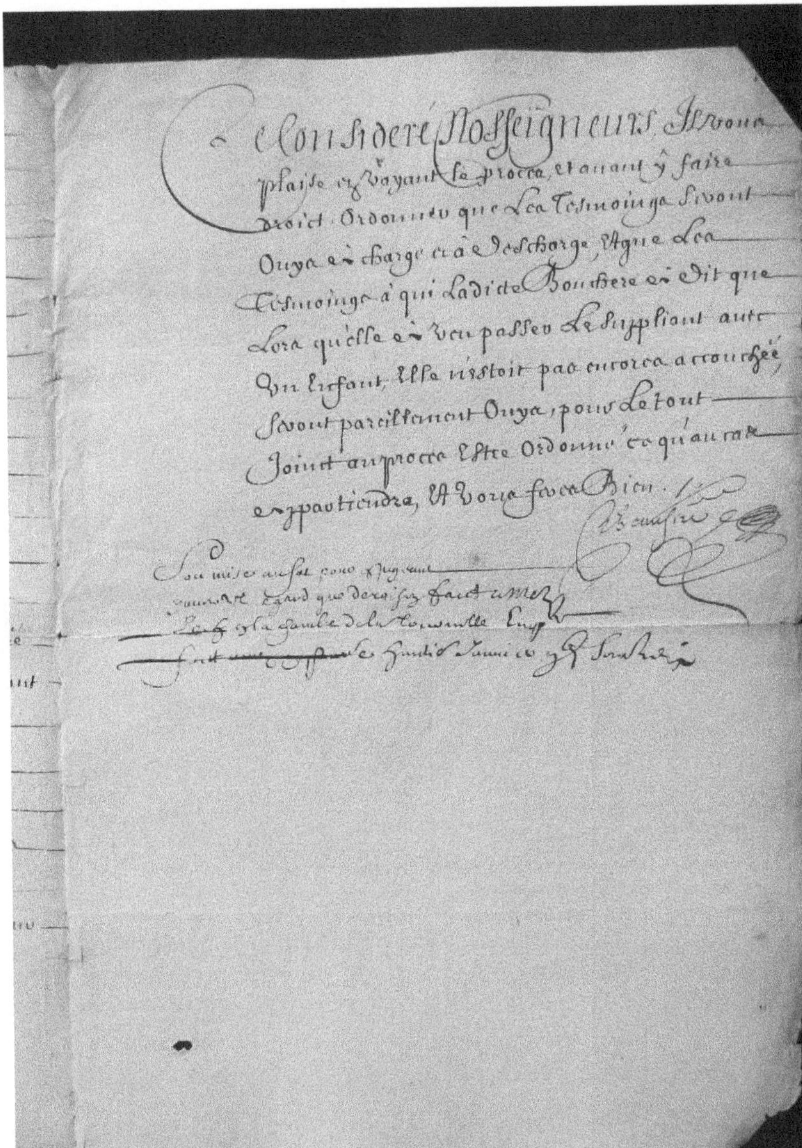

Ce considéré Nosseigneurs, Il vous plaise en voyant le procès, et auant y faire droict, Ordonner que les tesmoings seront ouys en charge et à descharge, et que les tesmoings à qui ladite Bouchere a dit que lors qu'elle a veu passer le suppliant avec un enfant, elle n'estoit pas encores accouchée, seront pareillement ouys, pour le tout joinct au procès estre ordonné ce qu'au cas appartiendra, et vous ferez bien.

Beaussire

Soit mise au sac pour en jugeant y avoir esgard que de raison. Faict à Metz [illegible] la chambre de la Tournelle [illegible]
Faict [illegible] le huictiesme janvier [illegible]

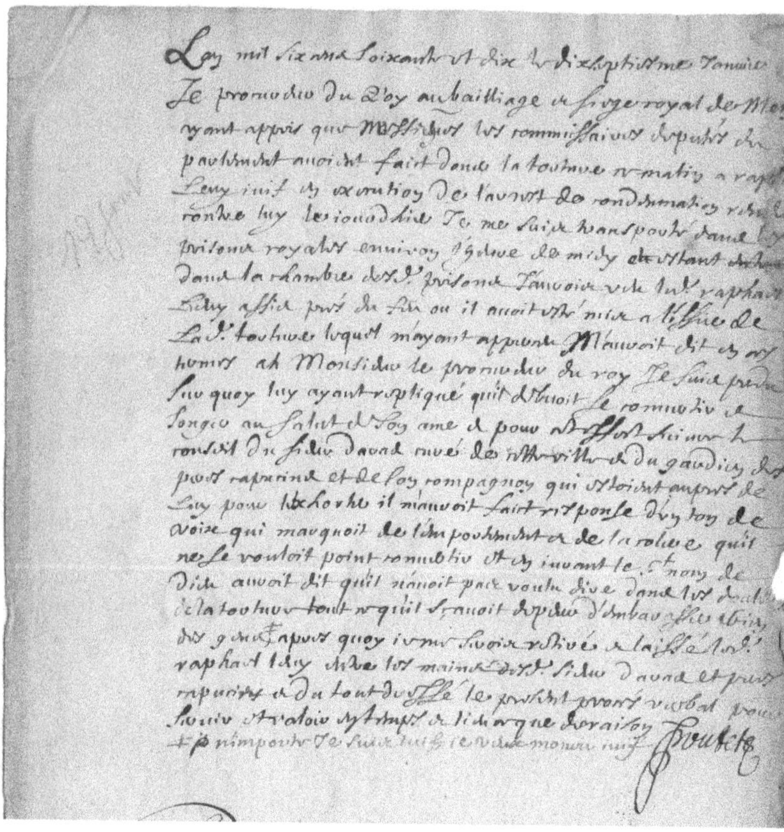

L'an mil six cent soixante et dix le dix septiesme Janvier
Je procureur du Roy au bailliage et siege royal de Metz
ayant appris que messieurs les commissaires deputés du
parlement avoient fait donner la torture ce matin a raphael
Levy juif en execution de l'arrest de condemnation rendu
contre luy le iour d'hier Je me suis transporté dans les
prisons royales environ 3 heure de midy et estant entré
dans la chambre desd. prisons J'auroie veu led. raphael
Levy assis pres du feu ou il avoit esté mis a l'issue de
lad. torture lequel m'ayant apperceu m'auroit dit en ces
termes ah Monsieur le procureur du roy Je suis perdu
sur quoy luy ayant repliqué qu'il debvoit se convertir et
songer au salut de son ame et pour cet effect suivre le
conseil du sieur david curé [illegible] et du gaudiers des
peres capucins et de ses compagnons qui estoient aupres de
luy pour l'exhorter il m'auroit fait responce d'un ton de
voix qui marquoit de l'emportement et de la colere qu'il
ne se vouloit point convertir et en iurant le st nom de
Dieu auroit dit qu'il n'avoit pas voulu dire dans les douleurs
de la torture tout ce qu'il scavoit de peur d'embarrasser bien
des gens apres quoy je me suis retiré et laissé led.
raphael levy entre les mains desd. sieur david et peres
capucins et du tout dressé le present proces verbal pour
servir et valoir en temps et lieu que de raison
[illegible] Je suis juif je veux mourir juif

[illegible signature]

Raphaël Lévy's will (January 17, 1670). Archives départementales de la Moselle, B 2144.

Metz, 1656, Merian's map. The Seille parade ground, where Raphaël Lévy was put to death. Documents messins, Société d'histoire et d'archéologie, DR.

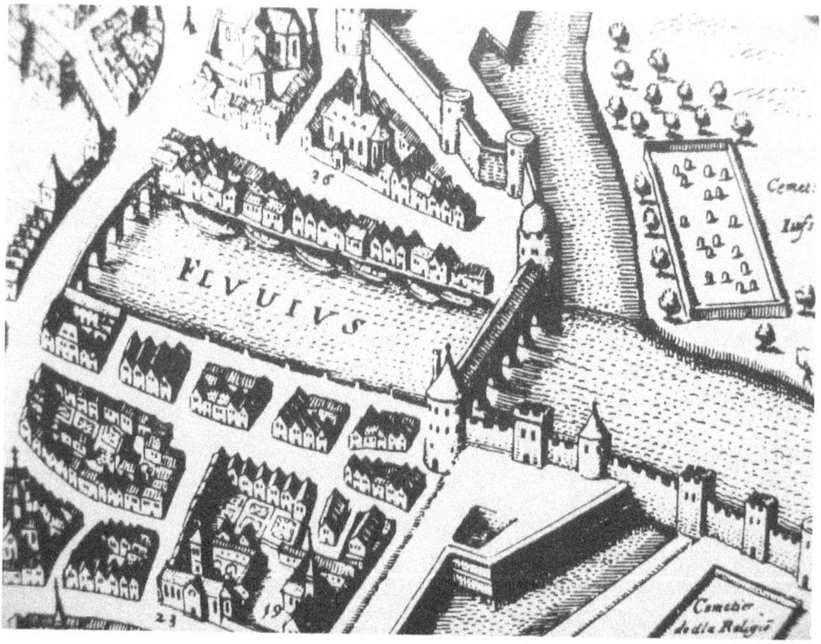

Metz 1656. Merian's map. Jewish Quarter (South Bank). Archives départementales de la Moselle, B 2144.

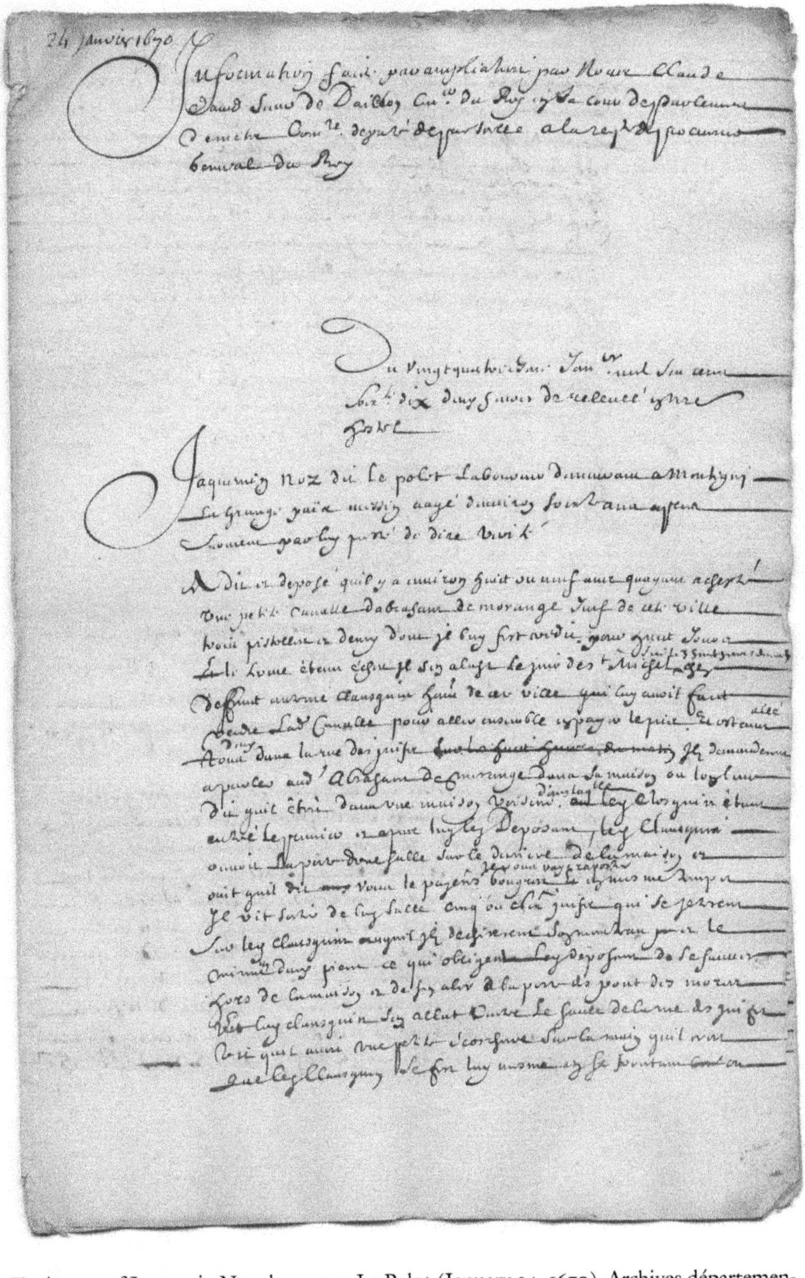

Testimony of Jaquemin Noz, known as Le Polot (January 24, 1670). Archives départementales de la Moselle, B 2144.

quotam contre la muraille. Et quinze jours apres le deposant
estant revenu en ce ville il parlat aux Abraham de Morhange
le fils de Gedeon qu'il avoit achepté de luy, et ayant eu ce
que Levy [illegible] Il luy donna [illegible] un
chapeau dont ayant voulu scavoir la cause le [illegible] luy
respondit qu'il ne la luy diroit jamais. Ce qui a donné sujet
au deposant de croire que [illegible]
avoit eu une somme d'argent des juifs pour ne pas dire les
choses qu'elle avoit veues dans la maison ou ils
luy deschirerent son manteau. Ne scavoir se souvenir dans
quelle maison c'estoit, mais a ouy dire que ce fut celle de
Mayeur Schambe [illegible] que luy dit que ce
temps la les juifs celebroient la feste des trompettes
qu'est tout ce qu'il a dit, lecture faite de sa deposition a
persisté ~~Signé~~ marqué

Daniel Daillon

Du vingt huitiesme Janvier [illegible] soixante
dix quatre heures de relevée en notre hostel

Nicolas Boëmey tixerand demeurant en ceste ville place de Chambre
agé de quarante ans ou environ apres serment par luy fait
de dire verité

A dit qu'il y eut dix ans le huictiesme juillet dernier qu'estant
a l'office un ~~dimanche~~ a la Cathedrale de ceste ville parce qu'il
estoit dimanche ce jour la, Il laissa un fils qu'il avoit pour lors agé
de cinq ans et demy nommé Edme devant sa porte apres luy avoir
donné un liard pour achepter des cerises, et estant de retour de
l'office il demanda son enfant a sa femme qui luy dit qu'elle ne l'avoit
point veu depuis une heure ce qui obligea le deposant de le chercher
dans toutes les maisons voisines ou ne l'ayant point trouvé. Il
obtint le lendemain permission du major de la ville de le faire
crier au son du tambour ce qu'il fit dans tous les carrefours
sans apprendre aucunes nouvelles de son enfant ~~[illegible]~~ [illegible]

Five The Trial of Raphaël Lévy, New Herod

In the diary kept by an unknown Metz Jew, there is a passage describing a strange episode that was not mentioned during the trial. After Raphaël voluntarily returned to Metz and was imprisoned there, a rumor apparently began to circulate: "It was said that the child had been found in the home of a Jew, hidden in a barrel sealed with nails in order to extract its blood."[1] This macabre discovery aroused the populace, which threatened to attack Jews indiscriminately. The Jewish population avoided a bloodbath thanks only to the protection of the intendant. The charge of ritual murder stimulated the imagination, triggered hallucinations, and drove witnesses to invent the most irrational fantasies throughout the duration of the affair. The rumor mentioned in the anonymous diary captured the full horror of the situation, reminiscent of the fantastic prints depicting the murder in Trent, which still lived in memory. We do not know where the rumor originated or how it related to Raphaël. We do not know who might have heard it, or why the alleged barrel had not been found quickly when Jewish homes were searched, since they were all located in the same area of the city. This story of a child sealed inside a barrel awaiting a barbaric end was not mentioned by Amelot de La Houssaye, Olry Terquem, or Joseph Reinach, but the image was a terrifying one, which left an indelible impression, influenced public opinion, incited hatred of Jews, and no doubt contributed to the execution of Raphaël Lévy, who could do nothing to counter it.

In fact, everything seems to have been permitted. Appearing before judges who raised no objections, asked for no clarifications, and even seemed to encourage stories of this sort, witnesses told the most bizarre tales. They generally dated back a number of years, yet the witnesses remembered the facts with remarkable precision (except for certain crucial details, often of a material kind). These fables, which had nothing whatsoever to do with Raphaël Lévy, contributed to the judgment against him by encouraging a range of irrational associations and inferences. Throughout the trial, evocative comparisons were introduced. They too had nothing to do with the case itself, but their emotional charge was such that they were bound to influence the judges. For several weeks, witness after witness appeared with what each thought was damning proof of Raphaël's guilt. For instance, on December 2, 1669, Didier the Egyptian recalled that four or five years earlier he had been assigned to travel to Verdun with a Jew who wished to convert. This Jew allegedly told him that "the Jews liked to take young Christian girls who still had their virginity and draw blood from their feet and arms, and that they used this blood, but he did not remember for what." In what respect did these words allegedly spoken years earlier advance the investigation, since this was hearsay based on no tangible proof and served only to sow doubt about Raphaël's denials? Furthermore, the hearsay was based on the words of a man who was about to convert to Catholicism and was ostensibly attacking his former co-religionists.

Let us examine two more depositions that the judges agreed to hear even though they did not concern the Lévy case and had no connection to the charge of Jewish ritual murder. They were taken, rather, in connection with the case against Mayer Schwabe and others, which will be discussed at greater length in the next chapter. On January 24, 1670, Nicolas Boêmey recalled:

> Six years ago, having gone to the cathedral of this city to hear the sermon because it was Sunday, he left a son named Brice, who was then five and a half, on his doorstep after giving him some money to buy cherries. And upon returning from the sermon, he asked his wife about the child, and she said that she had not seen him for an hour, so that the deponent was obliged to look for him in all the neighbors' houses. Not finding him, he obtained permission from the city's mayor the next day to have the boy's name cried out by the drummer, which he did at every intersection without learning any news of the child. [...] He has not seen him or heard any news of him.

That is the end of Boêmey's story. Marguerite Close, his wife, followed him:

> Said that six years ago remembered that it was a Sunday that she lost a son who was then five and a half, who left the house at around half past noon to buy some cherries in the neighborhood, and when her husband returned from the sermon he asked where the child was, which caused her to notice that he had gone missing. [...] And, not having found him, the next day they had his name cried out by the drummer at the city's intersections and then went looking for him in all the surrounding villages without learning anything. Since which time she could not imagine what had become of him, nor would she be able to accuse anyone of having taken him.

These disturbing accounts of a couple's loss of a child who went off to buy cherries and never returned are highly emotional. Like Didier's parents, this mother and father went from place to place in search of the boy, called on their neighbors for assistance, and hoped desperately that they might find him. But the child had disappeared and would never return. We will never know what happened to him. Was he lost? Was he kidnapped? Was he attacked by wild animals? Did he fall down a well? Did he drown in a pond? The record is silent. Unlike the Le Moynes, the mother in this case says she "wouldn't be able to accuse anyone of having taken him." The husband does not even mention this possibility. This is a man who went to mass on Sunday and listened to the priest's sermon; as a practicing Catholic he is presumably immune to this sort of fabrication. Neither parent imagined their child might have been the victim of a crime, much less a ritual murder. No menacing Jew figures in their narratives. To be sure, the clerk does not tell us how the judges reacted to this tale; nor does he indicate the extent to which this and similar stories may have influenced their judgment of Raphaël's guilt, despite the illogic of linking the two events. In any case, the judges do not seem surprised by the testimony; nor do they reject it, and the archives contain no explicit record of any questions they might have asked, even though the questions they raised about other aspects of the investigation were carefully noted by the clerks.

Another deposition was taken on January 30, 1670, and although it too had nothing to do with Raphaël Lévy, it may have struck the judges as offering some fragile corroboration of the charges. According to Humbert Brouillard:

> About ten or twelve years ago, when he was a soldier in Sieur Laubusel's company, which was stationed in this city, while passing by the rue des Juifs, he saw that the cellar of one of the city's Jewish homes was being emptied, the owner of which he did not know, and he noted that mixed in the dirt that was being removed from said cellar, there was the head of a dead person, which the deponent took in his hand and threw to the ground, and from there he went to the guard house and told the corporal that he had seen and handled said head, whereupon the corporal ordered him to investigate and gave him two soldiers from the company, and all three went to the rue des Juifs to the place where he had seen said skull, but they could not find it.

This story also remained buried in the mass of trial documents. Its terrifying details of Jewish depravity would have delighted a writer such as Édouard Drumont, who might have seized on it for his crusade had he known of its existence. Notice, however, that this deposition also describes an event said to have taken place many years earlier—ten or twelve years, to be exact. Furthermore, it concerns a Jew whose name the witness does not know and who does not seem to have been prosecuted despite the apparent discovery of a skull in his cellar. Finally, notwithstanding all this material evidence, the case does not figure in any judicial archive. In other words, the deposition asks us to believe that a skull was seen, that the report was investigated by soldiers who would certainly have filed a report with their superiors, and yet nothing came of it. Was this colorful tale purely and simply an invention? Was the skull, if there was one, a child's skull? The witness does not say this, even though he claims to have held the skull in his hand before "throwing" it to the ground. The discovery of this skull was obviously intended to recall the discovery of little Didier's skull in the forest of Glatigny. But once again, this testimony, meant to be damning for Raphaël, seems like a tall tale, which in any case has nothing to do with ritual murder. If it was included among the trial documents, it was solely to create a climate of suspicion; with so many similar stories brought to light by the trial, how could the alleged crime not also be true despite the absence of tangible proof (other than the testimony of the few witnesses who stood by their stories)?

Gilles Le Moyne, little Didier's father, was convinced of Raphaël Lévy's guilt. In a plea to parlement on behalf of himself and his wife in mid-January 1670, he insisted, throughout his statement on the ritual murder aspect of the case, on calling for the most extreme punishment. Lévy stood for all Jews, whom Le Moyne saw as people bent on "deicide because they are enemies of the Christians." Thus the boy's murder was depicted as a reenactment of the murder of Jesus, a primal scene that the Jews were condemned to repeat forever. Gilles Le Moyne ridiculed Raphaël's protestations of innocence, which he saw as intended solely to "save his synagogue and to claim that they do not murder or sacrifice any Christian because their law prohibits it." Presenting themselves several times as "poor supplicants," the Le Moynes claimed to be seeking justice: "Poor supplicants, they lost their only child, and they might have been half consoled if the death of this poor innocent boy had occurred in any way other than by the hand of this new Herod, thirsty for his blood in order to sacrifice it to the inhumanity and barbarity of his synagogue."

No previous witness had formulated the charge of ritual murder in such unambiguous, vehement language. The allegations mentioned earlier, at least one of which (the case of the young virgin) implied a ritual murder, were not made until much later in the trial and had no direct relationship to the Lévy affair. For Didier's parents, who were in fact the people responsible for keeping an eye on their child, Raphaël Lévy was a new Herod who had sacrificed their son for the sake of his synagogue, reenacting the deicide that for Christianity was the central event in the history of the world. Was it because the Le Moynes felt guilty that they stated out loud an allegation that had previously remained unspoken?

Raphaël Lévy had refuted the idea of ritual use of Christian blood as early as December 14, 1669, to no avail: "Never, he exclaimed, do Jews use Christian blood or any other human blood or brute animals, and even when Jews want to eat meat, they soak it in water for an hour in order to drain the blood from it, besides which they salt the meat and leave the salt for another hour to make sure that all the blood is drawn out, after which they remove the salt and dispose of it along with the water in which their meat soaked."

This is an accurate description of the ritual whereby Jews make meat kosher. It also underscores the refusal of Jews to eat any food containing blood, which Raphaël offered as proof of his innocence. He implies that any observer of good faith would reject the charge of ritual murder on the grounds that the ingestion of blood is alien to Jewish religious beliefs. Lévy stuck to this defense; he invoked religion to deny the charges against him. As he said on December 18, 1669, "Nothing horrifies Jews as much as things of this sort." To the end he insisted that "Jewish law does not call for martyrs." He denied kidnapping the child, and on January 17, 1670, just before the torture began, when asked "whether the dead Rabbi advised them to abduct children to make martyrs of them," he answered in the negative. His plight had forced him to become an amateur historian and sociologist, so that when he was interrogated on December 18, 1669, he tried to explain why he thought the charges against him had been made: "Said that, since they are of a different faith from the Christians and are so few in number wherever they live, they find that they are always accused falsely by wicked people who wish them ill. And that is why they offer special prayers to God that they not be accused of kidnapping children, because when a child is lost, people frequently spread the rumor that the Jews took it, even though no such thought ever occurred to them."

In other words, Raphaël worked out his own sociological explanation for the terrible charge against him: that the permanent minority status of the Jews in the midst of an often hostile population made them the perfect scapegoats. He emphasizes an important point: the crucial role of ordinary people in dramatizing the allegation. Throughout the trial, it was among "the populace" that rumors originated and "the populace" that lashed out against the Jews, whom people envied or feared. And it was "the populace" that resorted to violence. Raphaël was aware of this and blamed his neighbors more than his judges, who he believed were trying to do their duty under constant pressure from a threatening "populace." His most zealous accusers were in fact his immediate neighbors, people who knew him and had rubbed shoulders with him for years. To be sure, a number of his close neighbors, including the miller and the servant girl, remained loyal to him to the end and even testified in his behalf. But Raphaël was quite viscerally aware of the traditional antagonism that so many Jews have experienced in various times and places.

What emerges from the testimony of these various witnesses is a radical hostility to Jews. For Gilles Le Moyne, the crime was nothing less than a reenactment of the death of Jesus, for which he held the Jews responsible. Then as now, he implies, these implacable "enemies" of the Christian religion had but one desire: like their former king Herod, they were after the blood of Christian children for use in their synagogues. Le Moyne, who had surely studied his catechism in Counter-reformation Lorraine, was thus able to invoke the name of Herod as a symbol of the mysterious Orient, a man accused in the Gospel according to Matthew of ordering the massacre of the innocent, the children of Bethlehem. Although this monstrous deed was not mentioned in any of the other Gospels, Matthew portrayed the king of the Jews as a brutal ruler who ordered a large number of executions.[2] In the Christian imagination, Herod was Satan, the Antichrist—a profoundly disturbed and megalomaniac personality, in sharp contrast to the evident modesty of Raphaël Lévy. Yet in the eyes of Gilles Le Moyne, he symbolized the power of the Jews (although Jews frequently condemned Herod). Recent historiography has gone some distance toward restoring Herod's reputation: he built the fortress of Massada, imagined the city of Caesarea and its port, rebuilt a majestic Temple, and displayed great talent as a state builder. To Christians, however, he symbolized unlimited power and was a tyrant who devoured children. Raphaël unfortunately became his threatening modern incarnation.

In his plea of January 1670, Didier's father argued that Raphaël "wants to insinuate that they do not massacre or sacrifice Christians and that their law prohibits this. His explanation is wrong, considering the sacrifice of Abraham and the Old Testament, which shows that their synagogue observes and does the opposite. It is enough for said petitioners to make convincing allegations, which cannot be refuted by Jewish allegations taken from the Talmud of the Infidels, whose only purpose is to oppress Christians and foster hatred of them, including comparing them to dogs."

Gilles Le Moyne, Raphaël's principal accuser, was the only witness to cite Abraham's sacrifice as undeniable proof that Jews are capable of sacrificing children. This idea is linked to that of the *Kiddush Ha-Shem*, the sacrifice of children in desperate situations, for instance during crusades, in order to avoid conversions, as may have happened in Germany and even in Metz. This hypothesis is supported by the near simultaneity of Jewish martyrdom and the accusation of ritual murder.[3] In his final attack on Raphaël Lévy, Gilles Le Moyne drove his point home by reviving, in the middle of the seventeenth century, Christian fantasies rooted in the sacrifice of Jacob by Abraham.

Le Moyne was also the only witness to attack the "Talmud of the Infidels," which he indicts along with the Old Testament as the source of what he believes to be the Jews' inveterate hatred of Christians. As the father of the vanished child, Le Moyne was a central figure in the case, but oddly enough he does not seem to have testified in person and never directly confronted Raphaël Lévy. His petition to parlement was not submitted until late in the case, on January 12, 1670, the day after Lévy's attorney Beausire delivered his brilliant summation, in which he pointed out the magnitude of the contradictions in the testimony of any number of witnesses. Le Moyne may have felt it all the more urgent to intervene because Beausire had openly denounced "everything that religious zeal and hatred of the Jews conjured up to condemn them." Le Moyne's statement was intended to refute the attorney's courageous exposition of the consequences of ineluctable religious conflict. His violent attack struck home effectively because it was formulated in almost scholarly terms: he was the only person in the case to use the Talmud as proof that Jews hate Christians. How did this humble peasant know about the Talmud? How was a resident of the tiny, remote village of Glatigny even aware of the existence of such a work? We will never know. His petition, which also mentioned Herod, was followed a few days later by the torture and execution of Raphaël Lévy. It can therefore be read as an explicit call for vengeance.

On January 16, 1669, Lévy was subjected to a particularly horrible session of torture. The climate in Metz was close to that of religious warfare, although the Church as an institution did not participate. Raphaël was questioned to find out

> whether he, who is an elder among the Jews, was not aware that on Good Friday and other days they mock the passion of the son of God of the Catholic religion.
>
> Said no and added that all who spread such rumors are the dregs of the populace, ignorant of their [Jewish] law and what they practice.

Raphaël not only denied the existence of the incriminated practices to the end; he also took care to single out "wicked people" among the Christians, among the "dregs of the populace," who wished "harm to the Jews." To the end, Raphaël Lévy insisted on the innocence of many Christians. For instance, he described the mayor of Boulay as "honest" and "generous." The young serving girl also remained loyal to him, a girl who, in her own words, "professes the apostolic and Roman Catholic religion." Later, when pressed again to turn against the Jew in a climate of aggressive hostility, she courageously replied that "she has nothing to reproach said Raphaël Lévy for." Among other "Just" Christians of the time were Catholic witnesses on behalf of Raphaël who were never heard by the court; they included the miller, who never wavered in his support, as well as the two cobblers from Boulay whom he had met on his way back to that town to participate in Rosh Hashanah services. Clearly, Raphaël never extrapolated from Gilles Le Moyne's attitude to conclude that all Christians were against him. He reserved his enmity for "wicked people" and refused to endorse the idea of a visceral hostility between Jews and Christians.

Some time after the trial ended (the precise date is unknown), the king echoed these tolerant sentiments:

> The king forbids and prohibits acceptance or belief of any such stories, as is clearly stated in the bull He dispatched, which states: "It sometimes happens that a few Christians, who bear hatred toward Jews, hide or lose their own children, whereupon they spread the rumor that the children were taken, abducted, murdered, and sacrificed by Jews, who eat their hearts and drink their blood, and because of these wicked tales and baseless stories said Jews, though innocent, are arrested prosecuted, imprisoned, and since it is well-known that these and other, similar rumors are false, given that the Jews do not sacrifice and do not serve any sacrifice and do not eat or drink blood, especially of animals with cloven hooves, no Christian shall for these reasons bear witness against nor be heard as a witness against any Jew."

Unfortunately, it was already too late for Raphaël Lévy, but this royal decree, which put an end to various other trials stemming from the Lévy affair, is a clear repudiation of the myths to which some Christians still ingenuously adhered. By a strange coincidence, the king also used the adjective "wicked" to describe credulous and malevolent Christians, as distinct from all those who, like the Most Christian King himself, remained impervious to such myths.

One reason so many prejudices emerged in this trial is that, for many of the people involved, religious ideas broadly structured their perception of the world and their relation to time and space. As we have seen, the timing of Raphaël's travels was determined by religious holidays, and in a broader sense the Jewish calendar governed the everyday lives of Lévy and his co-religionists. The religious calendar also governed the lives of the Catholics of Lorraine in this age of Counterreformation, which witnessed many changes in religious practice. We see this in the testimony of a number of witnesses. Boêmey recalled that it was upon his return from church, where he had heard a sermon, that he wondered about the prolonged and worrisome absence of his son, who had gone off to buy cherries. His wife also stated that it was when her husband came home from church that she first became aware of her son's disappearance. Most of the witnesses dated various episodes in the case in relation to religious events such as Michaelmas (which figured in a charge of desecration of the host at Passau in 1477) or All Saint's Day, an important holiday in the Catholic tradition.

It is also striking to observe how the anonymous Jew identified various actors in the case as Catholics in his diary. On the very first page, he refers to the "Lorraine cavalryman and other Catholics" who entered the city of Metz at the same time as Raphaël, who later met "two Christian individuals" on his way home. Then he reported that "rumor had it that a Catholic peasant had lost his child" and that "this Christian" had gone to Metz with his wife.[4] Similar identifications are found throughout the presentation of the affair. All the witnesses are explicitly identified as such: "Two Catholics testified," "a Catholic woman" came to give a deposition, "a Christian from Les Étangs also came to say . . . ," while another had "heard from a Catholic man named Clausquin." Somewhat later, we read that "Christian women spread rumors on several occasions," while "another Christian testified" and "another Christian and his servant claimed to have seen. . . ." In the diary (but not in the trial documents), Raphaël Lévy himself identifies certain witnesses in this way: "He can prove, he claims, by the miller of Boulay and three Catholics whom he met as well as other Christians. . . ." References to Catholics and Christians occur frequently in the diary, but Catholics are never distinguished from Protestants, who were numerous in the region (perhaps the author of the diary was unaware of the distinction). This is particularly striking since that author presents the chronology of the case entirely in terms of the Jewish calendar. Hebrew months are repeatedly used as markers, as are the religious holidays that influence the everyday behavior of the actors. Although the Church did not become involved in the case against Raphaël, what one sees is a confrontation of two religions living side-by-side in mutual distrust, as if religion were a structural factor in shaping an antagonism, or at any rate an insuperable separation, conducive to irrational outbursts and belief in myths such as ritual murder. In Christian eyes, Jews were remote and alien beings.

Raphaël Lévy refused to defend himself by alleging that a visceral hostility existed between Christians and Jews. He studied the record of his own case and, like Captain Dreyfus after him, became literally the most competent expert on it, yet he refrained from accusing his neighbors as a group. He limited himself to attacking the logic implicit in the testimony of his accusers, demolishing their arguments step by step. He displayed a surprising tenacity and pugnacity, and it is clear that he read the dossier carefully, analyzed it logically, and identified all the factual errors, contradictions, and even barely perceptible shifts in vocabulary. He tirelessly attacked the prejudices underlying certain hostile judgments and sent letter after letter and petition after petition to the various authorities dealing with the case. For instance, in one astonishing (undated) petition to parlement, Raphaël Lévy, like Alfred Dreyfus after him, and with equal force, protested against the failure to include certain evidence in the trial record, in violation of the rules of legal procedure:

> All the details have been hidden from him, because said minutes were not communicated to him, nor were any of the subsequent documents that might have been used to deduce his innocence. Mere reading aloud of the minutes cannot give him all the information he needs for his defense, especially since he does not understand French perfectly, much less the terminology of the Palais [i.e., legal language]. [...] The petitioner is well aware that witness reports and other documents of this kind are secret in criminal trials, but the minutes of the testimony concerning the recovery of the body [of the child Didier] should not be a secret document. [...] It is therefore just and reasonable that he

> receive these minutes and other non-secret documents made subsequently, even of his interrogation, so as to identify any evidence that might help to prove his innocence and in particular to determine whether the individuals who discovered and found this body are not relatives of said Lemoine [*sic*] and his wife or otherwise suspect, since they notified the court only long after the fact, during which time they had ample opportunity to arrange the body, clothing, and other items as they saw fit.

Raphaël's tenacity is astonishing. He admits that he does not understand French well, much less the legal language used by the court, yet he understands the procedural rules governing criminal trials. His request to the court is formulated in sophisticated language: "so as to identify any evidence that might help to prove his innocence." He hopes to undermine the testimony of the Le Moynes and to shed light on the strange way in which the body was discovered while no authorities were present. The parents "notified the court only long after the fact," so that "it might please the court to order the constable to proceed to the spot and prepare a report on the state in which [the body] was found." In short, Raphaël reproached the court for allowing itself to be manipulated by the Le Moynes and their friends after failing in its basic obligation to conduct an impartial investigation.

With vivacity and even humor, Raphaël also exposed the many contradictions in the testimony of the witnesses for the prosecution. On December 24, 1669, for example, he mocked the testimony of Idote Charpentier, who

> never saw him enter with a child and a gray-brown cloak on the day when the child is supposed to have been abducted from Glatigny [...] said above that she did not know the date or time when she saw said Jew pass by the Porte des Allemands, yet said witness stated that she saw the Jew's black hair without noting his face or height or the color of his horse, which was white, which shows the falsity of the deposition, since it was impossible during the time that she had to consider said Jew because she could not have noticed what he has just observed.

Charpentier had identified Lévy as the kidnapper of the child on the basis of his hair color while insisting that she could not recognize his face, just as Marguerite Gassin recalled that the person she saw passing by had black curly hair but "she could not remember whether it was the accused." Raphaël pertinently remarked "that he does not know what the witness means, because she says that she does not know him." How could the court accept such testimony when he pointed out several times, in the presence of other witnesses, that he did not wear a cloak that day ("The witnesses have testified out of envy and not to tell the truth, and he had no cloak and never wore a gray-brown cloak")? This piece of evidence turned out to be crucial, because Raphaël demolished the argument of the many witnesses who simply invented this cloak as proof of his guilt. Indeed, as other witnesses attested, he had been wearing a simple tunic, which afforded him no opportunity to hide a child. He pointed out himself that it "was quite cold" and that he "held his horse's reins on top of his tunic because he had no cloak." He returned to this point several times during the hearings because he believed that it offered clear proof of his innocence, since it was impossible to hide a child beneath a garment of this sort. He also demolished the testimony of Anne Godelet, whose imagination knew no bounds. Her fantastic testimony was based on unverifiable hearsay from a person she (naturally) could not identify. On December 2, 1669, carried away by passion, she testified as follows: "Also heard two days ago from a peasant in Walcheprick whose name she does not know that on the day when the child from Glatigny was lost, he met said Raphaël on his way to Metz on a white horse that was all in a lather, carrying in front of whom something that resembled a child, and he even saw the head as the Jew galloped past and his cloak was lifted by the wind."

The white horse all in a lather, the child's head peeking out for a fleeting moment as the wind blew the cloak aside. . . . Raphaël defended himself point by point. From the time of the first charges on October 24, 1669, he had repeatedly stated that the horse he was riding was white with a short tail, and he denied the description given by the cavalryman who claimed to have met him: "Said cavalryman stated that the horse on which said Jew was mounted had one ear cut off and that the Jew was more powerful and taller than the respondent and that he had a gray cloak, and the horse of the respondent, as has been acknowledged, has both of its ears, and the respondent was without a cloak."

Raphaël neglected no detail, no matter how small: he pointed out the simple fact, which anyone could verify, that his horse had both of its ears, so that any person of good faith should immediately conclude that this horse was not the one the cavalryman had seen and therefore he was also mistaken about the person. Similarly, the inconsistencies in the cavalryman's allegations should suffice to prove they were false, since he began by stating he had met Raphaël and the child but sometime later, before the judge, he admitted that he had not told the truth, that Raphaël was not the person he had encountered and had not signaled him with his eyes and hands as if to buy his silence—signals that were supposed to have been undeniable signs of the Jew's guilt.

On several occasions Raphaël attacked the crucial testimony of Blaisette Thomas, the butcher's wife, which the judges nevertheless found convincing. She stated that shortly after giving birth,[5] she saw Raphaël enter Metz through the Porte des Allemands with the little boy riding on the withers of his horse. On January 8, 1670, Raphaël stated

> that it had come to his attention that the butcher's wife who said she had seen the petitioner pass by with a child on his horse thirty-six hours after giving birth and that in his confrontation with the witness, she said that he was the person she had seen, told several people before and after the trial was heard in the *bailliage* that, when she saw said petitioner pass with a child, she had not yet given birth, and that investigation will reveal that she gave birth only one day before the allegedly kidnapped child went missing, the petitioner was supposedly seen entering the city with a child several days before the one in question was lost, which would be very relevant for the proof of his innocence.

Raphaël was determined to refute this key point, which would demolish the charges against him. This woman's testimony was crucial to the case. Indeed, as Lévy's lawyer argued, "the butcher's wife said that she saw the accused enter with the child at midday, which she interprets as between ten in the morning and one in the afternoon," but "by the testimony of the father and mother, the child was not lost until three in the afternoon." The butcher's wife's testimony collapsed when, according to the anonymous diary, "the husband stated that on Monday his wife had given birth and had remained in bed for two days. How could she have seen the pious man and the child when she was in bed, especially since her windows opened to the rear?" The court chose to ignore all of this and to believe instead this woman's highly fanciful testimony.

Raphaël also asked that non-Jewish witnesses be heard, for instance the miller who was with him constantly during the trip from Boulay to Metz as well as for much of the return trip to Boulay, which they entered at the same time.[6] He also suggested calling André Lemusnier as well as the two cobblers, Jean Mouseler and Jean Cordonnier, whom he met and greeted on his way back to Boulay. Or again, Jean Cherer, the Boulay surgeon, who was preparing to leave for Burgundy and whom Raphaël asked to be called as a witness a few days before his execution, but in vain. He submitted a petition to which he received no response: "It is very important," he wrote, "for the exoneration of the accused that said Cherer not leave before being heard."

Two centuries before Captain Alfred Dreyfus, Raphaël Lévy transformed himself into a handwriting expert and translator. He carefully examined how the two translators had rendered his words, displaying surprising expertise in equivalences between German and French. He rejected the translation of numerous words, protested against inaccuracies, and claimed that certain words that counted against him did not appear in his statements, including insults such as "dog" and "liar" and the phrase "I no longer make excuses for myself." Last but not least, he challenged the confusion between *gefunden* and *gebunden*—a point that would prove crucial. He stated that in the tenth of the letters that he gave to the servant girl, he had asked whether the child had been *gefunden*, that is, found. But both translators read this as *gebunden*, meaning bound or garroted. This translation was a key piece of evidence: if Raphaël knew that the child had been bound, if he possessed this information, then he was undeniably guilty. Although the servant, on questioning, confirmed Raphaël had never uttered the phrase "the child was bound," the judges believed they had at last found incontrovertible proof of the defendant's guilt.

There was one additional point, however, on which Raphaël admitted his testimony had changed, and this supported his accusers. Impressed by the strength of Lévy's character despite his violent hostility toward him, Amelot de La Houssaye was only too glad to point out this single lapse. Early in the investigation, on October 14, Raphaël testified that he had loaded the barrels of wine onto his son's horse, telling his son that he would catch up with him because "his horse would not be weighed down." But during the torture session of January 16, 1670, he testified "that it would have been impossible for him to carry a child in front of him because his horse was laden with oil and other provisions that he had bought in the city." Having exhausted all his arguments and feeling desperate, Raphaël thus contradicted himself on this one point, although he had previously remained on top of every detail of the case and refuted his accusers point by point. In the end, however, this contradiction does not seem to have weighed heavily in the final judgment; the judges did not pick up on it.

Raphaël Lévy was aware that his trial had been one-sided and biased. A few days before his death sentence, on January 8, 1670, sensing that the verdict would not be in his favor, he submitted yet another petition to "Our Lords of Parlement":

> Humbly begs Raphaël Lévy, Jew, voluntary prisoner in the royal prisons of this city, saying that, in the prosecution of the extraordinary case against him, he has been advised that the police lieutenant who has always been much inclined to hear witnesses against the accused and never for him, has heard all the witness who wanted to accuse the petitioner and carefully arranged for their depositions to be recorded in writing, but when others came forward prepared to say that they saw a man on horseback passing with a child but that it was not the petitioner, whom they know, he refused to hear them, saying that their testimony was of no use.

Not only would those witnesses for the defense remain unheard, but none of the Jewish witnesses would be called to testify. They were considered unsuitable, deemed in advance to be parties to the case who would conceal the truth simply because they shared Raphaël Lévy's faith. In other words, any number of witnesses, both Jews and non-Jews, were unable to testify in his defense. Despite all the implausible statements in the record, which both Raphaël and his lawyer pointed out, the charge of ritual murder, suddenly revived in a region from which it had vanished, definitively sealed his fate.

Six Good Friday at Mayer Schwabe's

A Desecration of the Sacred Host?

During the trial another myth resurfaced, one deeply rooted in the Christian imagination but unrelated to the charge against Raphaël Lévy. Oddly, this trial within the trial did not begin until December 2, 1669, despite Didier Le Moyne having vanished on September 25 and Raphaël Lévy first being interrogated in prison on October 14. In the meantime, a parade of witnesses had appeared, the child's skull was found, and the trial for ritual murder was proceeding apace. Then, on December 2, a new incident arose, which initially seemed to have nothing to do with the fate of the accused. Witnesses not previously interviewed suddenly appeared to testify about a mysterious gathering of Jews that had nearly ended in the murder of a respectable Christian citizen of Metz. Claude Daillon, the royal official who conducted the entire investigation, allowed these new witnesses to testify, even though they knew nothing about the disappearance of the child or the supposed role of Raphaël Lévy. Indeed, he paid close attention to their testimony throughout a series of hearings that he ultimately linked to the case against Raphaël Lévy. In fact, there was no logical reason for these witnesses to be heard in the order they were heard, and this lent something of a magical aura to the whole series of accusations.

Clémence Paquin, the widow of Antoine Clausquin, a tailor of Metz, was the first to testify:

> Said that she had heard from said deceased, her husband, that the late Chaucer, a plowman living in Pontiffroy, had asked him eight or nine years ago to borrow from the Jews of this city the sum of ten écus, which obliged him to go to the home of Mayeur [*sic*] Schwabe, Jew, on the day of the great Friday [Good Friday], at around ten or eleven in the morning. And having entered the house of said Schwabe, in a

> back room, he saw several Jews gathered around a large table, some of them armed with halberds and others with feathers in their hats, who were simulating the death and passion of the son of God. He did not tell her that he had seen anything on the table, but after being seen by said Jews, one of them set upon said deceased, her husband, with a large knife and tried to cut his throat, but he parried the blow and took it on his right hand, and at the same time, having been pulled by his cloak, he left it in the hands of the Jews and fled through the street door of said Schwabe's house, where his wife returned his coat, and, upon leaving said house, he met one Birier, Jew, who said to the late Clausquin that he had better not speak of the insult he had received and that there would be a coin of six risdalers for him, but said Clausquin refused to listen to him and went immediately to file a complaint with the police lieutenant. Since that time, neither the deponent nor her husband knew what became of the case, but she knew that her husband suffered for some time from the wound he had received on his hand, because she had seen it and helped him treat it.

That same day, Martin Cuny, a master cobbler also residing in Metz, followed Paquin to the stand:

> Said that eight or nine years ago, while descending the rue des Juifs on Good Friday at eleven or twelve in the morning, he encountered Antoine Clausquin, a tailor of Metz, who showed him his bloody right hand and told him that he had just been wounded in the home of Mayeur [*sic*] Schwabe, where he had seen several Jews gathered in a back room of the house in which there were three or four long planks in the form of a table and on these several lighted candles with a crucifix set in the middle, and that some of said Jews wore hats and the others hats decorated with feathers and were armed with halberds, pikes, and knives, and when these men saw him, the wife of said Schwabe pushed him into the room and shouted that he must be killed, and at the same time one of said Jews came at him with a knife and tried to cut his throat, but that he parried the blow and was wounded on the hand, and then, after trying to escape from their clutches, he left his cloak and fled through the door onto the street, where they threw his cloak after him, and during the time that said late Clausquin recounted to the deponent what had happened to him and showed him his wound, there arrived one Aaron [no other name known] and one Grand Birier, Jews, who told said Clausquin to enter a house to have his wounds bandaged

> and said that he would be given six white écus and told him to make no fuss, to which said Clausquin responded that he would never sell his blood and would file a complaint, and when said deponent asked said Clausquin why the Jews had mistreated him, he said that it was because he had taken their gathering by surprise, which they said he should not have seen, nor the things that they wanted to do. Added further that he had seen on the table a writing desk, paper, and that everything was arranged in such a way that it seemed that the Jews wanted to simulate the death and passion of Our Lord Jesus Christ. Does not know if said Clausquin then went to the police lieutenant to file his complaint but remembers hearing him say that he had done so, and nevertheless was never summoned by said police lieutenant to make a statement, and since that time has heard no more about the case. That is all he said.

These, then, were the ingredients of the drama: Good Friday, the most dramatic date in the Christian calendar, the passion of Jesus Christ, his interminable suffering, and the spilling of his blood, for which the Jews were held responsible. This event is solemnly commemorated in a highly ritualized manner, as Christians virtually relive in their own bodies the crucifixion of Jesus. Over the centuries this event had of course often been written about, depicted in painting and sculpture, and commemorated in musical compositions, some of which could be heard in the churches of Counterreformation Lorraine. The testimony of these two witnesses thus introduced the ultimate mystery of Christianity into the heart of a trial that had been dragging on for quite some time. This unexpected turn in the case suddenly transformed its nature by confirming a deliberate attack on the Christian people. Underlying the linkage between the two cases was the fact that Good Friday called to mind the Jewish Passover (or Pesach), during which Jews, according to the myth of ritual murder, sacrifice children in order to use their blood in the preparation of matzoh. To be sure, the date was wrong: the murder in the Lévy case was supposed to have taken place at the beginning of the Jewish year, in the "terrible months" of September and October, which were not associated in the Catholic imagination with ritual murder, since this was not a time when Jews made matzoh, the unleavened bread that commemorated their flight from Egypt and time of wandering in the desert.

The Schwabe case was better adapted to the Catholic calendar, because it coincided with the passion of Jesus. The testimony of the witnesses plunges us straightaway into the mysteries of the Catholic faith, allegedly simulated and mocked in a somber back room of Schwabe's house, dimly lit by candles that revealed a crucifix set upon a long table. Around the table, half-hidden in the shadows, we find a cast of strange characters transposed directly from some medieval print—Jews wearing caps or hats with feathers and armed with menacing halberds, like silhouettes from a nightmare. At the center of this chilling horror tale is blood—the blood of Jesus Christ, which the Jews have allegedly mocked for centuries, blood that Schwabe was said to have "collected in bowls and other vessels and shipped off by boat."[1] There is also the blood that flows from Clausquin's hand after it is wounded as he tries to protect his throat, from which even more blood would have flowed had the blow struck home. Clausquin, his wife testified, claimed to have refused to accept payment in exchange for his silence, for this would have amounted to "selling his blood." Implicitly, there was also the blood that the Jews had been about to draw from the crucifix by plunging their blades into it. And thus, as in Trent, the ritual murder case against Raphaël Lévy suddenly took a turn that brings us face-to-face with another charge that had long haunted the Christian imagination: the desecration of the host by the blade of a knife or sword in a general context of monetary exchange.[2]

We see immediately that the testimony of the first two witnesses differed on a number of important points. Clausquin's wife testified that, before he died, she heard him say that one Chaucer, also deceased, had sent him to borrow money from Schwabe, but Martin Cuny stated that it was Clausquin himself who told him about the incident without mentioning the role of Chaucer. Of course no one could challenge the word of Clausquin, who was dead, but his wife's hearsay testimony was accepted as if it came from the man's own mouth. Even more than the widow Paquin, Martin Cuny told a dramatic tale that inevitably electrified his audience: the Jews he had seen gathered in Schwabe's back room were armed not only with halberds, he said, but also with knives and pikes, well equipped for their murderous ends. On this particular Good Friday they not only mocked Christ but also, according to Cuny, attacked a crucifix, whose outline could barely be made out in the flickering candlelight. The presence of the crucifix revealed the meaning of this somber gathering. Mme. Paquin, Clausquin's wife—the same Clausquin who told the story of the incident to Martin Cuny—was unaware of all this, however. She also knew nothing of the writing desk on the table or of the mysterious papers strewn about the crucifix and had heard nothing about the crucial role played by Schwabe's wife, who had supposedly urged the Jews to kill Clausquin. In her story, Schwabe's wife seemed eager to save her husband by hastening after Clausquin to return his torn cloak. She had no idea that Clausquin refused to "sell his blood" as the price of his silence when Aaron and Birier offered him money to say nothing about the incident and reveal nothing about the abominable practices of the Jews. Nevertheless, the prosecutor ignored these discrepancies, which impugn the witnesses' testimony.

For several days, the astonishing Clausquin affair receded into the background, while the court turned its attention once again to witnesses against Raphaël Lévy. Then, on December 9, Gérard Mangeot, a gardener from Metz, took the stand:

> Said that seven or eight years ago he heard the late Antoine Clausquin, a resident of this city of Metz, say that upon going one Good Friday to the home of a Jew of this city, he found the doors closed and opened them until he came to a back room, in which he saw ten or twelve Jews armed with pikes and other weapons gathered around a creature that they wished to kill and had arranged as if they wanted it to represent the passion of the son of God, and that the Jews, upon seeing said Clausquin, one of them came and stabbed him with a pike, which forced him to run for his life, and said Clausquin added moreover that if the doors had not happened to be open to facilitate his escape, he would certainly have been killed, said to him that it seemed he was in the house of Mayeur [*sic*] Schwabe but did not dare to affirm this because he did not remember well, and told him also that he would file a complaint with the police lieutenant.

The role of Chaucer (now dead), who had supposedly asked Clausquin (also dead) to borrow money from Schwabe, had thus been expunged from the testimony of both Cuny and Mangeot, as if to certify their authenticity. As the witnesses succeeded one another, certain details of the story were accentuated, magnifying the wickedness of the scene. According to Mangeot, it was not simply "a number" of Jews who had gathered around the table but ten or twelve, a fairly exact figure that lent verisimilitude to the tale. Who could make up the presence of a dozen individuals? Mangeot was also the first witness to speak of the presence of "a creature" that the Jews "had wished to kill and had arranged as if they wanted it to represent the passion of the son of God." Although the widow Clausquin testified that her husband "did not tell her whether he had seen anything on the table," Martin Cuny said that Clausquin had seen a crucifix, while Mangeot insisted that Clausquin had told him there was a creature on the table that the Jews intended to kill in a simulation of the passion of Christ. The nature of the testimony thus changed: Mangeot somehow came up with the word "creature," which several medieval chroniclers had used in describing desecration of the host. This presumably lent authenticity to the Good Friday ceremony at Mayer Schwabe's, with a "child" in place of the profaned and battered host.[3] Thus the rumor, retold by one witness after another, swelled in significance. Certain dramatic details were accentuated, or invented, to enhance the verisimilitude of the tale. "A creature" suddenly conjured up by one witness established an implicit link to the case against Raphaël Lévy. If the Jews of Metz had for years mercilessly mocked the passion of Jesus by sacrificing a fresh victim, then there could be no doubt about their responsibility for the ritual murder of little Didier. Blood was indispensable to their ceremonies; this was the common thread of all of the stories involving alleged diabolic attacks on Catholics or Catholic symbols. Like the story of the mutilation of the crucifix, the story of this strange Good Friday ritual had a purely symbolic side. But if a "creature" had really been stabbed to death, like the Le Moyne child, then the Jews were certainly guilty of deicide as a people. The whole episode seemed contrived to persuade the judges of this. If a dozen Jews could make a martyr of a "creature," then Raphaël Lévy, who had yet to be sentenced to death, was obviously guilty of the murder of the Le Moyne boy.

After Mangeot, another witness, Mathieu Demange, also a plowman, took the oath and testified:

> Antoine Clausquin, a resident of this city of Metz, went one Good Friday to the home of Mayeur [*sic*] Schwabe, Jew of this city, he found the front doors closed, which he opened, and seeing no one, he also opened the door of a back room of the house, in which he saw nine or ten armed Jews gathered around a creature, which bore a resemblance to the passion of Our Lord, and one of said Jews, upon seeing him,

> came toward him and stabbed him with a pike, with which he did not say that he had been wounded, but this forced him to run for his life, and that if he had not found the doors open, he would have been killed. Deponent also said that said deceased Clausquin told him that he would file his complaints with the police lieutenant, but he did not know if he had done this, never having heard it spoken of since then. Which is all that he said he knew.

Clearly, this fourth witness gave testimony quite similar in every respect to Mangeot's, for instance that "nine or ten armed Jews" threatened the same "creature" on Good Friday. Four witnesses could not be wrong; all of them corroborated the significance of the Good Friday date, which Clémence Paquin had merely referred to in passing as "*grand vendredi*" instead of "*vendredi saint*" like the others, almost diminishing its symbolic charge.

On December 18, what had remained to that point only a latent possibility now entered the case as an intangible reality. Although the questioning bore on the testimony of the cavalryman, the cobblers, and the butcher's wife, Raphaël was quite unexpectedly asked whether "on Good Friday and other days, Jews do not simulate the passion and death of the son of God in derision of the Christian religion in secret places." Naïvely, and in utter ignorance of the Schwabe affair, Raphaël Lévy replied that "that was a question he had never heard them discuss and such things were never done." On December 24, he was again questioned directly about the Schwabe affair: during one of the longest interrogation sessions of the entire case, as witness after witness testified that they had seen Raphaël on horseback with little Didier, the four witnesses in the Schwabe case confirmed their original depositions. And the unthinkable occurred: Raphaël, dumbfounded, was confronted with the witnesses who had testified about the Good Friday gathering. He objected to these tall tales and insisted that they were devoid of all reality. Quite logically, he hammered on one idea: Martin Cuny based his deposition on the word of Clausquin, a man who had been dead for a long time, so "said witness should be punishable for not having reported what he knew to the authorities at that time, which shows that this is perjured testimony, that the Jews never do this kind of thing." Similarly, he objected to the testimony of Clémence Paquin, whose "deposition is a falsehood expressly invented to do harm to the Jews." When finally confronted with Mathieu Demange on December 14, Raphaël argued that his testimony was "perjury... against the Jews, just like the others who were deposed on the same event, because they kept silent until now, which shows that Clausquin never spoke of this to said witnesses." In thus coming to the defense of Schwabe, Raphaël unwittingly reinforced the link between the two cases, as the prosecution intended. The general atmosphere created by this diversion served the prosecution's case. Emboldened by the supposed parallel between the two cases despite the lack of any tangible connection, the prosecutor anticipated asking for a penalty in the Schwabe case as exemplary as the one that he was preparing to request against Raphaël Lévy.

Between December 24 and January 17, however, the affair within the affair disappeared. It did not come up again until after Lévy had been executed, as if no one had paid any attention to the four Schwabe-related witnesses, who had appeared along with all the other witnesses, surgeons, translators, and others who gave evidence against Raphaël. It was only after Lévy's fate was sealed, after he had been tortured and burned, that the authorities returned to the strange, evil Good Friday gathering of Jews in the home of Schwabe, which Lévy insisted had never occurred. Schwabe was now interrogated for the first time within the walls of the prison. This marked a turning point in the case, because he was now questioned not only about the ceremony in his home but also about the abduction of little Didier. The ritual murder and the crucifixion were now linked in the imaginations of the authorities as they had been previously in the minds of the witnesses. What we see now is a metamorphosis of the accusation of ritual murder: that charge now merged with another charge—ceremonial desecration of the host—which thus linked it to the death of Jesus Christ. This linkage dated all the way back to the Middle Ages, and it was represented on the stage in Metz and elsewhere as late as the eighteenth century.[4]

The questioning of Schwabe dealt first with the Lévy affair. Schwabe appeared as a syndic of the community, along with six other prominent Jews. Recall that he was one of seven Jews whom Louis XIV had authorized to wear the black hat. When asked if he and the six others had had a hand in the abduction, he replied simply that "he is certain that Jews do not practice such abductions." Subsequent questions also dealt with the abduction of the Le Moyne child, and he answered them all in the same way: "Said that he knew nothing about any of that and that they do not engage in such acts." Then came a question that served as a transition between the two cases: "Asked if said child, having been taken by said Jews, was not crucified in derision of the death and passion of Jesus Christ. Said that it was not." The Lévy affair suddenly took on a new dimension. To be sure, several witnesses had testified a short while earlier that the strange gathering that led to the wounding of Clausquin took place at Schwabe's house on Good Friday, but no mention was made of the kidnapping of Didier Le Moyne. On January 17, 1670, after the Lévy affair was ended, as it were, by his tragic execution, the prosecutor continued to link the two affairs as he pursued his case against Schwabe. Indeed, Schwabe and his accomplices had already been accused of trying to hide evidence of the kidnapping. The Schwabe affair now assumed a greater symbolic performance: he now occupied the central position formerly occupied by Lévy. And the alleged Good Friday ritual now became central, because it tied the case in with the deepest recesses of the Catholic imagination; the prosecutor asked if little Didier had not been "crucified in derision of the death and passion of Jesus Christ"—a verbatim repetition of the charge made by several of the witnesses who had claimed to know about the gathering at Schwabe's home.

When the prosecutor questioned Schwabe about "whether it was customary among Jews to simulate the death and passion of the son of God every year and particularly on Good Friday in contempt of the Christian religion, and whether, when they found no Christian child to do such things, they used a crucifix or other representations bearing a human figure," he no longer had the murder of little Didier in mind. The Schwabe he was after now was no longer the one who had allegedly attempted to protect Raphaël by searching for Didier's body; he was rather the Schwabe of the Good Friday gathering, the one who profaned the host, as was often recounted in Metz in the form of legends brought to life in the theater and passed on from generation to generation of Catholics. The death of Christ took the place of the death of the innocent Christian child, of the "figure" incarnating the resurrected Christ—a figure that was also, for many commentators, that of Christ on the cross.[5] On January 17, 1670, Schwabe answered: "Said that they do not practice this, that they are no longer at liberty to make sacrifices, and that when they were at liberty to do so, they sacrificed lambs and never human creatures."

The remainder of the interrogation focused solely on the Good Friday gathering and not the ritual murder:

> [Asked] if he, the respondent was not surprised seven or eight years ago on Good Friday in his house with several other Jews committing similar representations, impieties, and abominations?
>
> Said no, and no one could say that he was.
>
> Asked if said Clausquin did not surprise him, the respondent, with several other Jews in a room at the back of his house, [in which] they were armed with halberds and knives and had feathers in their turned-up hats, and all around a table on which there were lighted candelabras and a crucifix in the middle of the table where a creature was stretched out and tied in the form of a cross.
>
> Said that was false and that he never had a halberd or sword in his house, except for a silver-handled sword that he was given as collateral.
>
> [Asked] if at the moment said Clausquin was seen by said Jews, one of them went after him and tried to stab him in the throat, which blow was parried by Clausquin, who was wounded on the right hand,
>
> Said that never happened and that he never saw said Clausquin in his house.
>
> [Asked] if it was he, the respondent, who stabbed said Clausquin,
>
> Said no and that the supposed stabbing never happened.
>
> Asked whether, when said Clausquin had been wounded, he had not been grabbed by the cloak to stop him and had not left said cloak in the hands of the Jews and fled through the street door,
>
> Said that he knew nothing about any of that and that it was all lies.
>
> Asked whether the wife of the respondent did not take the cloak to said Clausquin at said door,
>
> Said no and that neither he nor his wife knew anything about any of that.
>
> [Asked] whether, when said Clausquin left his house, one Birier, Jew, did not tell him that if he did not speak of the insult he had received, he would be given six risdalers,
>
> Answered that he knew nothing about any of that.
>
> [Asked] whether said Clausquin did not encounter in the street outside the respondent's house a Christian to whom he complained of what had happened to him and showed him his wound, and whether

two Jews, namely Aaron and said Birier named above, did not arrive at that moment and did not ask said Clausquin to enter a house to have his wound bandaged and did not say that if he made no fuss he would be given six écus.

Although Schwabe insisted that "all these questions are pointless, because the thing never happened," the prosecutor inexorably followed the new lead. On his own he transformed the ordinary candles into threateningly tall, majestic candelabras and used words such as "impiety" and "abomination" to accentuate the insult to the Catholic faith. Allowing his imagination free rein, he asserted that "the creature was stretched out and tied in the form of a cross," which no witness had volunteered. The image of a creature "tied in the form of a cross" and soon to be martyred, crucified, by a group of Jews reinforced the indication that a crucifix was also present and confirmed that the Jews were indeed reenacting a deicide, which justified the most severe punishment.

On January 18, 1670, the confident prosecutor again summoned the witnesses in the case, who one by one recounted what they knew of the unsavory Good Friday gathering. The three witnesses who had testified on December 2 stood by their previous depositions without hesitation. In addition to Clémence Paquin, Martin Cuny, and Gérard Mangeot, a new witness, Jaquemin Noz, known as Le Polot, a plowman, also testified, but according to him the evil gathering of Jews took place not on Good Friday but on Michaelmas and at the home of Abraham Morhange rather than Mayer Schwabe. Schwabe pointed out the contradictions that proved his innocence and cast doubt on the integrity of the witnesses, several of whom owed him money. Mathieu Demange was his "mortal enemy," he said, owing to a murky transaction involving the sale of horses, and so was Mangeot, who was also his "mortal enemy for having refused to lend him money against collateral...said witness, because of this refusal, had several times threatened to beat the accused." Similarly, Cuny "was a wretched little man who for five sols would swear a hundred false oaths and who once threatened the accused and his wife because they refused to give him a coin of thirty sols." Even more than in the Lévy case, debtors' resentments against lenders seemed to have turned into criminal accusations. As mentioned earlier, Schwabe was a syndic, a prominent individual significantly above Raphaël Lévy in socioeconomic status. Because of his advantageous social position, he was involved in many financial dealings, and conflicts stemming from those relationships evidently led to charges that were taken at face value because they reflected traditional popular beliefs.

That same day, Schwabe's wife, Sybille Zay, was interrogated along the same lines as her husband. Once again, the prosecutor asked whether she knew Raphaël, whether she knew where he had hidden the child, in what way the child had been killed, and who scattered his things around the forest. Then, without any logical transition, he turned from the Lévy case to the mysterious gathering in her home, in which she was supposed to have played a major role:

> Asked whether the Jews were not accustomed to making sacrifices or representations of the death of Christ in derision of the Catholic religion,
>
> Said no.
>
> [Asked] whether, when they could not have a Christian child for said sacrifices, they did not use a crucifix or other representation of a human figure,
>
> Said no.
>
> Asked whether said Clausquin, on Good Friday seven or eight years ago, did not surprise a number of Jews in the home of the husband of the respondent, gathered in a back room, armed with halberds, some with turned-up hats, who were around a table on which there was a crucifix or other figure of a human creature, with lighted candles, a writing desk, and paper, all to represent the death and passion of the son of God in hatred and contempt of religion,
>
> Said no, that they never did such things and that she knew nothing about any of that,
>
> [Asked] whether she, who is answering, upon seeing said Clausquin, did not say in the German or Hebraic tongue that he had to be killed,
>
> Said no, that she never saw said Clausquin,
>
> Asked whether after what she said, one of said Jews did not approach said Clausquin and try to stab him in the throat, which blow Clausquin parried and was wounded on the right hand; which of said Jews struck said blow, and whether it was her husband,
>
> Said that all of it was false, with all due respect, and that she had never heard of any such thing,
>
> Asked whether, when Clausquin tried to flee after being wounded, the Jews did not grab him by his cloak and continue to attack him, and

> whether, having freed himself, he did not leave his cloak in their hands, which she returned to him at the door of her husband's house,
>
> Said as above that she knew nothing about any of that, and that it never happened,
>
> Asked whether, when said Clausquin was in the street, he did not complain to several people to whom he told things as they had happened, and whether they were not two Jews named Aaron and the Grand Birier, who told said Clausquin not to say a word, and that if he did not speak of what had happened, there would be a coin of six risdalers for him, and asked him to enter a house to be bandaged,
>
> Said that she [was] ignorant of all that and that it never happened.

A comparable dialogue then ensued with Mayer Birier, who also had no knowledge of the fate of little Didier and who also insisted that Jews did not kidnap children. When the prosecutor asked him "whether Jews do not simulate the death of Jesus Christ, particularly on Good Friday in derision of the Christian religion," he answered: "Jews never do that kind of thing." During the week of January 24–30, 1670, the prosecutor again summoned certain of the witnesses in the Schwabe case. He also took the testimony of the parents whose child had gone off to buy cherries and never returned, an incident that was unrelated to either the Lévy case or the Schwabe case but that made the omnipresent threat to children all the more palpable.

Jaquemin Noz, known as Le Polot, testified again and amplified his narrative considerably while adding new details:

> Said and deposed that about eight or nine years ago, having bought a small horse from Abraham Morhange, a Jew of this city, for three and a half pistoles, for which credit of eight days was offered, when the term arrived, he went on Michaelmas at eight in the morning to the home of the late Antoine Clausquin, a resident of this city, who had bought said horse from him, to go together to pay the price; and both having gone to the rue des Juifs, they asked to speak to said Abraham Morhange in his house, where they were told that he was in a neighbor's house, into which said Clausquin entered first and after him said deponent, said Clausquin opened the door of room in the back of the house and heard someone say: "You will pay, fellows," and at the same time he saw leaving said room five or six Jews who hurled themselves on said Clausquin, whose cloak they tore in two, which obliged said deponent

> to flee the house and leave by the Porte du Pont des Morts, and he and Clausquin ran up the rue des Juifs, saw that he had a small scrape on his hand that he thought said Clausquin had done to himself by rubbing against the wall. Did not remember what house this was in, did not hear that it was the house of Mayeur [*sic*] Schwabe, remembered only that he was told at that time that the Jews were celebrating the Feast of Trumpets [Rosh Hashanah]; which is all he said.

Noz confirmed that this mysterious gathering took place but unwittingly attested to Schwabe's innocence by stating that the meeting had not been held in his home. His testimony shows that this case was intertwined with a complex set of economic relationships involving the purchase and sale of animals, the granting of credit, and loans left unpaid. Note, too, that the violence of the scene is accentuated, since now it is "five or six Jews" who hurl themselves at Clausquin. Oddly, Noz denied that Clausquin had been wounded in this attack and testified instead that he had scraped himself "by rubbing against the wall"—a far cry from the dripping blood reported by previous witnesses. But what attracts attention most of all is the end of his deposition. Noz makes it clear that two religious calendars and two different sets of charges were slowly coming together. The terrifying gathering of Jews that had supposedly ended in an attack on Clausquin was now said to have taken place during the religious holiday in which Jews blow the *shofar*. Noz places the incident at Michaelmas, that is, the end of September, which does indeed correspond to the Jewish New Year, or the holidays of Rosh Hashanah and Yom Kippur, when the *shofar* is blown. For the first time, the original gathering of Jews, and the occasion of the second set of criminal charges against them, was set not on Good Friday, the Friday before Easter, which takes place in March or April, but rather on Michaelmas, when the *shofar* is sounded. Noz was also the first witness who did not mention an attack on either a person held prisoner or a crucifix. His testimony marks a departure from the theme of "mockery" of Catholicism. In it, the gathering of Jews who allegedly attack Clausquin has no religious significance.

This theatrical testimony was greeted with profound silence. The prosecutor took no notice of the fact that Noz's story proved Schwabe's innocence or of the fact that this strange gathering did not in fact take place on Good Friday. Noz's version did not influence the trial, which made sense only if the heavy religious overtones of the case were reaffirmed in support of the charge of deicide, which required that the meeting be held on the day of Christ's passion rather than on the Jewish New Year. Claude Daillon, the royal prosecutor, was determined to establish that the Schwabe gathering took place on Good Friday and therefore chose to ignore the testimony that it had occurred on the "Day of Trumpets," at the same time of year as the alleged ritual murder, which had led to the execution of Raphaël Lévy and might have led the accused in the Schwabe case to fear for their lives as well. The prosecutor therefore abandoned this line of questioning, although in his final interrogation of Raphaël Lévy, who had identified Schwabe and Salomon as "his best friends in Metz," he asked again "whether the Jews Salomon and Mayer Schwabe did not advise him to kidnap children for martyrdom," thus stressing the existence of a link between the two men that would be used to condemn both of them.

Fortunately for the prosecution, and as if by miracle, a new witness came forward on January 30. His testimony put an end to any doubts that the contradictions in previous witnesses' statements might have created. At just the right moment, Jacques Moitrier, a Metz merchant, appeared to restore the essential religious dimension of the Schwabe case:

> Said and deposed that about nine or ten years ago, he could not be precise about the year, but remembered that it was a Holy Thursday or Good Friday, that he had ordered the late Clausquin to go to one Lambert, a Jew of this city, to find out the final price of a horse that he, the deponent, had sold. Said Clausquin returned about an hour later with an answer, saying that he, the deponent, was the reason he had almost been killed, whereupon, the deponent having asked to know the reason, said Clausquin told him that he had gone to the rue des Juifs to speak to said Lambert, who was not at home, and then he saw several Jews going into the house of Mayeur [*sic*] Schwabe, whereupon said Clausquin followed them to see if Lambert was among them, and he saw said Jews go down into a low space at the back of the house of said Schwabe, where he saw said Jews whipping in crucifixion a man or other creature who resembled a human, and when the Jews saw said Clausquin, said Mayeur Schwabe came at him with a knife, with which he wounded or scratched his hand. Which wound the deponent saw on the hand of said Clausquin, who was so frightened and shaken that he could barely say what had happened to him. Remembered that it might

have been ten or eleven in the morning, and that said Clausquin had not been drinking wine. That is all he said.

This time the story filled the bill perfectly: the gathering, the witness indicated, had indeed taken place on Good Friday, not at Michaelmas, and this corresponded more or less to the Jewish Passover, and the Jews were seen "whipping in crucifixion a man or other creature who resembled a human," in a ceremony symbolizing the profanation of the host. Thus, in the good city of Metz, which had enjoyed the honors of the Sun King, whose intention was to take the Jews under his protection, those same Jews had, for want of a boy to sacrifice, whipped a man, re-enacting the deicide that condemned them for all eternity. The savagery of the scene had been magnified from one witness's testimony to the next, here reaching a crescendo perfectly attuned to the most morbid imaginings of the triumphant Counterreformation. It did not matter that no victim had been reported missing, that no judicial investigation had been launched into this diabolical gathering, and that a mock crucifixion carried out by a large number of Jews and known to so many witnesses had never been publicly denounced. Nor was there any interest in the numerous contradictions among the accounts of the various witnesses. Testimony continued to be taken in somewhat haphazard fashion for another week, until the prosecutor arranged a confrontation on January 25 among Aaron Halphen, Mayer Birier, and certain witnesses for the prosecution, who persisted in their charges against the Jews. Then the case was closed, the culpability of the defendants proven. And so the prosecutions came to an end.

On January 29, the prosecutor submitted a petition to the members of parlement: "The royal prosecutor general finds that the principal Jews are guilty and accomplices in the crime of which Raphaël Lévy was convicted and anticipates that the punishment should extend to all of them, including one Mayer Schwabe, currently held prisoner." In his mind, Halphen, Birier, and Schwabe, the principals in the mysterious Good Friday ceremony that had been the subject of all the recent session of the court, were thus "guilty and accomplices in the crime" of Raphaël Lévy. There could be no doubt that "the punishment"—that is, death by burning—must "extend to all of them" as well.

Seven Popular Threats and Royal Alliance

Although the individuals involved in the Lévy and Schwabe cases knew one another well and shared a common sociability, the imagination had free rein in Counterreformation Lorraine, a region of uncertain political status fought over by Louis XIV, the duke of Lorraine, and the emperor. Political authority was deeply divided, and nothing seemed capable of quelling the anxieties of the many witnesses who appeared before the court. A veritable madness, rooted in certain unshakeable Catholic prejudices, took hold of the population, with help from the local judicial authorities, abetted by the quick withdrawal from the case of the intendant, who—oddly in a city that symbolized the authority of the French monarchy—turned his back on Raphaël Lévy almost at once.

Raphaël was aware of this: "Those who are spreading rumors," he said, "are the dregs of the populace, ignorant of their law and of what they are doing." To him it was obvious that "the people spread such rumors whenever a child is lost."[1] Lévy's attorney agreed; for him, Raphaël was "absolutely innocent, being a criminal only in the mouths of the populace, which has turned against him for no reason solely because he is a Jew."[2] The anonymous diary writer who followed the events of the case closely was also constantly critical of the irrational behavior of the "populace." On October 13, 1669, when the rumor that the child had been found in a barrel sealed with nails began to spread, some people

> persuaded the child's mother to go with a large mob to the office of the intendant and demand to see the child. But the intendant managed to calm the crowd by convincing them that the story was a lie. This did not prevent emotions from running high, so high that on that day no

> Jew [*Israélite*] dared show himself in town or country. That emotion put the [Jewish] community in great danger. There were several reports that the populace (may God preserve us and give us peace) intended to rise up that night. Two prominent Jews went to the intendant to ask for help and protection. The intendant replied that he believed the reports and that, based on what he had seen in front of his house, he saw that the allegation was false. He had the crier announce, and published on public bulletin boards, that no one was to offend a Jew with verbal insults, much less blows, and anyone who violated this order was subject to a fine of ten *risdalers*. People were supposed to warn their family members. Fathers and mothers would be held responsible for the actions of their children, and masters and mistresses for the actions of their domestics and servants, and if fines were not paid, there would be prison sentences. Thank God, this proclamation quieted the populace, and no one dared speak out against the Jews.[3]

A short while later, in mid-January, Mayer Schwabe was imprisoned. When the bailiff and judge escorted him to his cell, they

> were followed by a great multitude of the populace. From this anyone can see the danger in which the [Jewish] community found itself. But God, praised be His name, did not withdraw his mercy from us. He saw to it that we found grace in the eyes of the intendant and filled his heart with pity for us. The same was true of the judicial officials, who urged the intendant to keep an eye [on] us and to ensure that there would be no riot. The intendant dispatched the major and a number of soldiers, and they kept the populace away. Then guards were stationed for eight to ten days with orders not to allow Christians to enter the rue des Juifs by night. After that period, he urged the gate guard to patrol the rue des Juifs hourly and make sure that no harm came to the Jews, and the next day, a Friday, he once again published and posted an order that no one speak against the Jews or, worse, beat them or otherwise mistreat them, the penalty for which was set at 100 *quart d'écus*. Fathers and mothers would be responsible for the actions of their children, masters for their domestics and servants. If the fine were not paid, there would be imprisonment. He also posted the same order throughout the surrounding area, which with the help of God somewhat calmed the turmoil among the people.[4]

These two remarkable texts illustrate the fear that has always haunted the Jewish people: the fear of riots and pogroms, of unrestrained, irrational violence. Confined to their ghetto, unable to go into town or venture out into the countryside, sitting in their homes, the Jews of Metz were protected by soldiers dispatched by the intendant at the behest of two Jewish notables, who hoped to avert violence. Thanks to the forceful intervention of the intendant, who "kept an eye" on a Jewish population terrorized by the charges against both Raphaël Lévy and Mayer Schwabe with repercussions for the entire community, the worst was avoided, and there was no popular uprising. The threat of a fine and, worse, imprisonment must have dissuaded more than one potential rioter. The intendant, who represented the Most Christian King, defended the law and order of the absolutist state that he served by keeping the peace and maintaining control of his territory. He twice saved the Jews from the popular fury aroused by the charges of ritual murder and desecration of the host "in derision of the passion of Christ." He immediately recognized that the rumor about the child having been found in a barrel was "false," that it was a "lie," and he took prompt action to correct it. It remains to be seen why this same intendant was less vigilant about the handling of the case against Raphaël Lévy itself. He was no doubt equally aware of the falseness of the allegations against Raphaël and might have intervened in the name of royal authority. Why was he so quick to turn the case over to local judicial authorities, who conducted the investigation on their own? There were clearly limits to royal protection. The state protected the Jews from popular violence but was reluctant to get involved in the prosecution of Raphaël Lévy.

There is more to the story, however. In Lorraine, the overlapping of local authorities was so complex that it led to a number of conflicts between representatives of the central government and provincial officials. For instance, when the master alderman summoned the bourgeois and clergy in early March to work out a common position vis-à-vis the king, who had been asked by Jewish notables to intervene in the case, the intendant reacted negatively to a meeting that had been called without his knowledge and that included merchants and butchers who were in competition with Jews. When he learned the third estate was nevertheless holding a second assembly, he informed other authorities and went to the meeting personally, accompanied by the captain of the guard, having made up his mind to dissolve this assembly of local notables. Indeed, he forcefully intervened more than once in the Schwabe case, opposing actions by the parlement of Lorraine. At the same time, a delegation of Jewish notables left for Paris to beg the king to intervene. In mid-March, to the immense satisfaction of the Jews, who were awaiting his arrival, the intendant returned to Metz and confirmed to the leaders of the Jewish community that he was going to "ask parlement for the trial documents, that his commission included orders to review the trial from beginning to end and to find out exactly what had happened."[5] Indifferent to his presence, the local judicial authorities arrested Wilstadt Liberman and also tried to arrest Abraham Spire, who was out of town. Both were accused of offering money to witnesses to go into the woods and look for the child. Later, on March 29, the court sentenced Schwabe to pay a large fine and imposed various sanctions on the other defendants. It also prohibited Jews from entering the city during Holy Week and ordered that its judgment be engraved on a copper plaque and affixed to a stone to be placed in a small square close to the rue des Juifs. Then "the trial record was placed in the hands of Monsieur l'Intendant, who reviewed it and questioned a number of Jews in order to find out what they had to say before giving his opinion to the king, who had ordered this review."[6] The intendant asked M. Lionne to explain the situation to the king and in the meantime ordered that the judgment of parlement be suspended. The deputies refused to accept this, however, on the grounds that the intendant's order did not bear the royal seal, and they decided to ignore it.

It was at the height of this emergency that Richard Simon published his courageous *Factum*, in which he wrote: "The Jews of Metz are today hoping for the same justice from the Most Christian King and his Council, who will easily discover all the calumnies that have to date been heaped upon their nation. These calumnies are based solely on false reports and made-up stories."[7] He accepted the traditional model of the royal alliance, underscoring what "the zeal or, rather, the fury of religion can do to the minds of the people and even of their leaders," which had "obliged any number of princes to support the Jews against the calumnies of the people." He sought the intervention of the king himself to save Mayer Schwabe and the other imprisoned Jews. To that end, he petitioned the king, just as a Jewish notable had gone to Frankfurt in October 1669 to plead Raphaël Lévy's case to the emperor, whose influence in the region was great, especially since the duke of Lorraine tended to side with the emperor against the king. The notable in question returned with an order signed by the emperor, who certified that Jews did not commit such crimes. Simon, on the other hand, turned to Louis XIV, the sovereign ruler of Metz, who had shown on several occasions that he was interested in protecting the Jewish community, in favor of which he had already introduced certain measures. Demonstrating remarkable knowledge of Jewish history, Simon wrote in his *Factum*:

> The Jews are accused every day of execrating Christians, and some go so far as to claim that prayers of this nature are part of their religion. But such blasphemies are alien to them, and they pray every Saturday and on other holidays for the kings and princes of whom they are subjects....The law that requires Jews to pray to God for their princes can be found in the Talmud in the treatise on fathers called *Pirke-Avoth*, chap. III. There, Rabbi Hanina says the following: Pray for the peace of the kingdom; because if men did not fear justice, they would devour one another. Moreover, in their prayer book entitled *Seder Tephilot*, one finds the prayer they say for their king and princes in their synagogues: "Bless, keep preserve, assist, raise up, enhance, and exalt our lord the king....May the King of Kings preserve him in his mercy and cause him to prosper...may He prolong the days of his reign...may the King of Kings in his mercy fill his heart and the hearts of his princes and advisors with pity, that they may do us good and do good unto our brothers, the Israelites, during his lifetime and may Judah be saved and Israel live in the certainty that the Redeemer will come to Zion."[8]

To defend the Jews, Simon thus pointed to the famous prayer for kings and emperors, which sealed the vertical alliance. He not only knew it intimately but also used it to prove, *a contrario*, the inanity of the charges against Raphaël Lévy and his co-defendants. For him, orthodox Jews who offered up this prayer on Saturdays and holidays could not be guilty of such crimes. Raphaël Lévy, who had gone to Metz to buy wine and a *shofar* for the Rosh Hashanah and Yom Kippur holidays, had to be innocent, because the ritual murder of a Christian child would have been an affront to the alliance between the Jews and the Most Christian King. He cited the immense confidence that the Jews of Metz had in their sovereign, for whom they prayed constantly and whose saving intervention they expected. Indeed, we know that in October 1657, a decade before the Lévy affair, Louis XIV, accompanied by the queen and dukes, went to the synagogue of Metz on Succoth and was received "with pomp and circumstance."[9] Despite Lévy's horrible end, the Jews of Metz continued to celebrate their king and honor the royal alliance. Long after his execution and other miscarriages of justice, "the Jews remember that the great king was just, benevolent, impartial, and fair in his treatment of them. They count him among the good sovereigns who protected them."[10]

The strategy of royal alliance,[11] for all its fragility, was thus incompatible with acts inimical to the values of the Most Christian King. Since, moreover, the king's ministers were pleased with the behavior of the Jews, who frequently assisted royal armies in the field by efficiently supplying them with food and horses, there was every reason to hope that the king would intervene. The Marquis de Louvois, minister of war, recommended intervention on behalf of Jews who assisted in France's military campaigns. With this advice from his ministers, and having already been informed about the case by the Marquis de Berny and his father, Hugues de Lionne, secretary of state for foreign affairs, the king quickly decided not to act on "the superfluity of ends and conclusions in the petitions submitted by the prosecutor general of Metz," which were based on accusations that the king considered to be untrue. Not only did he not expel the Jews, but he maintained all their privileges and prepared to lend assistance to a community that had been so useful to the monarchy. This was the point at which the Marquis de Berny received the delegation of Jews from Metz who had come to Paris to implore royal intervention, leading Berny to exclaim, "What do you want? Your Jew is dead. Why didn't you come to me sooner?"

On April 18, 1670, the king's Council of State issued a decree that was supposed to put an end to both cases:

> Concerning the petition presented to the king in his Council by the community of Jews residing in the city of Metz, alleging that their enemies, unable to find any cause for complaint in their conduct for so many years, sought to make them odious through the enormity of a crime of which they accused a Jew named Raphaël Lévy, a resident of Boulay, in Lorraine.
>
> They claimed that this Jew had kidnapped a Christian child in order to sacrifice him, and in order to make this very peculiar allegation

plausible, they used Gillot Le Moine [*sic*] and his wife, residents of Glatigny, who had lost a child that was later found, half-devoured, in the woods, as recounted by the surgeons who were dispatched to the scene....

On the depositions of certain witnesses, insignificant people, mandated and posted, and on the basis of mere conjecture and suspicion, the parlement condemned said Lévy to be burned alive, and this was done.

About which the petitioners, whose intention is not to take up the cause of a foreign Jew, would have remained silent, despite the harm to themselves done by this sentence, if their enemies had not sought to make use of it to oppress and ruin them. Among the witnesses who deposed against said Raphaël Lévy, some stated that they had heard from one Clausquin, whose profession was to sell horses, and whom they acknowledged to have died eight years earlier, that Mayer Schwabe, a Jew residing in the city of Metz, had tried to murder him, and upon these depositions, the court found against this Jew, who was made a prisoner and placed in a dungeon in which he languished for more than three months, despite the absence of sufficient evidence against him.

But all these persecutions are minor compared with the severe indictments brought by said parlement of Metz against the petitioners at the request of the same deputy prosecutor....

This quite irregular manner of proceeding forced the petitioners to throw themselves at the feet of His Majesty to implore his aid and ask him for protection, which the kings who preceded him and he himself has [*sic*] never refused, and to hear their plea....that the cruelties they are accused of inflicting on Christians are pure illusions, which have no basis other than the malice and envy of their enemies.

When all these things were humbly presented to His Majesty, he ordered Sieur Marquis de Berny, secretary of commands, to write to Sieur de Choisy, commissioner for the generality of Metz, to ensure that the petitioners receive justice, as they deserve.

In execution of which order, said Sieur de Choisy sought information about this case, and in order to familiarize himself thoroughly with the facts, he informed the parlement of Metz that it was the intention of His Majesty that the records of the trials of Raphaël Lévy and Sieur Mayer Schwabe, along with the information gathered against the petitioners on order of the deputy prosecutor, be brought to him....

But parlement issued a decree against the principal petitioners, some of whom were imprisoned without being told the cause of their arrest,

> while others are in flight to avoid such treatment, insofar as it is enough in Metz today to be Jewish to be accused, and enough to be accused to be found guilty.
>
> But the parlement of Metz, which seems more incensed than ever against the petitioners owing to the commission that it pleased His Majesty to entrust to Sieur de Choisy, was not content simply to have issued a decree against a number of Jews. It also, through a series of extraordinary prosecutions, and a quite irregular and hasty procedure, issued a judgment on March 29 last, condemning Mayer Schwabe to pay a fine of 3,000 livres and ordering the continuation of the trial of Abraham Spire. Furthermore, said judgment was to be engraved on copper and attached to a pillar of stone in the square of the rue des Juifs, which clearly shows that it was issued solely to make the petitioners odious and leave traces of the hatred and envy of their enemies....
>
> In view of the petition and said judgments of January 6, February 5, and March 29, all things considered, the king being in his Council, ordered said parlement of Metz to send immediately to His Majesty, via the diligence of his prosecutor general, the grounds for the judgment rendered against said Raphaël Lévy and all other proceedings, charges, and information gathered against said Jews.
>
> Meanwhile, His Majesty expressly prohibits said parlement from executing its judgment of March 29 last against Mayer Schwabe and others pending orders to the contrary from His Majesty.
>
> Done in Council of State of the king, His Majesty being present, at Saint-Germain-en-Laye, on the eighteenth day of April 1670.[12]

Despite this specific order, the parlement of Metz continued to ignore the king's wishes and intended to proceed with its prosecution of Spire, who was not explicitly mentioned by name in the council decree. It tried one last time to resist and convey to the king its reasons for the judgments against Lévy and against Schwabe and his co-defendants. Once again, two Jewish notables hastened to Paris to pursue the matter. They came away pleased that "the government regarded the whole case as a false indictment" and ordered the immediate release of all imprisoned Jews. In August 1670, Louis XIV prohibited any further prosecution of Spire, and in October 1671, displeased with parlement's obstructionist attitude, he ordered an acceleration of the procedure so as to be done with the case once and for all.

Among the trial documents that deal with the Lévy and Schwabe cases there is one, damaged and stained, undated and unsigned, that is nevertheless worth quoting:

> [Jews] were placed into and reduced to situations of extreme danger and peril to their property...as if they used and...have Christian blood and were...obliged to have it....The king...prohibited and banned faith and belief in such things, as the bull He sent on this subject clearly shows, when in the following terms He said: "It is sometimes the case that Christians who bear hatred toward Jews hide their own children, or lose them, and immediately maintain and spread the rumor that they were taken, kidnapped, murdered, and sacrificed by the Jews, and that they ate the heart and drank the blood of said children, and because of these wicked statements and worthless speeches said Jews, though innocent, are arrested, prosecuted, and imprisoned, and since it is clear to us that this and similar rumors are false, since the Jews do not sacrifice and do not use sacrifices and neither eat nor drink blood, especially of animals with cloven hooves, no Christian should on such grounds give testimony or be heard against any Jew...and if on grounds such as the above any Jews should have been arrested and imprisoned, they must be released at once."

More than anyone else, the Most Christian King, like the popes before him, quashed the wicked rumors that accused Jews of "eating the heart and drinking the blood" of Christian children. The king prohibited "faith and belief in such things." Noting the beliefs and traditions of the Jews, "who drink no blood," he came to a clear conclusion: "No Christian should on such grounds give testimony or be heard against any Jew." In this instance, Louis XIV thus honored the royal alliance, obliging local judicial authorities receptive to anti-Semitic prejudices that were widely shared in Lorraine to give way before his own hostility to such "false rumors."[13]

Despite the clear statement from the king, rumors of another alleged kidnapping by Jews began to circulate in 1673. In the village of Baudrecourt, not far from Metz, a woman accused a Jew of kidnapping her child. She went to the rue des Juifs and asked for money, threatening to "denounce everything" if she did not get it. The mayor questioned her, and she "admitted that her own statements were contradictory and that the whole story was a lie. He had her arrested and turned her over to the police lieutenant for prosecution." The people grew restive: "A [Catholic] man beat a Jew. The mayor had the man arrested and dispatched a letter to the king to let him know what was happening.... Meanwhile, the child was found, whereupon a recommendation was made to M. de Pompone [*sic*] on the king's behalf to write that the authorities had done well to incarcerate this man and prosecute him. He also ordered the police lieutenant to investigate the matter but not to publish his findings, which were to be submitted to the king." When the king, the queen, and the entire court arrived in Thionville on July 30, 1673, three Jewish notables went there to "compliment" the king, while "the enemies of Israel" also pleaded their case, attacking the agents of the king who had "refused to bring the Jew to justice." The king was in Metz only briefly, however, and did not have time to deal with the case. After a series of further developments and several interventions by Jewish notables, who remained wary, "an ordinance appeared: it stated that the king recognized that this man's extended prison term was for the time being punishment enough for him, but that if anyone heard him spread wicked rumors about the Jews, the government should immediately arrest him and turn him over to the police lieutenant, who should not publish his findings but submit them to the king, who will issue whatever order he deems appropriate."[14]

Once again, the royal intervention in this case is worth noting, as the following letter from Arnaud de Pomponne, minister of state, to Victorin de Lavogade, His Majesty's lieutenant in the government of Metz, shows:

> At Nancy, the XIIIe day of August, 1673,
>
> Monsieur,
>
> This morning I had the honor to read to the king the letter you sent me concerning what happened in Metz last Friday in connection with a woman who had lost track of her child, which people took as a pretext for accusing the Jews of kidnapping him, and even of attacking said Jewish community, and primarily two or three of them. His Majesty approved of your arrest of the man who slapped one of said Jews, and since He does not wish to tolerate similar disturbances, you can be of assistance by publicizing His will as you deem appropriate. His Majesty would like you to turn the prisoner over to the police lieutenant to investigate the incident, by way of the royal prosecutor, and would

like you to send a report of the findings to His Majesty. You may do the same if similar accusations arise without fear of being taken here for one of the circumcised. In the meantime, I beg you to believe, Monsieur, that I am your very humble and very affectionate servant.[15]

This text reveals the full extent of the royal intervention: the king refused to "tolerate similar disturbances." Arnaud de Pomponne even ordered His Majesty's lieutenant in Metz to take firm action in such cases "without fear of being taken for one of the circumcised." The emotions stirred by this series of allegations proved to be so intense, however, that it seemed impossible to put a stop to all the alarmist rumors. Not even prompt intervention by the sovereign was enough, and the king's minister is already joking that further interventions might lead people to believe that the king's lieutenant was "one of the circumcised."

In 1675 there was another allegation against the Jews, this one from the son of the executioner, who accused the Jews Lion and Zanville of abducting a child, "whom they hid under their cloak," the same method of concealment that several witnesses testified had been used by Raphaël Lévy to hide little Didier Le Moyne, even though Lévy wore only a tunic:

Thereupon, a large crowd gathered and attacked Lion and Zanville. The mayor, having got wind of all this, tried to save the Jews by having them arrested and thrown in prison and then asked the lieutenant to investigate. On the following Friday, he began his investigation and questioned several individuals. The Jews were found innocent by the court of the *bailliage*, and the executioner's son was imprisoned. All of this was reported to the king by the governor and the prosecutor general assigned to the parlement. The response was that the executioner's neighbor should also be arrested. Since this neighbor was not yet 12 years old, he was to be whipped by his father inside the prison, and the man [presumably the father] is to pay 15 *quarts d'écu* in damages and all court costs. He shall be publicly led to the courtroom, where he shall promise on his life that he will never do such a thing again. The judgment was sent to the king, who found that it was not sufficiently severe.[16]

Clearly, the Jews of Metz had enough confidence in the solidity of the royal alliance to appeal directly to the sovereign, go to Paris to press their case, contact the highest authorities, and even persuade them to intervene before it was too late to save at least Mayer Schwabe and his co-defendants. Faced with new rumors of kidnappings and an increasingly aggressive "multitude," moreover, the police lieutenant was increasingly firm in his actions against "wicked rumors" inciting physical attacks. These actions enjoyed the backing of the king, who wanted troublemakers to be punished more severely. All of this seems to have reinforced the traditional Jewish believe in the virtues of a vertical alliance with the sovereign, while at the same time heightening Jewish fears of the "populace," with which any hope of achieving an understanding seemed more and more illusory.

Nevertheless, the fear of severe royal sanctions was not enough to dissuade ill-intentioned individuals from repeating "wicked rumors." Consider yet another case from Metz, in 1667:

> When a Jew named Aaron leaned against the counter of Montaigu, the defendant, he alleges that Montaigu drove him away with insulting and offensive words, saying that he did not want people like him loitering in his shop, and that when they needed a rabbi, they used Christian blood, adding that when the son of said defendant was in the rue des Juifs, he reported that someone had set upon him as if to cut his throat and would have done so had he not run away. These are atrocious insults and slanders that Montaigu cannot and will not support, and who knows what demon inspired them, for he had been drinking wine. Whereupon said Montaigu, appearing before said notaries, said and declared that he had said these things falsely, impudently, and slanderously, that he repented of his words and begged pardon for them, and asked said Aaron and the Jewish community to forgive him, because said witness admits that his words were counter to the truth and said that he will never do it again, which declaration Salomon Joseph, syndic of their community, was willing to accept and to end all further prosecution.[17]

Thus we can clearly see that anti-Semitic incidents continued despite efforts by the authorities to prevent them. A Jew leans on the counter of a shop owned by a Catholic, and the traditional accusation suddenly springs from the mouth of the shopkeeper: the Jews "use Christian blood" and continue to attack young men, as evidenced by an attempt to cut the throat of his own son. Only in this case, the accuser, made aware of the risk of punishment by recent events in Metz, admitted that he had spoken under the influence of alcohol and withdrew his allegations, which were "atrocious insults and calumnies" instigated by the "demon." In the presence of a notary, he begged pardon of Aaron and the Jewish community and promised he would never do it again.

Although royal intervention could not prevent such accusations from recurring, it could anticipate them and limit their repercussions. Indeed, other incidents that occurred somewhat later showed that the absolutist state, for all its coercive power, could not by itself change people's habits or eliminate their prejudices. In 1683, for example, four Metz Jews were accused of kidnapping an eleven-year-old girl, but the girl soon confessed that she had invented the tale out of whole cloth to explain her absence from school. Then, in 1685, two Metz Jews were accused by a merchant from Nancy of "kidnapping a Christian child, whom they hid beneath their cloaks." But when a man from Nomeny refuted this testimony, the Nancy merchant, fearing prosecution, withdrew his charges.[18] In Metz during this period, the most implausible stories were hard to stamp out; it seems that Jews always hid their prey under their cloaks! Prejudices seemed to endure indefinitely. The decisive intervention of the royal government, determined to restore public order by putting an end to the Lévy and Schwabe cases, ultimately failed to do away entirely with charges of ritual murder, which remained deeply rooted in the depths of the Christian consciousness. The vertical alliance, though frequently effective, here encountered its limits.

Eight The Dreyfus Affair
A New Lévy Affair?

The last decades of the nineteenth century witnessed a spate of accusations of ritual murder, especially in Central Europe; between 1881 and 1900, no fewer than 128 such charges were made. In every case it was Jews who were suspected of murdering Christians, usually young children and often for the alleged purpose of preparing the Passover matzoh. Between 1891 and 1900, we count 79 cases of this type, especially in Austria-Hungary, Bulgaria, and Germany. Among the most famous of these, widely publicized in the press, were cases in Kutaisi (Georgia, 1879), Tisza-Eszlar (Hungary, 1882), Corfu (Greece, 1891), Xanten (Germany, 1891–92), Polna (Austria-Hungary, 1899–1900), Konitz (Germany, 1900–01), and, later, Kiev (Ukraine, 1911–13). This was a period of strong nationalist agitation, which caused turmoil and threatened the political equilibrium of a number of countries, and virulent anti-Semitism was widespread. Indeed, the first anti-Semitic congress met in Dresden in September 1892.

Jews were designated as alien enemies of the national community. Their mere presence was considered a danger for societies left fragile by the advent of modernity, which weakened tradition and led to internal state reorganization and external challenges to established frontiers. This sudden resurgence of the charge of ritual murder after a lengthy period of relative calm (since the end of the eighteenth century) resurrected the irrational climate of the Damascus affair. Christian anti-Semitism in Eastern Europe revived memories long associated with the death of Christ and the desecration of the host. Meanwhile, many Jews had become champions of modernity and enthusiastically assimilated into the societies in which they were living, so they were taken by surprise when Christianity once again became the cornerstone of national identity, threatening an end to their emancipation and expulsion from the imagined community of the nation.

France, for its part, had seen no charges of ritual murder for quite some time. As the place where the nation-state was invented, its national identity seemed relatively secure. Nevertheless, the country's surprising defeat in the Franco-Prussian War (1870) inaugurated a long period of uncertainty and questioning of its fundamental values and institutions. Fear of foreigners and spies gripped a public traumatized by the loss of Alsace and part of Lorraine. Accelerated secularization mobilized Catholics, who joined forces with nationalists hostile to the "Jewish and Protestant Republic," which they believed diluted France's Catholic identity. It was in this climate of external threat and rekindled Franco-French warfare that Capt. Alfred Dreyfus was arrested for spying in late 1894, tried, and sentenced to deportation. Years of silence followed, despite various little-noticed developments in the case. It was not until 1898, after Esterhazy (the actual spy) was found innocent and Zola published his famous article "J'accuse," that things began to take a different turn. Agitation by anti-Semitic nationalists attained heights never before seen, demonstrations were staged, and anti-Jewish violence spread across the country. During 1898 and 1899, France remained in a virtual state of siege, and the republican regime itself was threatened.

The most intense phase of the Dreyfus Affair coincided with an accusation of ritual murder in Polna, the so-called Hilsner affair, which attracted attention throughout Europe. Strangely, few specialists in the Dreyfus Affair have looked for a connection between these two cases. France, the home of the Dreyfus case, and Moravia (part of the Austro-Hungarian Empire), where the Hilsner affair unfolded, were both plunged into turmoil as they sought to preserve their identities in the face of German-speaking enemies. In both cases, German-speaking Jews emerged as ideal suspects.

On Saturday, April 1, 1899, just before Easter, the body of young Anezka Hruzova was discovered in a forest. She had been murdered. Suspicion quickly fell on Leopold Hilsner, a young Jew of twenty-three, who had been seen in the woods a short while before the murder. He was tried in Kuttenberg in September 1899, found guilty, and sentenced to be hanged. Tomas Masaryk denounced "the international superstition" concerning the Jews and ritual murder and maintained that it was an anti-Semitic myth based largely "on an economic motive." His letter, published in the *Neue Freie Presse*, aroused the ire of anti-Semitic students, who violently attacked him. Chalk in hand, Masaryk strode to the front of a room and, unable to make himself heard, wrote the following words on a blackboard: "The Polna affair is a product of Christian anti-Semitism, and I regard it as an attack on the nation. . . . The investigation is an offense to common sense and humanity."

Influenced by August Rohling's book *The Jew According to the Talmud*, which was published in 1871 and immediately translated into Czech, the press uniformly denounced "the Germanization of the Jews of Kolin," linked "the Jews and cannibalism," and asked whether "we must protect ourselves against the Jewish *seder*." Masaryk came in for a great deal of opprobrium, both from the press and from demonstrators who staged noisy marches in a number of cities. Meanwhile, Hilsner's defenders relied on a book by Hermann Strack, published in 1892, *The Jew and the False Accusation of Ritual Murder*, which demonstrated the absurdity of Rohling's accusations.

In this tense climate, and despite the threats to himself, Masaryk did not give up. He emphasized the "power of suggestion" and wrote that "the Polna trial is a psychological sequel to the trial of Dreyfus. . . . The superstition of ritual murder stands as an indictment of the people of Bohemia. . . . How can anyone accuse the Jews of engaging in a ritual involving such a barbaric murder?"[1] The Supreme Court of Vienna ordered that Hilsner be given a new trial, but he was convicted again of the murder of Anezka Hruzova and sentenced to death, although his sentence was later commuted to life imprisonment. He remained in prison for nineteen years until Emperor Charles I granted him a pardon.

Meanwhile, in Rennes, Alfred Dreyfus was also found guilty for the second time by a military tribunal. The two cases had many elements in common. What is more, the witnesses were aware of this. For instance, the prosecutor in the September 1899 trial compared the Hilsner case to the Dreyfus case. Dreyfus was also found guilty twice and also gained release by accepting a pardon (which Dreyfus did sooner than Hilsner). His innocence was recognized in 1918, but Hilsner remained in prison and, though pardoned, was still implicitly seen as guilty. At first glance, it may seem incongruous to link high treason to the crime of ritual murder. Contemporaries were under no illusions as to the connections, however; Dreyfus and Hilsner were often compared, as were Zola and Masaryk.[2] Dreyfus and Hilsner were indeed victims of similar machinations by nationalist and anti-Semitic reactionaries, who opposed the liberal order that Zola and Masaryk were defending with their open attacks on judicial corruption, falsified evidence, perjured testimony, and pervasive irrationality. Despite shared prejudices against the Jews, which one encounters in their writing, both Zola and Masaryk displayed enormous courage in standing up for the truth and calling for new trials to redress monumental miscarriages of justice.

The similarity between the two cases (and their protagonists) did not escape the notice of anti-Semites in Vienna. One speaker, addressing an audience that included the city's anti-Semitic mayor, Karl Lueger, denounced Hilsner's crime, while another went after Dreyfus. The *Neue Freie Presse* complained that "Vienna desperately needs a Zola." In France, too, nationalist and Catholic ideologues insisted that ritual murders really did occur. Abbé Chabauty sought to prove this as early as 1882,[3] while in 1886, Édouard Drumont wrote about them at length in *La France juive*. In that same year, Jab devoted a long chapter to the case in Trent and concluded that "every Jew, *even today*, is required by Jewish law to eat and drink Christian blood at Easter and also needs Christian blood for use in circumcision and other religious rituals." Ritual crime, he added, "is still practiced today wherever there are observant Jews. . . . But the claim that Jews still draw our blood and deprive us of our lives in fact seems somewhat harsh."[4]

In 1889, a French translation of August Rohling's *The Jew According to the Talmud* was published, lending weight to these accusations. In 1890, a Dr. Martinez brought out a pamphlet entitled "The Jew Is the Enemy" in which, on the basis of the Trent case and the authority of Drumont, he charged that "Jews murdered countless Christians, especially children, in order to obtain their blood."[5] When the Dreyfus Affair erupted, the stage was already set. On November 6, 1894, *La Croix*, a leading anti-Semitic nationalist newspaper, denounced "the traitor" on page one: "In Germany as in France, every trial of a Jew is cut short in one way or another. This explains the extraordinary silence of the entire German press about trials for ritual infanticide. . . . Yes, they are cursed, and we are Christians."[6] Throughout the Dreyfus Affair, the same newspaper returned again and again to accusations of ritual murder. Countless articles on the subject were filled with the most terrifying details, and they were often linked to the charges against Dreyfus. On April 12, 1898—Easter—*La Croix* described a passion play in Paris and noted that when Judas appeared in the hall, people shouted, "Dreyfus!" On April 28, the newspaper denounced the "abduction of a Catholic child by a Jewish woman in Jerusalem on the day before Easter" and added that "the ogress wanted to sacrifice [the girl] to the Teutales of the Talmud. The story then turned to the case of Father Thomas, who had allegedly been "bled by the Jews of Damascus," and concluded with the prayer: "May this martyr deliver us from the Dreyfusards, who steal the souls of our children in the name of their sacred laws!"

Shortly after the trial in Rennes and Dreyfus's pardon and release from prison on September 26, 1899, *La Croix* discussed the work of Gougenot des Mousseaux, *Le juif, le judaïsme et la judaïsation*, which was all about ritual murders supposedly committed by Jews. It devoted a full page to the "ritual murder in Polna," using the report in *La Libre Parole* to denounce the lenient treatment of the accused in Xanten: he was acquitted. A short while later, the paper expressed fear that Hilsner, too, would escape capital punishment thanks to the irresistible occult power of the Jews, who, in Eastern Europe as in France, had intervened to protect their own, with the pardon of Dreyfus by the president of the Republic as a case in point, since he had been found guilty a second time in Rennes.[7] An advertisement for "Masonic Murder, Ritual Crime, Jewish Treason," a pamphlet published by the Ligue Antisémite, included frightening images of two ritual crimes, one at Tisza-Eszlar and the other at Trent, depicting Jews armed with huge knives literally bleeding naked youths and collecting their blood in basins.[8] Just below this, on the same page, we find a caricature of "the traitor Dreyfus." The pamphlet itself tried to show how, during the Damascus affair, European Jews had given money to employees of the French consulate to induce them to destroy evidence: "Is this not exactly what happened in the Dreyfus Affair? . . . Doesn't this verdict seem expressly designed for today's Dreyfusard Jews?" For the authors of the pamphlet, the same was true of Hilsner: "Though briefly distracted by their other martyr, Dreyfus, the Jews quickly collected the gold needed for the usual campaign of corruption. Despite the confessions (as in France), they obtained a new trial (as in France)."[9]

The Jewish press also compared the two events but argued that Jews had been unjustly accused in both cases. Throughout the long years of the Dreyfus Affair, and even somewhat earlier, *L'Univers israélite*, the *Archives israélites*, and the *Revue des etudes juives* all dealt repeatedly with accusations of ritual murder. Historians of the Dreyfus Affair have neglected this aspect of the story. Yet articles about ritual murder were frequent in these years, including reports of the various cases in Central Europe and historical studies of earlier instances. For example, we find discussions of Jews who were put to the stake in Endingen in 1470 after confessing under torture, and of a child in La Guardia who was supposedly killed for ritual purposes by five Jews.[10] There was an article about a report drafted by Lorenzo Ganganelli for Pope Benedict XIV in the eighteenth century, which absolved Jews of all charges of ritual murder and should have put an end, once for all, to "a popular imagination haunted by the mystical idea of blood."[11]

During the Dreyfus Affair, the number of articles about ritual murder increased. At the height of the affair, the subject became almost an obsession—and in that "anti-Semitic moment" Jews were in serious danger.[12] The letters of Heinrich Heine on the Damascus affair were also published,[13] and there was special interest in the Polna case, which the Czechs themselves had compared with the Dreyfus Affair[14] while also denouncing persecutions that were taking place in Konitz (Prussia) for the same reason.[15]

An even more important voice was the *Archives israélites*, which frequently linked the Dreyfus Affair to contemporaneous accusations of ritual murder in Central Europe. On the day after the Rennes verdict, the journal published this note: "A jury in Kuttenberg has returned a verdict that is in some ways similar to the verdict of the military tribunal in Rennes. By a vote of 11 to 1, it found Hilsner not guilty of murdering the victim himself, but all 12 jurors found that he had participated in the crime and therefore sentenced him to death."[16]

In both cases, Henri Prague argued, the accusers had relied on forgeries to prosecute innocent men: "The forgeries in the case of Capt. Dreyfus are direct descendants of the false charges made against our coreligionists in the Middle Ages, which made them out to be killers of Christian children. . . . The forgery has been modernized and adapted to the conditions of contemporary life. Skeptical Parisians are unlikely to be persuaded by charges that Jews committed ritual murder."[17]

In the same vein, Isaïe Levaillant, the editor-in-chief of *L'Univers israélite*, wrote: "The man who was court-martialed was not strictly speaking Capt. Dreyfus or even the Jew Dreyfus, it was the Jew in general as he has always figured in the Catholic imagination, the deicide Jew, the well-poisoning Jew, the host-desecrating Jew, and the ritual murdering Jew."[18]

There was no question that "the Dreyfus Affair is strictly identical to the charges of well poisoning and ritual murder that our forefathers faced" in the Middle Ages.[19] Countless articles published during the time in which France was gripped by a fever of anti-Semitism turned on the theme of a return to the irrationalism of the Middle Ages, with its beliefs in well poisoning and ritual murder; the credulity, fanaticism, myths, tall tales, and idle gossip that characterized the medieval period returned with a vengeance to the heart of modernity.[20]

For both the anti-Semitic and the Jewish press, then, it was self-evident that there was a connection between the charge of ritual murder and the charge of treason against Dreyfus. The theme of ritual murder became ubiquitous in this period, which was also the period of the Dreyfus Affair. The coincidence is striking, yet historians have ignored it. This was the context in which Isidore Loeb was the first to blast "the credulity of the public," the "falsifications of history," and the "absurd myth that we kill Christian children in order to drink their blood."[21] Salomon Reinach wrote an enthusiastic preface to the French translation of Hermann Strack's attack on Rohling's writing.[22] In *Histoire des Israélites* Théodore Reinach discussed "the horrible tragedy of Raphaël Lévi [*sic*] of Boulay, burned in 1670 following a false charge of ritual murder."[23] Finally, in 1898, his brother Joseph Reinach, the most persistent of the Dreyfusards, published *Raphaël Lévy: Une erreur judiciaire sous Louis XIV*. Within a very short period of time, all three Reinach brothers thus raised the issue of the Lévy affair, and two of them discussed the case at length.[24] Joseph even wrote the first book on this affair in more than two centuries—unlike the Calas affair, it had vanished from the national memory. This very rigorous work consisted of a lengthy introduction, a reproduction of the accusatory text that was attributed by contemporaries to Amelot de La Houssaye, and a reproduction of the pro-Lévy response by Richard Simon, along with various items from the court record, all of which were published for the first time. We do not know how he obtained these documents, which are not readily accessible and which he used as indirect evidence of the innocence of Capt. Dreyfus. He commented critically on the documents; pointed out the contradictions in La Houssaye's account; noted the important role played by Simon, whose theological works he apparently knew; and even cited some of Graetz's comments on the Lévy affair. The work required meticulous research,[25] which demonstrates this politically committed Jew's deep involvement in the case. When he died, *L'Univers israélite* wrote that "Joseph Reinach had very clear ideas about the Jewish question, which make him typical of the 'assimilated' Jew. After the emancipation of the Jews, Judaism became merely a religious denomination, and since Reinach was not a believer, he had ceased to identify with Judaism but had never abandoned his concern with the fate of Jews."[26] Confirmation of this point can be seen in the crucial role he played in the Dreyfus Affair as well as the way in which he linked that injustice to the injustice done to Raphaël Lévy centuries earlier.

The Dreyfus Affair thus focused attention on both the remote Lévy affair and the contemporary Hilsner affair, along with other accusations of ritual murder in the final decades of the nineteenth century. Joseph Reinach was the most political of the three brothers, the one who had long played an important role in French politics, who had been a confidant of Gambetta and a key figure in the Opportunist Party, which dominated the political scene at the time. If he published a book about a case to which few people had paid attention for two hundred years, it was because he believed he could use it as a weapon on behalf of another innocent man who had been unjustly condemned: Alfred Dreyfus. The book prefigured his celebrated and monumental *Histoire de l'affaire Dreyfus*. One of the captain's most faithful supporters, a close friend of the Dreyfus family who devoted himself to proving the innocence of the accused at the risk of endangering his political career by alienating the voters of Digne, which he represented, Reinach, though not a historian, used his impressive study to counter his most implacable enemy, Édouard Drumont, the man who led the national mobilization against the Jews.

The author of *La France juive* threw himself into his mission. Thanks to *La Libre Parole*, whose articles were reprinted by much of the national and local press, Drumont spread his anti-Semitic venom with undeniable brio and boundless imagination. Driven by hatred, he put together a movement of a scope never before seen in France. Much of its vitriol was aimed squarely at Joseph Reinach, who was treated to the most scandalous insults. Reinach became Drumont's primary target, the object of his increasingly vicious attacks. Countless caricatures depicted him as a terrifying animal of one sort or another. Reinach displayed admirable courage in the face of an adversary who did not shrink from the vilest of threats. He encouraged Auguste Scheurer-Kestner, with whom he was in constant dialogue, to assume the role that Voltaire had played in the Calas affair by unmasking the injustice done to Dreyfus as Voltaire had exposed the injustice done to Calas. Toward the end of 1897, as he was preparing to publish his book on Raphaël Lévy, Reinach wrote to Scheurer-Kestner, whom he addressed as "Mon cher Arouet" (Arouet was Voltaire's real name): "Attached you will find some excerpts from Voltaire, which may be useful to you at some point. Here you will find the same arguments and the same stupidity that both of you have met, fought, and defeated."[27] He sent him excerpts from Voltaire's letter to d'Alembert, which contains the following: "Is there any example in the annals of history and crime of such a parricide, committed with no plan, no interest, and no cause?" Reinach added: "Just like Voltaire in the Calas affair. Calas was dead, he had been broken on the wheel, and it was certainly not to restore his confiscated property to his female [*sic*] that Voltaire did back then what you are trying to do today. . . . Therein lies the patriotic, superior, general interest, which is what justice is all about."[28]

While insisting on the Calas affair, Reinach was certainly also thinking of the Lévy affair, about which he was writing his own study at the time, as well as the Dreyfus Affair. The Lévy affair preceded the Calas affair, but Voltaire had ignored it, even though Lévy's alleged crime also had "no plan, no interest, and no cause." Voltaire never mentioned the tragic fate of Raphaël Lévy, although he certainly knew about the unjust conviction because he had carefully read Richard Simon's *Factum*. Indeed, while writing his *Dictionnaire philosophique*, he relied on this text for information about tortures to which Jews had been subjected.[29] The

Calas affair (1762) fell between the Lévy affair (1669) and the Dreyfus Affair (1894): three events separated by a century. The comparison was inevitable, especially since, when the *Archives israélites* published the first translation of the Yiddish diary by an anonymous writer who believed in Lévy's innocence,[30] it was preceded by an article by Olry Terquem, of which Joseph Reinach was surely aware but which he did not include in his own selection of texts about the case, as if he wished to reserve for himself the pleasure of being the first to compare the unfortunate Capt. Dreyfus to three earlier heroes, Lévy, Calas, and the chevalier de La Barre. Terquem had written at length about this connection: "We have collected here the stories of the last three judicial murders committed in France in the name of religion: a Jew in the seventeenth century! No one protested; the case went unnoticed! A Protestant and a Catholic in the eighteenth century! But Voltaire and his friends were there, the time had come. The cup was full. In '89 it overflowed."[31]

In a sense, Dreyfus was thus merely the last in a line of injustices, and for Terquem these injustices led straight back to the French Revolution. By acting decisively on behalf of Dreyfus, Reinach and the Protestant senator Scheurer-Kestner were following in the footsteps of Voltaire. Both could have claimed him as an illustrious predecessor. But in a context of extreme violence, the clash between Reinach and Drumont soon took an unexpected turn: an explicit link was drawn between the Lévy and Dreyfus affairs.[32] The Dreyfus Affair was thus placed in a new light, linked to the myth of ritual murder—a myth that, as we have seen, had been revived in Central Europe and recently insinuated itself into France, with the previously forgotten Lévy affair as the prime example. Or, rather, it would be more accurate to say that the Lévy affair had been forgotten by everyone except Drumont and his acolytes, who seized on it to raise in France an issue that was so effectively causing turmoil in Central Europe. In Drumont's incredibly violent book, *La France juive*, published in 1886, he predicted that France would face an anti-Semitic crisis within a few years and then did his best to make sure that his prediction came true. It was Drumont who created the political climate in which something like the Dreyfus Affair could take place by denouncing day after day the presence of Jews in the army, personally provoking some of them, and spreading the idea that Jews were likely to commit treason.

Nothing was lost on Drumont. He fed his rage on a wide range of sources and devoted many pages of his celebrated screed, millions of copies of which were sold, to the case of Raphaël Lévy.[33] We will never know how he learned of this event from the distant past. Zealous and meticulous, he obtained a copy of Amelot de La Houssaye's vehement attack on Lévy, the *Abrégé du procès fait aux Juifs de Metz*, which he cites. He also claimed to base his argument on another seventeenth-century text hostile to Lévy as well, Emmanuel Michel's *Histoire du parlement de Metz*. Drumont, who devoted his life to anti-Semitism, was an astonishing bookworm who unearthed the most hostile treatments of the Jews he could find and delighted in what he read. He even cited the text that Simon wrote hastily in support of Lévy and the Jews of Metz, only to dismiss its conclusions peremptorily. As usual, Drumont amassed a huge volume of documentation. He was a man obsessed by anti-Semitism who neglected nothing that might help his cause. Did he perhaps learn of the Lévy affair from the *Archives israélites*, which he scoured systematically for useful material?[34]

In any case, Drumont's lengthy discussion of the Lévy affair in his widely read *La France juive* focused the attention of anti-Semites on the case. Four years later, in 1890, Henri Desportes published *Le Mystère du sang chez les Juifs de tous les temps*, which included a preface by Drumont in which he again discussed the Lévy affair: "The record of the trial of Raphaël Lévy must exist somewhere in Metz, unless the Jews managed to make it disappear."[35] Desportes devoted an entire chapter of his book to the "Metz crime." He, too, referred to the *Abrégé du procès fait aux Juifs de Metz* to demonstrate the truth of the charge against Raphaël Lévy. He delved even more deeply into the details of the affair than Drumont did. He considered the problems with the translation of Lévy's notes and with contradictions in the testimony given by witnesses. Yet he concluded that France "was no longer living in 'barbarous times' and was in fact the most civilized country in the world. Will the Jews dare to say again that they have never been legally convicted of murdering Christian children?" He also attacked Théodore Reinach, who continued to characterize Lévy's death as "judicial murder." In conclusion, he wrote that "the halo they place on the head of such a man clearly demonstrates the value that Jews attach to ritual murder: this barbaric custom is certainly not limited to a few fanatics."[36]

As the title of his book implied, Desportes thus believed that Jews, with the approval of the Jewish elite to which the Reinach brothers belonged, continued to practice this "barbaric custom" in the modern era. In this context, the Dreyfus Affair can therefore be seen as a substitute for the charge of ritual murder. Like the latter, it demonized all Jews, characterizing them as animals thirsty for blood, throwbacks to ancient times, and alien to the soul of France, which they eagerly betrayed. Nothing could stop the increasingly prevalent practice of comparing the two affairs. In 1897, four years after the beginning of the Dreyfus Affair, Jean de Pavly, a retired teacher at Lyon's École du Sacré-Coeur, published a report that reflected the official position of the Church on the subject, ending with the remark that the charge of ritual murder "is today due solely to the bad faith of a few scoundrels who believe that anything goes when it comes to tormenting Jews. The courts cannot be harsh enough in their treatment of these wretches, whose perfidious insinuations have no purpose but to impel the populace to exceed the bounds of decency."[37]

Though written by a Catholic writer, this text had no effect. In response to the vicious attacks of the anti-Semites, Joseph Reinach therefore published his *Raphaël Lévy. Une erreur judiciaire sous Louis XIV*. Esterhazy had just been found innocent, and Zola had published his "J'accuse." Anti-Semitic crowds were gathering in cities, molesting Jews, and forcing the police and army to intervene to prevent violence. Intellectuals banded together to form the Ligue des Droits de l'Homme et du Citoyen as a counterweight to the anti-Semitic and nationalist Ligue de la Patrie Française. Drumont, Guérin, and their acolytes were everywhere. Nationalist, Catholic, and anti-Semitic organizations seemed to dominate the public arena by virtue of their ability to mobilize large numbers of people in all strata of French society. The small band of loyal Dreyfusards who remained devoted to the captain's cause as he struggled to survive on Devil's Island carried on their lonely fight while waiting for the intellectuals and later Jaurès and the Socialists to become involved. Joseph Reinach, along with Scheurer-Kestner, the vice president of the Senate, Mathieu Dreyfus, and Bernard Lazare led the fight and threw themselves body and soul into action on Dreyfus's behalf. Reinach would later become the historian of the affair, and his writing on the subject remains indispensable. Clearly, his book on Lévy was an important weapon in the struggle. Since anti-Semites linked the two cases, Reinach was defending Dreyfus when he demolished the case against Lévy. Right at the beginning of his book, before getting into the voluminous documentary evidence, he wrote that "histories of judicial errors are never pointless. They force people and even judges to reflect on the issues, if only briefly. It is impossible to read the history of Raphaël Lévy without finding in it food for thought."[38]

Reinach systematically demolished the conclusions of Amelot de La Houssaye, from whom Drumont and Desportes took their inspiration. He showed that "the blood libel" against the Jews was an irrational, superstitious belief and that the charges stemming from it incorporated this false assumption in a chain of logical deductions. He cited the work of Strack, which Drumont did not mention, and showed how all the popes had solemnly condemned this type of accusation, which was nevertheless repeated by would-be voices of the Catholic camp such as *La Croix* and Drumont. He made rigorous use of the Yiddish diary written by an anonymous contemporary of Raphaël Lévy and published the first full translation in the *Archives israélites*. Above all, Reinach relied heavily on the account of the case written by Richard Simon, a theologian and Hebrew scholar, in response to a request from his friend Salvador, with whom he studied the Hebrew Bible and Talmud. Simon proved Lévy's innocence, and his text was given to the Marquis de Berny, who promised to bring it to the attention of Louis XIV. Reinach then showed how Louis XIV considered the case in council and issued a decree, which he signed personally, ordering an end to the parlement's prosecution of three Jews accused of conspiring with Raphaël Lévy. He quoted any number of decrees issued by the King's Council and the Council of State, which Drumont and Desportes preferred to ignore because they ran counter to their thesis. And he pointed out the role of the Marquis de Louvois, which, along with all the other evidence, showed that the French government intervened forcefully to protect the Jews from the vengefulness of the parlement of Metz: "The parlement finally understood what Louis XIV desired and laid down its arms once and for all."[39] Reinach demonstrated his very detailed knowledge of the case, which he explained with the same skill he would later demonstrate in recounting the history of the Dreyfus Affair.[40] Implicit allusions to the latter are everywhere in Reinach's account of the Lévy affair. He notes the contestable role of experts,[41] emphasizes the defendant's "innocence and nobility" and refusal "to confess anything," and discusses the character and stamina of this "stubborn Jew."[42] When he wrote that "the assumption of jurisdiction in the case by the Council of State was tantamount, *de jure* if not *de facto*, to nullification of Raphaël Lévy's conviction and of all subsequent prosecutions," did he not already have the intuition that the same thing would someday happen to Dreyfus—although he would have to wait much longer for his innocence to be acknowledged by the appellate court in 1906, following the failure to obtain an acquittal in the Rennes trial of 1899?

Soon after Reinach's book appeared, Drumont published a stinging response in *La Libre Parole*. "When it comes to rehabilitating criminals," he wrote, "Joseph Reinach is not content to work on new cases. He also dabbles in old ones. While putting together a tissue of forgeries in an effort to whitewash Dreyfus by attacking the honor of innocent men, he has also been attempting to rehabilitate a Jew by the name of Raphaël Lévy, about whose guilt there cannot be a shadow of a doubt." Drumont discussed the Lévy trial at length, arguing that the delaying tactics of Jews at the time stood no chance of success in seventeenth-century France, as opposed to modern Austria-Hungary, where they had been able to intervene successfully, as Drumont saw it, in the Tisza-Eszlar case. He ended his diatribe by warning his readers that thanks to the efforts of Joseph Reinach, "you can be sure that Dreyfus will someday end up with a myth of his own."[43]

In the dramatic context of 1897–98, the Jewish press welcomed Reinach's book, which implicitly reinforced his commitment to Dreyfus. In *Archives israélites*, Henri Prague wrote:

> The very moving and soberly eloquent book published this week by Joseph Reinach, a deputy, excerpts of which we have before us, is a welcome arrival at a time when we hear reports of judicial errors from many quarters, the most distressing of which is surely the one inflicted upon the unfortunate prisoner who has been deported to Devil's Island. . . . When you finish this book, which is rendered cruelly topical by present circumstances, you will say to yourself that although times have changed, the stratagems that wicked people use to achieve their ends have scarcely varied, and sectarian passion—call it religious hatred, racial hatred, or professional jealousy—is still powerful enough, even

today, when the sun of civilization spreads its light so widely, to tilt the scales of justice and shake even the most righteous consciences.[44]

Isaïe Levaillant had a similar reaction to the book. In *L'Univers israélite* he wrote:

M. Reinach has obviously deliberately avoided facile comparisons and scrupulously limited himself to the role of historian. But whether he intended it or not, his book touches on some of today's most acute concerns. What emerges from his work is the most opportune lesson that in every epoch religious hatred, which perverts the mind and obscures the conscience, has created the kind of unhealthy climate in which judicial sins inevitably arise, as if this were their natural environment. . . . Can we say that judicial errors of the sort of which Raphaël Lévy was the victim have become impossible? Alas, the present, far from differing from the past in this regard, resembles it so closely that it can shed light on and explain what we are seeing today. The forms of justice may have changed. Torture may have been abolished. The right of every accused to defend himself as he sees fit may have been formally established. But the prejudices that blind man's judgment and the passions that distort his conscience remain the same. Jews, in France at least, are no longer accused of ritual murder. But they are believed to be capable of similarly odious crimes solely because they are Jews. Indeed, we may even ask whether the judicial error committed against Lévy would have been so easily corrected today—or, rather, not corrected, because it was irreparable, but at least recognized and proclaimed to have been a mistake. . . . What a happy chance it would be if the court martial judges could reflect on the lesson that emerges from the experience of Raphaël Lévy.[45]

What else was there to say? Levaillant took the pessimistic view that justice had probably regressed since the seventeenth century, that the fate of Dreyfus was even more arbitrary than that of Lévy, even though Dreyfus did not risk torture or burning. An equally pessimistic Henri Prague concluded that "justice was more easily and rapidly obtained a century ago under an absolute monarch than under a democratic republic that claims to be a government of justice, equity, and enlightenment."[46]

If only the court-martial judges had been able to take in the lesson of the Lévy affair, pertinently rediscovered by the captain's indefatigable champion Joseph Reinach! Unfortunately, this was not to be, and Alfred Dreyfus was once again found guilty. He would have to wait until

1906 to see the judicial error rectified—much longer than it took in the Lévy case (though of course Lévy himself did not live to see it).

*

In fact, despite the verdict of the appellate court in 1906, many continued to believe that Dreyfus was guilty, just as many adepts of the radical right continued to believe that Drumont was correct to insist that Raphaël Lévy had also been guilty. Indeed, many of the same people insisted on the guilt of both men. For instance, in 1914, Albert Monniot, one of Drumont's most faithful supporters, published a work entitled *Le Crime rituel chez les Juifs*, with a preface by his master, who insisted on the close connection between Monniot's book and his own *La France juive*. Monniot invoked the authority of both Drumont and Henri Desportes on the first page of his book. He denounced the work of Strack and of Théodore Reinach, whom he accused of "disguising"[47] the truth by denying the existence of ritual crimes. Oddly, he said nothing about the more systematic work of Joseph Reinach, whose *Histoire de l'affaire Dreyfus* was the only book of his mentioned. He returned repeatedly to the Dreyfus Affair, arguing that the captain was guilty beyond a shadow of a doubt.[48] After discussing the alleged ritual murders in Norwich and Blois, he came to Metz and the Lévy case. His conclusion was clear: "One decree or a hundred decrees, in the seventeenth century or the nineteenth, nothing counts but Israel's eternal denials. Naturally, a Reinach—Théodore—turned up to characterize the execution of Raphaël Lévy as judicial murder."[49]

Thus in 1914 and after, right-wing nationalists and anti-Semites still considered it appropriate to link the two cases. Drumont's followers, who remained active in the first half of the twentieth century, endlessly cited the Lévy affair as justification for their hatred of Jews. In 1923, Jean Drault, one of the most impassioned of Drumont's disciples, repeated word for word Amelot de La Houssaye's accusations against Lévy, "a rabbi of fifty-six, with dark, kinky hair, a big black beard, and the eyes of a vulture. He was quite certainly one of those mysterious agents of the Kahal who deal in Christian blood, as was proven in the Damascus investigation in 1840. . . . Thus under Louis XIV justice was more impartial in dealing with a murderous Jew than under the glorious Third Republic."[50]

Albert Monniot and Jean Drault were not the only followers of Drumont who did everything they could to link the cases of Raphaël Lévy and Alfred Dreyfus despite all the proof that both men were innocent.[51] From the seventeenth century to this day, the anti-Semitic tradition has drawn on these two cases to justify the hatred of Jews and the desire to banish them from French soil. Whether their alleged crime was ritual murder or treason endangering the country's Catholic identity, anti-Semites aimed to get rid of these foreigners in their midst—foreigners whom they held responsible for all of the country's woes.

Conclusion

It is unlikely that any murder took place in Metz or its environs in the final months of 1669. To this day, the death of little Didier Le Moyne remains a complete mystery. Wrongly accused and brutally tortured, Raphaël Lévy refused to confess to imaginary crimes. He somehow found the strength to refute, one by one, the witnesses against him and never betrayed his faith or his people. Because of his courage in facing the stake, he was regarded as a holy man and posthumously accorded the title of "rabbi," although his knowledge of the Torah was rudimentary. The Jewish community of Metz and the surrounding villages, orthodox in its religious orientation and united by strong social bonds, identified with him, preserved his memory, honored his martyrdom, and has ever since continued to avoid the accursed woods of Glatigny at night.

Nevertheless, Raphaël Lévy remains an unknown hero. He has never achieved the renown of a Jean Calas or an Alfred Dreyfus. His name is not mentioned in history textbooks. No statue has been erected in his honor. He does not figure in the French national memory or in the memory of French Jews outside the region of Metz. Yet the importance of his story goes beyond local history. It marks a critical moment in the construction of the nation-state. Faced with resistance from local notables, France was unable to impose its conception of law and order in Metz, which was nevertheless considered to be a "good city" that "covered the state." Local officials and members of parlement heeded only their own prejudices. The long resistance of the periphery to the imposition of state order in this disputed region sealed the fate of Raphaël Lévy. Nothing could save him, neither the royal alliance between king and Jews, long in disrepair, nor the improvised assistance of

Lévy's co-religionists, nor the testimony of those rare Catholic neighbors who tried to come to his aid.

The neglected history of this charge of ritual murder therefore deserved to be rediscovered, especially since it was intimately associated with another myth, that of desecration of the host, the crime that Mayer Schwabe and his friends, armed with daggers and pikes, were supposed to have committed in a dark back room. These two closely related stories turn out to have been singular events in the history of modern France, which by and large turned its back on the Middle Ages and its fear of witches, demons, and black magic. It is astonishing that these events should have occurred in the late seventeenth century, a period renowned for its cultural and scientific achievements. It is as if the Counterreformation needed an Other, hostile to its idea of order, alien to its faith, and standing outside of Christian tradition. Although Protestants would soon be excluded from the nation, they remained within the Christian tradition.

The fate of Raphaël Lévy would soon be submerged by the tides of history. A little more than a century later, the French Revolution led to the integration of French Jews into the French nation. The Lévy affair, falling as it did between the frequently oppressive Middle Ages and the Jacobin regeneration—that latter-day "exodus from Egypt"—vanished from memory. Forgotten by nearly everyone, this extraordinary affair was nevertheless enthusiastically taken up by the counterrevolutionary right. Anti-Semitic nationalists regularly seized on the case to illustrate the perfidy of the Jews—the same Jews that the Revolution and now the Republic transformed into citizens entitled to the honors of the nation even though they continued to plot against its soul. The fact that the Lévy affair resurfaced so emphatically during the Dreyfus Affair is a sign of its exceptional status. Drumont and others enthusiastically argued that ritual murder prefigured the betrayal of the nation by Jews who continued to hate Catholic France. For a brief moment, France seemed to revert to the Middle Ages, with all its fantasies and fears, and in Algeria there were even crusades of a sort, which led to the massacre of many Jews. When the Republic finally recognized the innocence of Captain Dreyfus, at last affording the wrongly accused Jew the protection of the state (as the absolutist monarchy had done more than two hundred years earlier), the Lévy affair was once again consigned to oblivion and erased from the national memory. Perhaps it is the contemporary retreat of the state, accompanied by an explosion of prejudice and a return to violence and even murder, that once again makes it important to discuss the tragic fate of Raphaël Lévy.

Notes

Introduction

1. This exchange took place in the presence of Bernard Lyon-Caen, Pierre-André Meyer's cousin; and Henry Schumann, a local scholar who had arranged for the meeting to take place. It was recorded in photographs by Xavier Lambert, a journalist at the *Républicain lorrain*.

2. On this astonishing meeting, see Lambert, "Les 'héritiers' d'une erreur judiciaire se rencontrent," *L'Est républicain*, February 23, 2001, *Les Dernières Nouvelles d'Alsace*, February 23, 2001, and *Tribune juive*, no. 51, 2001. See also the account given by Lyon-Caen in the *Revue du Cercle de généalogie juive*, no. 66, summer 2002.

3. AD Moselle B 2144.

4. Personal communications from Lambert, Meyer, and Schumann.

5. Lemoine, "Double drame au pays messin au temps de Louis XIV," *Renaissance du vieux Metz*, bulletin no. 122, January 2002.

6. Lemoine, "Double drame," pp. 8 and 10.

7. Ibid., p. 10. Note that in her draft she wrote: "His father, giving in to pressure from the mayor, Sieur Payer, and other prominent individuals. . . ."

8. Letter to Meyer, January 19, 2001.

9. Lemoine, "Double drame," p. 10.

10. Letter from Lemoine to Schumann. On January 2, 2004, she wrote another letter in which she again wished him a happy new year (private archives of Henry Schumann). Lemoine died at the end of June 2004. See *L'Est républicain*, June 30, 2004. In his article, Lambert wrote: "With the death of Mme Lemoine, the survivors of Raphaël Lévy are now the only direct repositories of this extraordinary story." Schumann expressed regret that he had not been able to attend the funeral wearing "a *kippa* as a token of gratitude." Personal communication.

11. Private archives of Pierre-André Meyer. I thank him for permission to publish these excerpts.

12. In a letter to the journalist Lambert, Bertin Diteshem, who for twenty-eight years served as one of the administrators of the Jewish community of Metz, remarked that "the affair that she [Bernadette Lemoine] investigated is still remem-

bered by the Jewish community of Lorraine, and especially that of Metz." Private archives of Xavier Lambert.

13. See Gavin Langmuir, *Toward a Definition of Antisemitism* (Berkeley: University of California Press, 1990).

14. Gavin Langmuir, *History, Religion and Antisemitism* (Berkeley: University of California Press, 1990), p. 266. Langmuir associates his interpretation of anti-Semitism with Raymond Boudon's more general theory in *L'Idéologie* (Paris: Fayard, 1986). For Langmuir, "non-rational Christian beliefs in life, death, and the infinite presence of Jesus of Nazareth inspired non-rational beliefs about the Jews" (p. 367).

15. Joshua Trachtenberg, *The Devil and the Jews* (New York: Harper Torchbooks, 1966); Jeremy Cohen, *The 3 Friars and the Jews* (Ithaca, NY: Cornell University Press, 1990), and Cohen, *The Evolution of Medieval Anti-Judaism* (Ithaca, NY: Cornell University Press, 1982); Langmuir, *Toward a Definition*; Alan Dundee, ed., *The Blood Libel Legend* (Madison: University of Wisconsin Press, 1991); Robert Chazan, *Medieval Stereotype and Modern Antisemitism* (Berkeley: University of California Press, 1997).

16. Israël Jacob Yuval, *Two Nations in Your Womb: Perceptions of Jews and Christians in Late Antiquity and the Middle Ages* (Berkeley: University of California Press, 2006), pp. 160ff. The classic article is still that of H. H. Ben-Sasson, "Kiddush Ha-Shem," *Encyclopaedia Judaica*, vol. 10. David Biale has argued that Jewish and Christian traditions regarding blood maintained a more general "symbiotic relationship," which led to "apocalyptic violence." For him, even the act of circumcision is linked to the charge of ritual murder, as shown by the examples of Endigen and, even more, Trent. See *Blood and Belief: The Circulation of a Symbol Between Jews and Christians* (Berkeley: University of California Press, 2007), pp. 83 and 99. These works belong to a current in modern historiography that has rediscovered violence between Jews at various points in time. See, for example, Michael Stanislawski, *A Murder in Lemberg: Politics, Religion and Violence in Modern History* (Princeton: Princeton University Press, 2007). On this work, see Pierre Birnbaum, "Tirez sur le rabbin!" *Critique*, October 2007.

17. For an overview of recent controversies on this subject, see Jeremy Cohen, *Sanctifying the Name of God: Jewish Martyrs and Jewish Memories of the First Crusade* (Philadelphia: University of Pennsylvania Press, 2004).

18. John M. McCulloh, "Jewish Ritual Murder: William of Norwich, Thomas of Monmouth and the Early Dissemination of the Myth," *Speculum* 12 (1997), pp. 698–740. See also Jeffrey Jerome Cohen, "The Flow of Blood in Medieval Norwich," *Speculum* 79 (2004).

19. The classic article is by Robert Chazan, "The Blois Incident of 1171," *Proceedings of the American Academy for Jewish Research*, 1968, *36*. For a more recent account, see Susan Einbinder, "Pucellina of Blois: Romantic Myths and Narrative Conventions," *Jewish History*, spring 1998.

20. On this case, see Moïse Schwab, "Le meurtre de l'enfant de choeur du Puy," *Revue des études juives* 33 (1896).

21. Ronnie Po-chia Hsia, *The Myth of Ritual Murder: Jews and Magic in Reformation Germany* (New Haven: Yale University Press, 1988), p. 3.

22. Hillel Kieval, "Middleman Minorities and Blood: Is There a Natural Economy of the Ritual Murder Accusation in Europe?" in Daniel Chirot and Anthony Reid, eds., *Essential Outsiders: Chinese and Jews in the Modern Transformation of Southeast Asia and Central Europe* (Seattle: University of Washington Press, 1997), p. 212.

23. Some historians, such as John McCulloh, op. cit., believe that this event became well known even before the Norwich case. Although the latter occurred earlier, it was not recounted by Thomas of Monmouth until 1155, and the Würzburg tragedy influenced the structure of his account of little William's disappearance.

24. Po-chia Hsia, *Myth of Ritual Murder*, p. 36. See also J. Kracauer, "L'Affaire des Juifs d'Endingen de 1470. Prétendu meurtre de chrétiens par des Juifs," *Revue des Etudes juives* 16 (1898).

25. Later, in 1759, Pope Clement XIII condemned similar charges after receiving a report from Cardinal Ganganelli, who later became Pope Clement XIV. Cecil Roth, ed., *The Ritual Murder Libel and the Jew: The Report by Cardinal Lorenzo Ganganelli* (London: Woburn Press, 1935). See also Marina Caffiero, "Alle origini dell'antisemitismo politico. L'accusa di omicidio rituale nel sei-settecento tra autodifesa degli ebrei e pronunciamenti papali," in Catherine Brice and Giovanni Miccoli, eds., *Les racines chrétiennes de l'antisémitisme politique (fin XIXe–XXe siècle)* (Rome: Ecole française de Rome, 2003), pp. 52ff.

26. Here I am following the account in the fine book by Ronnie Po-chia Hsia, *Trent 1475: Stories of a Ritual Murder Trial* (New Haven: Yale University Press, 1992).

27. See Chapter 8 below.

28. Po-chia Hsia, *The Myth of Ritual Murder*, pp. 81–83, 162, 197, 203.

29. On blood in Jewish and Christian ritual, see Jean-Paul Roux, *Le sang. Mythes, symboles et réalités* (Paris: Fayard, 1988), chap. 9. On the Eucharist in the Middle Ages, see Miri Rubin, *Corpus Christi: The Eucharist in Late Medieval Culture* (Cambridge: Cambridge University Press, 1991); and Caroline Walker Bynum, *Wonderful Blood: Theology and Practice in Late Medieval Northern Germany and Beyond* (Philadelphia: University of Pennsylvania Press, 2007), chaps. 4–8. On this theme generally, see *Le sang au Moyen Âge*, Les Cahiers du C.R.I.S.I.M.A., no. 4, 1999.

30. Jean-Louis Schefer, *L'hostie profanée. Histoire d'une fiction théologique* (Paris: POL, 2007), p 386. See also Jeremy Cohen, *Christ Killers* (Oxford: Oxford University Press, 2007). James Clifton shows how numerous painters, among them Giovanni Bellini, explicitly relate the body of Christ and the Eucharist and the cup that the angels use to collect the blood of Christ to the vessel employed in the mass. See "A Fountain Filled with Blood: Representations of Christ's Blood from the Middle Ages to the Eighteenth Century," in James Bradburne, ed., *Blood: Art, Power, Politics and Pathology* (New York: Prestel, 2002), p. 72. Note that in representations of ritual murder, Jews always use a cup to collect the blood of the martyred child who symbolizes Christ. On pictorial representations of the desecration of the

host and the body of Christ by Jews, see also Miri Rubin, "Sacrifice and Redemption in Christian Iconography," in Bradburne, ed., *Blood,* pp. 93ff.

31. Robert Stacey, "From Ritual Crucifixion to Host Desecration: Jews and the Body of Christ," *Jewish History*, spring 1998.

32. A recent literature proposes to look at the Middle Ages in terms of a postcolonial model, with the Jew as "internal Oriental." See Jeffrey Jerome Cohen, ed., *Postcolonial Middle Ages* (London: Macmillan, 2000).

33. Bettina Bildhauer, "Blood, Jews and Monsters in Medieval Culture," in Bettina Bildhauer and Robert Mills, eds., *The Monstrous Middle Ages* (Toronto: University of Toronto Press, 2003). This article lays out a thesis on which Bildhauer would expand in her later book, *Medieval Blood* (Cardiff: University of Wales Press, 2006).

34. Miri Rubin, "Desecration of the Host: The Birth of an Accusation," in Diana Wood, ed., *Christianity and Judaism*, Studies in Church History (Oxford, 1992) and especially *Gentiles' Tales: The Narrative Assault on Late Medieval Jews* (New Haven: Yale University Press, 1998).

35. Schefer, *L'hostie proclamée. Histoire d'une fiction théologique*, p. 38.

36. Ibid. Miri Rubin also describes this work by Uccello in her *Gentiles' Tales*, pp. 148 ff., as does Bettina Bildhauer, "Blood, Jews and Monsters in Medieval Culture," pp. 46 ff.

37. Caroline Walker Bynum cites many accusations of desecration of hosts by Jews in Germany, which follow the same pattern. See *Wonderful Blood*, pp. 58–59, 68–72, 241–243.

38. Quoted in Schefer, *L'hostie profanée*, pp. 43–44. Marie-Christine Pouchelle notes that there was a medieval legend according to which the wounds of a murdered person would bleed in the presence of the murderer. "Le sang et ses pouvoirs au Moyen Âge," in Arlette Farge, ed., *Affaires de sang* (Paris: Editions Imago, 1988), p. 27.

39. Ibid., pp. 271–273.

40. Rubin, *Corpus Christi*, p. 137.

41. Jody Enders, "Theater Makes History: Ritual Murder by Proxy in the Mistere de la sainte Hostie," *Speculum* 79 (2004), pp. 992ff. The author notes that a new edition was published in Aix as recently as 1817.

42. Quoted in Schefer, *L'hostie profanée*, pp 93–94. Jody Enders restores the original version: "*Cy prent L'hostie et la cloue d'un clou en une coulonne; et le sang en coule à terre*" (He took the host and nailed it to a column, and the blood flowed down to the ground"), p. 1007.

43. Schefer, *L'hostie profanée*, pp. 92ff.

44. Enders, "Theater Makes History," p. 1009.

45. Yuval, *Two Nations in Your Womb*, p. 208.

46. As David Biale remarks, "by desecrating the host and making it bleed, as well as by extracting the blood of Christian children for their own ritual needs, the Jews literally performed a 'substantialization' of Christian beliefs in transubstantiation and in the spiritual value of blood." *Blood and Belief*, p. 112.

47. Schefer, *L'hostie profanée*, pp. 174, 240ff.

48. I want to thank Pascal Faustini for transcribing the trial documents as well as for his persistent and generous assistance in collecting certain local documents. I also thank Pierre-André Meyer, Hillel Kieval, Ronnie Po-chia Hsia, and Miri Rubin for their invaluable advice. Jean Baumgarten and Maurice Kriegel carefully read the manuscript prior to publication. Additionally, I want to thank Denis Maraval, Jeanne-Marie Émond, and an anonymous reader for Éditions Fayard for their invaluable assistance in the preparation of the manuscript.

Chapter 1

1. Olivier Chaline. *Le règne de Louis XIV* (Paris: Flammarion, 2005), p. 311ff.

2. Jean-Christian Petitfils, *Louis XIV*, Perrin, 1995, p. 707.

3. Here I am following Chaline, *Le règne de Louis XIV*, chap. 5, as well as Joël Cornette, *Chronique du règne de Louis XIV* (SEDES, 1997). The richest work on this aspect of the period is still Casimir Gaillardin, *Histoire du règne de Louis XIV* (Paris, 1874). See especially vol. 3, in which Gaillardin analyzes the cultural and scientific activity of the period. The historiography of the Age of Louis XIV is exceptionally rich. It is therefore all the more striking to note the almost total silence about Jews. To be sure, the small Jewish minority played only a limited role, but historians have ignored it almost completely. See, for example, Pierre Goubert, *Louis XIV et vingt millions de Français* (Paris, 1966); Pierre Gaxotte, *Le siècle de Louis XIV* (Paris: Hachette, 1968); Philippe Erlanger, *Louis XIV* (Paris: Fayard, 1966); Anthony Levi, *Louis XIV* (New York: Carroll and Graf, 1994); Jean-Christophe Petitfils, *Louis XIV* (Paris: Perrin, 1995); Ian Dunlop, *Louis XIV* (London: Chatto and Windus, 1996). Similarly, neither François Bluche, *Le Grand Règne* (Paris: Fayard, 2006) nor Chaline, *Le règne de Louis XIV*, has a single word to say about the Jews in their vast tomes on Louis XIV. Roland Mousnier seems to be the only historian to have written a well-informed chapter on Jewish life in the Age of Louis XIV. Indeed, he devotes four lines to the Raphaël Lévy affair; see *Les institutions de la France sous la monarchie absolue* (Paris: PUF, 1990), p. 324.

4. Voltaire described the construction projects that the king launched in this period, as well as the pleasures and decorations of the court. He, too, calls attention to the year 1670, when the king decided that he would "no longer dance in public." See *Le siècle de Louis XIV*, in *Œuvres complètes de Voltaire* (Paris, 1819), vol. 2, p. 112.

5. Monsieur de Larrey, *Histoire de France sous le règne de Louis XIV* (Rotterdam, 1721), vol. 4, pp. 58–59.

6. Gaillardin, *Histoire de Louis XIV*, vol. 3, pp. 573ff.

7. Michel Nassiet, *La France au XVIIe siècle* (Paris: Belin, 2006), pp. 82ff.

8. Bernard Vonglis, *"L'Etat c'était bien lui." Essai sur la monarchie absolue* (Paris: Editions Cujas, 1997).

9. Quoted in ibid., p. 21. See also John Hurt, *Louis XIV and the Parlements: The Assertion of Royal Authority* (Manchester: Manchester University Press, 2002).

10. Annette Smedley-Weill, *Les intendants de Louis XIV* (Paris: Fayard, 1995),

p. 227. See also Pierre Goubert, *Le siècle de Louis XIV* (Paris: Editions de Fallois, 1996), chap. 5.

11. André Laingui, "Justice pénale, police et répression au Grand Siècle," in Henri Méchoulan and Joël Cornette, eds., *L'Etat classique* (Paris: Vrin, 1996), pp. 226–233. See also Arlette Lebigre, *La justice du roi* (Paris: Albin Michel, 1988).

12. Quoted in René Bour, *Histoire de Metz* (Metz: Editions Serpenoise, 1979), p. 137.

13. G. Cabourdin, *La Lorraine du néant aux Lumières* (Wettolsheim: Edition Mars et Mercure, 1977), pp. 9–28; and *Histoire de la Lorraine: les temps moderns* (Nancy: Presses Universitaires de Nancy, 1991). On these conflicts, see Jonathan Spangler, "A Lesson in Diplomacy for Louis XI: The Treaty of Montmartre, 1662, and the Princes of the House of Lorraine," *French History* 17(3), 2003.

14. For a detailed narrative, see Justin Worms, *Histoire de la ville de Metz* (Paris, 1863), pp. 218–222.

15. Bour, *Histoire de Metz*, p. 148.

16. There is one local study of the role of intendants in neighboring Alsace: Georges Livet, *L'intendance d'Alsace sous Louis XIV, 1648–1715* (Paris: Les Belles Lettres, 1956).

17. François-Yves Le Moigne and Gérard Michaux, "Metz défend l'Etat," in François-Yves Le Moigne, ed., *Histoire de Metz* (Privat, 1986); and Le Moigne, "Hommes du Roi et pouvoir municipal à Metz 1641–1789," in François-Yves Le Moigne, *La Lorraine, passionnément* (Metz: Editions Serpenoise, 1993), pp. 12–22.

18. AD Moselle, 17J, 4.

19. Emmanuel Michel, *Histoire du parlement de Metz* (Paris, 1845), BNF, Mfiche L1-MM2.3486, pp. 19, 31, 88, 144, 153, and 159.

20. See the careful analysis of this interplay of powers in Metz by Patricia Behre Miskimin, *One King, One Law, Three Faiths: Religion and the Rise of Absolutism in Seventeenth-Century France* (Westport: Greenwood Press, 2002), chap. 2.

21. Marie-José Laperche-Fournel, *La population du Duché de Lorraine de 1580 à 1720* (Nancy: Presses Universitaires de Nancy, 1985).

22. See Alfred Soman, *Sorcellerie et justice criminelle: le Parlement de Paris, 16e–18e siècles* (Hampshire: Ashgate, 1992), chap. 12, p. 181, which emphasizes lynchings, stonings, and other violent acts against alleged witches. See also Robin Briggs, *Witches and Neighbors: The Social and Cultural Content of European Witchcraft* (New York: Viking, 1996), p. 8.

23. For a systematic presentation of various historical explanations, see Nachman Ben-Yehuda, "Problems Inherent in the Socio-Historical Approaches to the European Witch Craze," in Brian Levack, ed., *Witch-Hunting in Early Modern Europe: General Studies* (New York: Garland, 1992). See also Robert Muchembled, *Sorcières, justice et société aux XVIe et XVIIe siècle* (Paris: Imago, 1987).

24. This is the hypothesis that Robin Briggs proposes in various works.

25. For Alfred Soman, "where the government was weak, zealots could act as they pleased, and thousands of citizens were tortured until they confessed and

were then sent to the stake. This is what happened in Scotland in many parts of the Holy Roman Empire, not only in Germanic principalities but also in some French-speaking provinces not yet incorporated in the kingdom of France: Franche-Comté, Orraine, the present-day department of the Nord, and a good part of Pas-de-Calais. . . . But where the government was strong enough to resist such pressure—in England, France, and Spain—there were relatively few trials, and by 1625 they were a thing of the past." See Soman, *Sorcellerie et justice criminelle*, chap. 14, p. 29.

26. Robin Briggs. *The Witches of Lorraine* (Oxford: Oxford University Press, 2007), pp. 373ff. See also pp. 19ff.

27. William Monter, *A Bewitched Duchy: Lorraine and Its Dukes, 1477–1736* (Paris: Droz, 2007).

28. Given the absence of archives, we do not know the number of trials for witchcraft in the Metz region. See Briggs, *Witches of Lorraine*, pp. 36ff, and André Brulé, *Sorcellerie et emprise démoniaque à Metz et au Pays messin (XIIe–XVIIIe siècles)* (Paris: Harmattan, 2006).

29. On the witches of Lorraine, the role of magic, and belief in demons, see Dom Calmet, *Histoire ecclésiastique et civile de Lorraine* (Nancy, 1738), vol. 3, p. 28. E. Delcambre, *Le concept de la sorcellerie dans le duché de Lorraine au 16e et 17e siècles* (Nancy, 1948–1951), vol. 1, pp. 151, 212–213; and, by the same author, "Les procès de sorcellerie en Lorraine. Psychologie des juges," *Revue d'histoire du droit*, 1953, pp. 389–420. L. Gibert, "La Sorcellerie au pays messin," *Pays Lorrain*, 1907, 35, as well as the work of Robin Briggs, who examined four hundred witchcraft trials in the region.

30. Robin Briggs, *Communities of Belief: Cultural and Social Tensions in Early Modern France* (Oxford: Clarendon, 1995), p. 8, and by the same author, *The Witches of Lorraine*, pp. 74ff.

31. Monter, *Bewitched Duchy*, p. 134. The author recounts many cases in Lorraine in which pigs were accused of killing children and hanged. See p. 33.

32. See Alfred Soman, *Sorcellerie et justice criminelle*, chap. 11.

33. Briggs, *Witches and Neighbors*, p. 19.

34. Ibid., p. 280.

35. Etienne Delcambre, "Psychologie des inculpés lorrains en sorcellerie," in Brian Levack, ed., *Witch-Hunting in Continental Europe* (New York: Garland, 1992), vol. 5, pp. 396ff.

36. Briggs, *Witches and Neighbors*, p. 308.

37. Robert Mandrou, *Magistrats et sorciers en France au XVIIe siècle* (Paris: Plon, 1968), pp. 426ff. See the critique by Pierre Chaunu, "Sur la fin des sorciers au 17e siècle," *Annales: économies, sociétés, civilisations* 24 (1969). See also Robert Muchembled, *Les Derniers Bûchers* (Paris, 1987).

38. Jean-Claude Diedler, *Démons et sorcières en Lorraine. Le bien et le mal dans les communautés rurales de 1550 à 1660* (Paris: Editions Messene, 1996), pp. 10–19. See also Monter, *Bewitched Duchy*, p. 133.

39. Diedler, *Démons et sorcières en Lorraine*, p. 173. In the neighboring province

of Alsace, with its complex political status, witch hunting also declined after 1640. Indeed, some women accused of witchcraft were found innocent and their accusers were condemned instead, in 1657, for example, and again in 1685 in Colmar. The last witch was burned in Sélestat in 1641, in Colmar in 1650, and in the republic of Strasbourg in 1660. See Joseph Klaits, "Witchcraft Trials and Absolute Monarchy in Alsace," in Levack, ed., *Witch-Hunting in Continental Europe: Local and Regional Studies*, pp. 157–160.

40. Michel de Certeau, *La possession de Loudun* (Paris: Archives/Julliard, 1970), and *L'écriture de l'histoire* (Paris: Gallimard, 1975), chap. 3.

41. Keith Thomas also calls attention to the connection between reinforced religious beliefs and the decline of the irrational: *Religion and the Decline of Magic: Studies in Popular Belief in Sixteenth and Seventeen Century England* (London: Weidenfeld and Nicholson, 1971), p. 663.

42. Ibid., p. 657.

43. See Stephen Haliezer, "The Jew as Witch: Displaced Aggression and the Myth of the Santo Nino de La Guardia," in Mary Elizabeth Perry and Anne Cruz, eds., *Cultural Encounters: The Impact of the Inquisition in Spain and the New World* (Berkeley: University of California Press, 1991), pp. 147–152. The author shows that in Spain during the Inquisition, witches were rarely prosecuted. Jews became the key target, and their magical powers were revealed by the supposed ritual murder of the Child Saint of La Guardia (1490), which was widely discussed for centuries, and indeed until quite recently, in Catholic Spain. It was alleged that the perpetrators of the crime imitated the Passion of Christ in order to mock it.

44. Anna Foa, "The Witch and the Jew: Two Alikes That Were Not the Same," in Jeffrey Jerome Cohen, ed., *From Witness to Witchcraft: Jews and Judaism in Medieval Christian Thought* (Wiesbaden: Harrassowitz Verlag, 1996).

45. Carlo Ginzburg, *Ecstasies: Deciphering the Witches' Sabbath* (London: Penguin Books, 1991), p. 72.

46. Diedler, *Démons et sorcières en Lorraine*, p. 70.

47. Pierre-André Meyer, *La communauté juive de Metz au XVIIIe siècle* (Metz: Editions Serpenoise, 1993), p. 80.

48. René Taveneaux, "Réforme catholique et Contre-Réforme en Lorraine," *L'Université de Pont-à-Mousson et les problèmes de son temps* (Nancy, 1974).

49. In 1679 in Montfort-L'Amaury, two soldiers who had blasphemed and said impious things about crucifixes had their right hand cut off and were then hanged on the public square before being burned at the stake. Alain Cabantour, *Histoire du blasphème en Occident. XVIe–XIXe siècles* (Paris: A. Michel, 1998), pp. 230 and 234.

50. François-Yves Le Moigne and Gérard Michaux, "Metz défend l'Etat," pp. 251–255. See also Henri Tribout de Morembert, "La prédication à Metz," in *Bossuet. La prédication au XVIIe siècle* (Paris, 1980).

51. Michel Pernot, "Etude sur la vie religieuse dans la campagne lorraine à la fin du XVIIe siècle," *Annales de l'Est*. Mémoire no. 39, 1971, pp. 91 and 111.

52. François-Yves Le Moigne, "Fastes et servitudes d'un diocèse-frontière sous la

monarchie absolue," in Henri Tribout de Morembert, ed., *Le diocèse de Metz* (Paris: Letouzay et Ané, 1970).

Chapter 2

1. Roger Clément, *La condition des Juifs de Metz sous l'Ancien Régime* (Paris, 1903), pp. 24–25.

2. M. Ginsburger, "Les Juifs de Metz sous l'Ancien Régime," *Revue des Etudes Juives*, 1905, p. 128.

3. Clément, *La condition des Juifs de Metz sous l'Ancien Régime*, pp. 25–27.

4. Martine Lemalet, "Juifs et intendants au XVIIe siècle," *17e Siècle*, April–June 1994, p. 298. See also the same author's observations on royal benevolence toward the Jews in "Les Juifs et l'Etat classique," in Henri Méchoulan and Joël Cornette, eds., *L'Etat classique* (Paris: Vrin, 1996).

5. Clément, *La condition des Juifs de Metz sous l'Ancien Régime*, p. 34.

6. Here I am following Nathan Netter, *Vingt siècles d'histoire d'une communauté juive (Metz et son grand passé)* (Paris: Librairie Lipschutz, 1938), p. 51. See also Gérald Cahen, "Les Juifs dans la région lorraine des origines à nos jours," *Le Pays Lorrain*, 1972, 53rd year, pp. 59–66.

7. Abraham Cahen, *Le rabbinat de Metz pendant la période française (1567–1871)*, 1886. BNF. Mfiche LD 183-19, p. 28. See also the dossier "Les Juifs de Lorraine," *Archives juives*, 2nd semester 1994, no. 27/2.

8. Pierre Mendel, "Les Juifs à Metz," *Annales de l'Est*, 1979, no. 3, p. 255.

9. Robert Anchel, "La vie économique des juifs de Metz aux XVIIe et XVIIIe siècles," in *Les Juifs de France* (J. B. Janin, 1956), p. 170. A century later, Louis XVI confirmed these letters patent and reviewed their history:

> Letters-Patent confirming privileges previously granted to Jews living in the City of Metz: Louis, by the grace of God, king of France and Navarre. Jews residing in our City of Metz having humbly informed us that they have lived in this City since the thirteenth century, and that, since it has passed under French rule, they have sought to prove their zeal and demonstrate the obedience and devotion they owe to their new Sovereigns, which has earned them the most favorable treatment on the part of our predecessors; that King Henri IV, of glorious memory, by the original Letters-Patent of 24 March 1603, took them and placed them under his protection and special safeguard and allowed them to trade and do business. . . . That these same motives were recalled in the generous Letters that this Monarch granted them on 18 October 1605, whereby he confirmed in part a new regulation that had been proposed to remove all difficulties that might exist between them and the inhabitants of the City. That Louis XIII, his successor, on 24 July 1632 granted them Letters-Patent confirming the preceding, as well as permissions that the Governors and Lieutenants-General of the Metz Region had granted them to purchase certain houses in said City, in the quarter of St. Ferroy within certain defined boundaries; and this in consideration of the services they had rendered to the garrison of Metz during the civil wars when it could not be paid. That in the year 1654, during the sojourn of Louis XIV in Metz, he favorably received the supplications pre-

sented to him to obtain confirmation of the graces and privileges that they held from his Predecessors; and that in his Letters of 25 September 1657, which he dispatched to that end, he declared that, having been informed particularly that the Jews had contributed their efforts and their gold both to the good of the City of Metz and to all the regular and special taxes and had even assisted from time to time the soldiers of the Garrison, so that he had every reason to be pleased with them; that by these same Letters, Louis XIV confirmed, approved, and ratified the aforementioned, with the intention that the Jews of said City and their descendants fully and peacefully enjoy the content thereof without harassment for any cause or reason. . . . That the late King Louis XV, our most honored Lord and forebear, twice afforded them the special effects of his protection, first upon his accession to the throne by Letters Patent of 31 December 1715 by which he confirmed and ratified various Letters Patent given in their favor and ordered that they and their descendants enjoy fully and peacefully all the privileges, usages, liberties, franchises, customs, and prerogatives contained therein. . . . We do hereby confirm, approve, and ratify the said Letters-Patent; it is our will and pleasure that they be executed in form and content so that the Jews established in said City and their descendants may continue to enjoy as in the past all their effect and content, without trouble or difficulty on any pretext or occasion whatsoever. Louis. Versailles, 3 February 1777 [Quoted in Nicolas Lançon, *Recueil des Loix, coutumes et usages observés pas les Juifs de Metz . . . en exécution des Lettres-patentes du 20 août 1742* (Metz, 1786). BNF 8°Ld 183.1].

10. Nathan Netter, *Vingt siècles d'histoire d'une communauté juive,* p. 54. See also Bernhard Blumenkranz, ed., *Histoire des Juifs en France* (Toulouse: Privat, 1967), p. 81.

11. Frances Malino, "Competition and Confrontation: The Jews and the Parlement of Metz," in Gilbert Dahan, ed., *Les Juifs au regard de l'histoire. Mélanges en l'honneur de Bernhard Blumenkranz* (Paris: Picard, 1985), p. 340.

12. Claude Rosenfeld and Jean-Bernard Lang, *Histoire des Juifs en Moselle* (Metz: Editions Serpenoise, 2001), p. 52. Similarly, Pierre-André Meyer argues that "the Jews were initially resented by the people of Metz as a foreign presence imposed on the city by an external authority. That authority had transformed Metz into a military city, which meant vastly increased expenditures. . . . Since the existence of the Jewish community was closely linked to the militarization of the city, attitudes toward the militarization probably affected attitudes toward the Jews." *La communauté juive de Metz au XVIIIe siècle,* p. 80. Robert Anchel observed earlier that "the fact that many Metz Jews were involved in supplying the troops stationed on France's eastern border earned them praise from several kings, from Henri IV to Louis XIV." See "La vie économique des Juifs de Metz," p. 177.

13. Clément, *La condition des Juifs de Metz sous l'Ancien Régime*, p. 37.

14. Ibid., p. 214.

15. Jean Daltroff, "Histoire des cimetières de la communauté juive de Boulay et proposition d'une approche pédagogique d'un lieu de sepulture," *Cahiers des Pays de la Nied*, no. 139, June 2003.

16. Jean Houdaille, "La population de Boulay (Moselle) avant 1850," *Population*, Nov.–Dec. 1967, p. 1061.

17. Matthieu Kedzierski, *La communauté juive à Boulay. Des origines à nos jours*, Lycée Fabert, Terminale L2, Metz, 1995.

18. Paul Bajetti, "La communauté israélite de Boulay," *Cahiers des Pays de la Nied*, 1986, no. 5, pp. 24–25. See also Paul Bajetti, *Boulay sous la domination Lorraine*, AD Moselle, BH 12479.

19. Frédéric Guir, *Histoire de Boulay* (Metz, 1933), p. 74. See also Claude Rosenfeld and Jean-Bernard Lang, *Histoire des Juifs en Moselle*, pp. 222–225.

20. AD Moselle, bundle 3 E 2737, folio 13. I thank Pascal Faustini for providing me with this document and other information about the life of Raphaël Lévy. See also Faustini, *La communauté juive de Metz et ses familles (1565–1665)* (published by the author: October 2001), p. 228.

21. Ginsburger, in his "Mémoriaux alsaciens," remarks that the son Raphaël Isaac ha-Lévi is named as a martyr in a number of Alsatian *Memorbücher* of the eighteenth century: Ribeauvillé, Haguenau, Bouxwiller, Niedernai, Issenheim, and Muttersholtz. See *Revue d'Etudes Juives*, vol. 40, 1905, p. 239. Pascal Faustini has found a reference to Raphaël in the *Memorbuch* of Coblence, dated 25 Tebet 5430.

22. Simon Schwarzfuchs, *Un obituaire israélite, le Memorbuch de Metz*, Metz. AD Moselle 1971, notices 430, 468, 827. Juda Leib, known as Lion, who was born in 1655, was probably in Boulay and died in 1721 in Metz, married a woman named Rosette (or Reizele in Yiddish). He had at least one son, named Raphaël, and a daughter, Blimlé (*Blumele* = little flower). The repeated use of the word *haver* in reference to Raphaël Lévy seems to be intended to depict him as a Jew who respected the rules of Halakhah. In Germany, from the fourteenth century on, the epithet *haver* "indicated official recognition of the teachings of the Torah." See "Haver," *Encyclopaedia Judaica*, vol. 7, p. 1491. In the original manuscript, which is preserved at the AIU, Raphaël Lévy is still more explicitly referred to as a *hassid*, that is, a pious Jew. Both epithets attest to his strict observance of the Law.

23. AD Moselle. B2144. Documents from the trial of Raphaël Lévy. In the remainder of this book, I rely almost exclusively on these trial documents and will indicate only the day of the trial in citing lengthier quotations. The archival reference will not be repeated in every note.

Chapter 3

1. *Mémoires de Gluckel Hameln* (Paris: Editions de Minuit, 1971), pp. 216–225 and 246. See Natalie Zemon Davis, *Juive, catholique, protestante. Trois femmes en marge au XVIIe siècle* (Paris: Le Seuil, 1997), pp. 17–79. See also Judith Baskin, "Jewish Women's Piety and the Impact of Printing in Early Modern Europe," in Margaret Mikesell and Adèle Seeff, eds., *Culture and Change: Attending to Early Modern Women* (London: Associate University Press, 2003). Baskin emphasizes how pious Gluckel found the Metz Jewish community to be.

2. Simon Schwarzfuchs, *Un obituaire israélite*, no. 611.

3. Historians generally do not accept Gluckel's account at face value; see Robert Liberles, "She Sees That Her Merchandise Is Good and Her Lamp Is Not Extin-

guished at Night: Glikl's Memoir as Historical Source," *Nashim* 7 (spring 2004), p. 18. See also Gérald Cahen, "Les Juifs de Metz du temps de Gluckel Hameln 1700–1724," http://judaisme.sdv.fr/histoire/villes/metz/gluckel/gluckel.htm.

4. Abbé Grégoire, *Essai sur la régénération physique, morale et politique des Juifs* (Paris: Flammarion. Champs, 1988), pp. 150 and 153.

5. Meyer, *La communauté juive de Metz au XVIIIe siècle*, pp. 83–85.

6. Cahen, "Les Juifs dans la région Lorraine," p. 114.

7. We also lack sources to distinguish more precisely between Judeo-German and an Alsatian dialect of Yiddish or some other regional dialect, or perhaps an Ashkenazi pronunciation of German. On these issues, see Frank Alvarez-Péreyre and Jean Baumgarten, eds., *Linguistique des langues juives et linguistique générale* (Paris: CNRS Editions, 2003).

8. Note also Gédéon Lévy's response when Gondrecourt asked him for money. On December 2, 1669, he replied: "I have no money. Today is the Sabbath, I cannot give you any, but the Jews of Metz will recognize you."

9. An *aune de Metz* was a measure of length equivalent to 0.67 meters.

10. Some years earlier, in 1612, Emperor Mathias sent troops to put down an anti-Semitic riot in Frankfurt led by Vincent Fettmilch. See Riuka Ulmer, *Turmoil, Trauma and Triumph: The Fettmilch Uprising in Frankfurt am Main (1612–1616)* (Berne: F. Lang, 2001).

11. *Journal* of an unknown Metz Jew, *Archives israélites*, August 1841, pp. 484–485. Hence we cannot entirely agree with Bernhard Blumenkranz, who wrote that "the Jews of Metz failed to display Jewish solidarity in this case"; *Histoire des Juifs en France. Ecrits disperses*, p. 54.

12. Cecil Roth, "The Feast of Purim and the Origins of the Blood Libel Accusation," *Speculum* 8(4) 1933, pp. 520–521.

13. See "The Crucifixion of Haman," an astonishing note signed simply "E. W." and published in the *Journal of the Warburg and Courtauld Institute* 1 (1937), pp. 245–246. See the comments of Israel Jacob Yuval, *Two Nations in Your Womb*, pp. 166ff. See also E. Horowitz, *Reckless Rites: Purim and the Legacy of Jewish Violence* (Princeton: Princeton University Press, 2006).

14. The second translator, Paul Du Vallier, who backed up the translation condemning Raphaël, was also a converted Jew formerly known as Mardochée Wallich. He was the son of the Jewish doctor in Metz. See Meyer, *La communauté juive de Metz,* p. 84. As Heinrich Graetz has shown, Du Vallier became "a wicked man, a traitor." See *History of the Jewish People* (Philadelphia: Jewish Publication Society of America, 1949), vol. 5, p. 175.

15. Note that Dom Calmet confused the *tefillin,* or phylacteries, with the *tallith* (prayer shawl). He wrote, "As they led him off, he tied two leather belts, knotted in the middle, around his head and left arm. This is what the Jews call Thaled, the knots of which contain the Commandments of the Law." *Histoire ecclésiastique et civile de la Lorraine*, p. 755.

16. *Archives israélites*, Sept. 1841, pp. 610–611. Note that certain phrases remained

in Hebrew characters in the original publication in the *Archives*, disappearing only from the later publication. Joseph Reinach, *Raphaël Lévy, Une erreur judiciaire sous Louis XIV*, p. 170.

17. *Archives israélites*, July 1841, p. 417.

18. *Archives israélites*, February 1842, p. 83.

Chapter 4

1. Yuval, *Two Nations in Your Womb*, pp. 178–179. The author argues that, for Christians, the presence of water meant the Jewish killers preferred blood to water, signifying baptism, and death to redemption. He added that the charge that the Jews used blood to make matzoh also indicated their preference for blood over water.

2. The account here is based on the trial documents, which can be found in the Archives départementales of the Moselle, B 2144. I also used the journal mentioned in the previous chapter, which was kept by an anonymous Metz Jew and translated into Judeo-German in 1841 by the Metz printer E. Hadamard for publication in a series of issues of *Archives israélites*. The original manuscript (AIU 216) was reprinted in 1927 in Budapest by Meir ben Abraham Halevy, a native of Jassy and a specialist in the history of Romanian Jews. Note that it was in a period of rising anti-Semitism that this text was reprinted by a Hungarian historian associated with the "Jewish science" movement, who no doubt saw it as a document that could illustrate the threat he saw gathering around him.

3. *Archives israélites*, August 1841, p. 484.

4. Reinach, *Raphaël Lévy. Une erreur judiciaire sous Louis XIV*, p. 74. Here I am following the text of Amelot de La Houssaye as it appears in Reinach's book.

5. Ibid., p. 77.

6. Ibid., p. 79.

7. Ibid., p. 118.

8. Graetz, *Histoire des Juifs* (Paris, 1897), vol. 5, p. 220.

9. *Lettres choisies de R. Simon* (Amsterdam, 1730), BNF Z 15118. Letter VIII, vol. 1, pp. 82–83, 87. See also vol. 2, letter 1, pp. 6–7. One can also use the recent edition published by Minerva (Frankfurt, 1967).

10. Ibid., vol. 1, letter XXV, p. 225.

11. Ibid., vol. 2, letter II, p. 14.

12. Ibid., vol. 3, letter XXVII, p. 8.

13. Bertram Eugène Schwarzbach, "Le témoignage de Jona Salvador sur les Juifs de Paris au XVIIe siècle," *Revue des études juives*, July–Dec. 1996, p. 471. See also François Cuisinier, "Richard Simon et les Juifs de Metz," *Cahiers Elie Fleur* (21) 2001–02, which also gives an overview of the affair.

14. *Lettres choisies de R. Simon*, vol. 2. Letter VIII, p. 53. See Myriam Yardeni, "La vision des Juifs et du judaïsme dans l'œuvre de Richard Simon," *Revue des études juives*, Jan.–Mar. 1970. On the meeting between Simon and Salvador, see also Paul Auvray, *Richard Simon, 1638–1712. Etude bio-bibliographique* (Paris: PUF, 1974),

pp. 26–27; and *Les juifs présentés aux chrétiens: cérémonies et coutumes qui s'observent aujourd'hui parmi les juifs, par Léon de Modène. Suivi de Comparaison des cérémonies des juifs et de la discipline de l'Eglise, par Richard Simon*. Introduction and notes by Jacques Le Brun and Guy Stroumsa (Paris: Les Belles Lettres, 1998).

15. Bertram Eugène Schwarzbach, *Voltaire and Richard Simon*, thesis for M.A. in philosophy, Columbia University, 1964, p. 52. See also Chapter 8 of this volume.

16. Graetz, *Histoire des Juifs*, vol. 5, p. 220.

17. My commentary here is based on the original version of the text in the BNF, 4° LD 184 5.

18. Simon, *Factum servant de réponse au livre intitulé Abrégé du procès fait aux Juifs de Metz* (Paris, 1670), http://fr.wikisource.org/wiki/Factum_servant_de_r%C3%A9ponse_au_livre_intitul%C3%A9_Abr%C3%A9g%C3%A9_du_proc%C3%A8s_fait_aux_Juifs_de_Metz#cite_note-1, p. 3.

19. Ibid., p. 7.

20. Ibid., p. 11.

21. Ibid., p. 10.

22. François Gayot de Pitaval, *Causes célèbre et intéressantes avec les jugements qui les ont décidées* (Paris, 1734), pp. 244–245. BNF 16° F 3121 (2).

23. Ibid., p. 274.

24. Ibid., pp. 269 and 274.

25. Abbé Grégoire, *Essai sur la régénération*, p. 55.

26. Ibid., pp. 182–183.

27. It should be noted, however, that a few years after writing the *Essai*, Grégoire was more categorical in the "motion in favor of the Jews" that he submitted to the Constituent Assembly late in 1789: "In the dark centuries of the Middle Ages, the Jews were accused of all the scourges with which heaven had afflicted earth. They were charged with crimes, always presumed but never proven, such as immolating Christian children and poisoning fountains, wells, and even rivers. . . . Does hate reason?" *La Révolution française et l'émancipation des Juifs* (Paris: EDHI, 1968), p. 10.

28. Curiously, he does not mention either Pitaval's book, which appeared in 1734, or the work of Dom Augustin Calmet, *Histoire ecclésiastique et civile de la Lorraine*, although it was published in 1757 and clearly set forth the particulars of the case while favoring the thesis of Lévy's guilt. See vol. 3, pp. 753–756. BNF FB.12682.

29. On Terquem, see Philippe Landau, "Olry Terquem (1782–1862). Régénérer les Juifs et réformer le judaïsme," *Revue des études juives*, Jan.–June 2001; and Pierre Birnbaum, *L'aigle et la synagogue. Napoléon, les Juifs et l'Etat* (Paris: Fayard, 2007), pp. 234–237.

30. Orly Terquem, "Raphaël Lévy (de Boulay)," *Archives israélites*, June 1841, p. 375.

31. Jonathan Frankel, *Damascus Affair: "Ritual Murder," Politics and the Jews in 1840* (Cambridge: Cambridge University Press, 1992), calls attention to the prominent role of Adolphe Crémieux, who confronted French authorities overtly favorable to the charges against the Damascus Jews. Ernest Alby, *Des persécutions contre*

les Juifs (Paris, 1840), pp. 71–72, in a strange book in which he speaks out against the persecution of the Damascus Jews, quotes them with approval as follows: "In 1572, on the fine summer's night of Saint Bartholomew's day, we witnessed an astonishing massacre of women and children. That night, Catholics made a human sacrifice in the name of the Church and shed rivers of France's noblest and most generous blood. Yet you speak of unleavened bread dipped in blood, which you have never seen or touched, when you have communed in the flesh and blood of your friends and relatives the Huguenots! How can you imagine the ceremony that you attribute to us, involving the crucifixion of a child on Good Friday—a ceremony that has never existed anywhere but in your wicked imaginations?" He also denounced the Damascus trial but never mentioned the Lévy affair.

32. *Archives israélites*, Feb. 1842, pp. 84–86. Note that Joseph Reinach did not publish this poem in his *Raphaël Lévy* after the journal.

33. Michel, *Histoire du Parlement de Metz*, p. 170.

34. It appears to have been mentioned only rarely. For example, I. Bédarride, in a work well known at the time, *Les Juifs en France, en Italie et en Espagne*, 1859, p. 378, alludes to it only briefly. In his eyes, "such a strange sentence for this period dispenses with the need for reflection. It shows clearly enough what the state of public opinion was in regard to the Jews of Alsace in the seventeenth century." Note the error: the affair did not take place in Alsace.

35. Justin Worms, *Histoire de la ville de Metz*, p. 13.

36. *Archives israélites*, vol. 24, 1863, pp. 502–503.

37. Oddly, these passages are missing from the French translation of Graetz's work that I cited previously. They can be found in the English translation, *History of the Jewish People*, vol. 5, pp. 174–176.

38. Édouard Drumont, *La France juive* (Paris: Flammarion, 1886); Reinach, *Raphaël Lévy*; Henri Prague, "Raphaël Lévy, un martyr en Lorraine," *Archives israélites*, 1898, vol. 58. See Chapter 8.

39. See Chapter 8.

40. André Spire, *Souvenirs à bâtons rompus* (Paris: Albin Michel, 1962), p. 33. André Gillois turned Spire's story into a radio play based on invented dialogues that revealed the drama of the affair. For instance, he ascribed this line to Mangeotte Villemin: "The Jews took Didier from me, and now they're going to kill him and eat him." *Les grandes familles de France* (Paris: Jean-Jacques Vital, Radio-No. 3 Editions, 1953), p. 96.

41. The deafening silence was, however, broken in 1938 by Rabbi Nathan Netter, who gave a short but detailed discussion of the "depressing tragedy" of Glatigny, based largely on the work of Joseph Reinach. See Nathan Netter, *Vingt siècles d'une communauté juive*, pp. 60–67. Roger Clément, *La condition des Juifs de Metz sous l'Ancien régime*, p. 59, discussed the case and emphasized the bias of the court. More recently, Bernhard Blumenkranz has discussed the case briefly in a number of places, e.g., *Juifs en France. Ecrits dispersés* (Paris: Les Belles Lettres, 1989), pp. 52–54. He also provides a *Bibliographie des Juifs en France* (Privat), pp.

192 ff. Zosa Szajkowski also gives a bibliography, somewhat dated but fairly complete: *Franco-Judaica: An Analytical Bibliography of Books, Pamphlets, Decrees, Briefs and Other Printed Documents Pertaining to the Jews in France 1500–1788* (New York: American Academy for Jewish Research, 1962), p. 119. The Lévy affair is mentioned briefly in the article "Blood Accusation" in the *Jewish Encyclopedia*, vol. 3, p. 267, but not in the article "Blood Libel" in *Encyclopedia Judaica*, 1972, vol. 4. E. Vacandard, in his article "La question du meurtre rituel chez les Juifs," a Catholic refutation of such practices, does not discuss the case. See *Revue du clergé français*, no. 401, Aug. 1, 1911. Many contemporary anti-Semitic texts continue to attack Raphaël Lévy; these will be discussed in Chapter 8. In addition to these, various articles have treated the case and found Lévy innocent. In 1931, A. Rosambert published "Les crimes rituels" in the *Revue Lorraine d'Anthropologie.* He denounced these legends, discussed various cases such as the one in Trent, and devoted several pages to the Lévy affair, "a trial for ritual crime that took place in the Age of Louis XIV" (p. 52). His brief presentation was summarized even more succinctly by Paul Lang, "Les Juifs de Lunéville et la petite histoire," *Revue juive de Lorraine*, no. 131, 1936. See also the brief notes by Paul Hegenauer, "Un drame judiciaire au Grand Siècle: L'affaire Raphaël Lévy," published in three articles in the *Journal des communautés*, April, May, and June 1957. See also the substantial but brief article by Pierre-André Meyer, "Un cas d'accusation de meurtre rituel à Metz au XVII è siècle," *Archives juives*, 1989. More recently, André Brulé included several pages on the Lévy affair in a more general work on witchcraft in Lorraine, on the grounds that "witchcraft lurks in the background of this case." See *Sorcellerie et emprise démoniaque à Metz*, p. 413. The one recent academic study available is a very well-informed article by Patricia Behre, "Raphaël Lévy, a Criminal in the Mouth of the People," *Religion* 23 (1993), included in her *One King, One Law, Three Faiths: Religion and the Rise of Absolutism in Seventeenth Century France* (New York: Praeger), 2001. Behre rightly emphasizes the relations between the religious and economic aspects of the case.

Chapter 5

1. Raphaël Lévy (of Boulay). Translation of a diary of this trial. *Archives israélites*, July 1841, p. 423. No commentator mentions this passage, not even Reinach—or Drumont!

2. See esp. Areh Kasher, *King Herod: Persecuted Persecutor* (New York: Walther de Gruyter, 2006), pp. 408ff. See also Emmanuel Haymann, *Hérode le Grand: Crimes et splendeurs sur la colline de Jérusalem* (Lausanne: Faure, 2005). On Herod and Christianity, see Peter Richardson, *Herod, King of the Jews and Friend of the Romans* (Columbia: University of South Carolina Press, 1996), chap. 12.

3. Yuval, *Two Nations in Your Womb*, chap. 4.

4. Raphaël Lévy (of Boulay). Traduction d'un *Journal* de ce procès, op. cit., *Archives israélites*, July 1841, p. 418.

5. Recall that at the time many midwives were seen as witches.

6. The author of the anonymous diary says the miller and two cobblers were

heard on October 15. See *Archives israélites*, July 1841, p. 424. We find no trace of this hearing in the trial documents, however.

Chapter 6

1. The anonymous journal writer mentions this accusation, of which no trace can be found in the trial documents. *Archives israélites*, Jan. 1842, p. 15.
2. See the Introduction.
3. See Introduction.
4. See Introduction.
5. Jean-Louis Schefer, *L'hostie profanée*, pp. 375–387. See Introduction.

Chapter 7

1. Statements of December 18, 1669, and January 16, 1670.
2. Statement of January 12, 1670.
3. *Journal*, op. cit., *Archives israélites*, July 1841, p. 423.
4. *Journal*, op. cit., *Archives israélites*, Sept. 1841, pp. 607–608.
5. *Journal*, op. cit., *Archives israélites*, Feb. 1842, p. 75.
6. Ibid., p. 79.
7. Richard Simon, *Factum servant de réponse au livre intitulé Abrégé du Procès fait aux Juifs de Metz*, op. cit., p. 7.
8. Ibid.
9. Quoted in Netter, *Vingt siècles d'histoire d'une communauté juive*, p. 52.
10. M. Charleville. Grand Rabbin de Versailles, "Louis XIV et les Juifs," *Archives juives* (48) 1887, p. 303.
11. On this theme, see Yosef Yerushalmi, "Serviteurs des Rois et non serviteurs des serviteurs. Sur quelques aspects de l'Histoire politique des Juifs," *Raisons politiques*. August–October 2002. See also Pierre Birnbaum, *Prier pour l'Etat. Les Juifs, l'alliance royale et l'Etat* (Paris: Calmann-Lévy), 2005, chap. 1.
12. This council decree was published in the appendix to J. Reinach, *Raphaël Lévy*, pp. 197–202.
13. Bernadette Lemoine, "Double drame au pays messin," p. 4, observes that many people simply ignored the royal and papal warnings against believing false rumors about Jews: "Did our ancestors in Lorraine know about these protestations from on high? Not very likely."
14. *Journal*, *Archives israélites*, Feb. 1842, p. 82.
15. AD Moselle, 17 J 26.
16. *Journal*, *Archives israélites*, Feb. 1842, p. 83.
17. Quoted in Pierre-André Meyer, "Un cas d'accusation de meurtre rituel à Metz au XVII è siècle," in *La communauté juive de Metz au XVIIIe siècle*, p. 63. See also Gilbert Roos, *Relations entre le gouvernement royal et les Juifs du nord-est de la France au XVIIe siècle* (Paris: Honoré Champion, 2002), p. 163. The author quotes other, similar cases that occurred later.
18. Roos analyzes the cases that followed the Lévy case in ibid., pp. 162–163.

Chapter 8

1. The two Masaryk quotes are taken from Ernest Rychnovsky, ed., *Thomas Masaryk and the Jews* (New York: B. Pollak, 1941), pp. 11 and 233.

2. See Hillel Kieval's many works on this theme, such as "Death and the Nation: Ritual Murder as Political Discourse in the Czech Lands," *Jewish History*, vol. 10, spring 1996, pp. 75–91; *Languages of Community. The Jewish Experience in the Czech Lands* (Berkeley: University of California Press, 2000), chaps. 8 and 9; and "Neighbors, Strangers, Readers: The Village and the City in Jewish-Gentile Conflict at the Turn of the Nineteenth-Century," *Jewish Studies Quarterly,* vol. 12, 2005, pp. 61–79. I want to thank Hillel Kieval for alerting me to comparisons of Dreyfus and Hilsner and Zola and Masaryk. See also Michael Curtis, "The Hilsner Case and Ritual Murder," in Robert Garber, ed., *Jews on Trial* (Jersey City: KTAV Publishing House, 2004), pp. 49–65; and Steven Beller, "The Hilsner Affair: Nationalism, Anti-Semitism and the Individual in the Habsburg Monarchy at the Turn of the Century," in Robert Pynsent, ed., *T. G. Masaryk (1850–1937)* (London: Macmillan, 1989), vol. 2, pp. 52–73. Karl Kraus also established a parallel between the Hilsner and Dreyfus affairs, but his "self-hatred" takes us a long way from Masaryk's position. For Jacques Le Rider, "his 'media critique' of the Dreyfus and Hilsner affairs led nowhere and rehashed the commonplaces of *Kulturkritik,* which was always eager to unmask the depravity of the mass-circulation press but not very persuasive when it came to defining the role of intellectuals vis-à-vis one of the major problems of European societies in the twentieth century: anti-Semitism." See Le Rider's "Critique de la presse à grand tirage ou hyper-assimilation à la norme culturelle? Les réactions de Karl Kraus, dans *Die Fackel*, au procès pour 'crime rituel' de Polna et à l'Affaire Dreyfus," in Juliette Guilbaud, Nicolas Le Moigne, Thomas Lüttenberg, eds., *Normes culturelles et construction de la deviance* (Geneva: E.P.H.E. Droz, 2004), p. 207. On the reemergence of the theme of ritual murder in Europe at the end of the nineteenth century, see Francesco Crepaldi, "L'omicidio rituale nella 'moderna' polemica antigiudaica di *Civiltà Cattolica* nella seconda metà del XIX secolo," in Catherine Brice and Giovanni Miccoli, eds., *Les racines chrétiennes de l'antisémitisme politique (fin XIXe siècle–XXe siècle*), op. cit., pp. 65ff.

3. Abbé Chabauty, *Les Juifs, nos maîtres!* (Paris, 1882).

4. Jab, *Le sang chrétien dans les rites de la synagogue moderne*, 1886. BNF. A 20507, pp. 208 and 280.

5. Dr. Martinez, *Le Juif, voilà l'ennemi. Appel aux catholiques* (Paris 1890), BNF 8° Lb57-10062.

6. *La Croix*, Nov. 6, 1894.

7. *La Croix*, April 12 and 28, 1898, and Sept. 26, 1899. See also the editions of May 22, 1895, Nov. 19, 1896, April 2 and June 1, 1898, and Aug. 24 and Sept. 27 and 29, 1899. Pierre Sorlin quotes some of these texts and writes, "The belief in 'ritual murder' was constant in publications of the Bonne Press." *La Croix et les Juifs (1880–*

1899) (Paris: Grasset, 1967), p. 142. See also pp. 296–297. In Catholic circles, note also the pamphlet by R. P. Constant, *Les Juifs devant l'Eglise et l'histoire,* published in 1897 to prove, following Drumont, that ritual murders were real and occurred in many places, from Trent to Damascus and down to the present time. Constant, *Les Juifs devant l'Eglise et l'Histoire,* 1897. BNF Microfiche. 8-H-6171.

8. Publicity poster for the pamphlet *L'assassinat maçonnique. Le Crime rituel. La Trahison juive*, BNF Fol M Pièce 20.

9. *L'assassinat maçonnique, Le crime rituel, La trahison juive* (Paris, 1905), p. 37. BNF 1.1-MFC, pp. 37 and 56.

10. J. Kracauer, "L'Affaire des Juifs d'Endingen de 1470," pp. 236–237. In the same issue, see also the remarkable study by Isidore Loeb, "Le saint enfant de La Guardia," pp. 203–232. See also Loeb, "Brelan d'accusations," *Archives israélites*, June 1895; and Schwab, "Le meurtre de l'enfant de chœur du Puy, 1320." In 1881, Loeb also wrote a long essay on the Hirtzel Lévy affair, which took place in Colmar in 1754. Falsely accused of theft, Lévy was tortured to death, only to be rehabilitated less than a year later. Isidore Loeb, *Hirtzel Lévy. Mort martyr à Colmar en 1754* (Versailles: Imprimerie Cerf et fils, 1881).

11. "Un *Mémoire* de Laurent Ganganelli sur la calomnie du meurtre rituel," *Revue des Etudes juives* 18 (1889), pp. 178–185.

12. Pierre Birnbaum, *Le moment antisémite. Un tour de la France en 1898* (Paris: Fayard, 1998).

13. *L'Univers israélite*, July 22, 1898.

14. *Archives israélites*, Dec. 14, 1899, April 12 and Nov. 1, 1900.

15. Ibid., May 10, June 28, and Nov. 15, 1900.

16. Ibid., Sept. 20, 1899. On Oct. 12, 1899, the *Archives israélites* also wrote: "One must expect all sorts of maneuvers by those who would stop at nothing to destroy the Jews, as we saw in the Tisza-Eszlar case and in the Dreyfus Affair."

17. Ibid., Oct. 20, 1898. According to Henri Prague, "The goal of the anti-Semites was to destroy the reputation of the Jews and turn the public against them. The notorious and mythical crime of ritual murder smacks too much of the Middle Ages and the Orient to succeed in this part of the world. Only the indictment of a Jewish officer for treason was capable, in this age of overweening chauvinism, to set the imagination aflame and arouse popular passions." *Archives israélites*, Sept. 22, 1898. See also the issue of Oct. 12, 1899, in which Prague argued that Drumont used the charge of ritual murder in Polna to renew his anti-Semitic agitation after the failure of his efforts in the Dreyfus Affair. On Feb. 8, 1900, the *Archives* denounced the Pope's silence in both the Dreyfus Affair and the Polna case, which "left the way open for implacable monks." In the same journal, Prague again compared the forgeries in the two cases on Feb. 15, 1900. Reviewing the ritual murder charges in Polna and Konitz on June 21, 1900, he stressed once more the idea that both represented "the eruption of latent hatred" as in the Dreyfus Affair. On Nov. 22, 1900, after Hilsner was sentenced to death a second time, Prague compared this to the two convictions of Dreyfus.

18. *L'Univers israélite*, Sept. 1, 1899.

19. *Archives israélites*, Sept. 13, 1899.

20. See for example *L'Univers israélite*, Jan. 28, 1898, and *Archives israélites*, Nov. 25, 1897; Feb. 3, 10, and 17, 1898; Feb. 16, 1899; and March 15, 1900. The theme of a reversion to the Middle Ages, a commonplace in the Jewish press of the period, can also be found in the writings of Joseph Reinach. See for example *Histoire de l'Affaire Dreyfus,* by Robert Laffont, introduction by Hervé Duchêne (Paris, 2006), pp. 264, 731, and 978.

21. Isidore Loeb, *Le Juif de l'histoire et le Juif de la légende* (Paris: Leopold Cerf, 1890), BNF 8° 5524.

22. Salomon Reinach, preface to H. L. Strack, *Le sang et la fausse accusation du meurtre ritual* (Paris, 1892). For Reinach, "the very idea of Jewish ritual murder is a tissue of absurd contradictions, because the Jew is horrified by blood, cadavers, and anything rendered impure by death. . . . This is a myth, a fraud" (p. xl). His preface was reprinted as an article in *Revue des Etudes juives* 25 (1892), under the title "The Charge of Ritual Murder."

23. Théodore Reinach, *Histoire des Israélites depuis la ruine de leur indépendance nationale jusqu'à nos jours* (Paris: Hachette, 1914), p. 276. In his article "Juifs" in the *Dictionnaire universel de géographie* (Paris: Hachette, 1884), p. 92, he discusses these "ridiculous fairy tales" and "absurd" and "odious accusations" by citing not only the examples of Trent and Damascus but also the case of Raphaël Lévi (*sic*). In 1913, Théodore Reinach spoke to the congress about religious progress and denounced "the odious attempt in the twentieth century to revive one of the most vicious slanders against Judaism, the charge of ritual murder." *Archives israélites*, July 24, 1913.

24. On Joseph Reinach, see Corinne Casset, "Joseph Reinach avant l'affaire Dreyfus. Un exemple de l'assimilation politique des Juifs de France au début de la IIIe République," diss., Ecole des Chartes. 1982; and Jean El Gammal, "Joseph Reinach et la République," diss., Université Paris X, 1982. Perrine Simon, "Contribution à l'étude de la bourgeoisie juive à Paris, entre 1870 et 1914," DEA diss., Institut d'Etudes Politiques, 1982. None of these authors discusses Reinach's book on the Lévy affair, however. On the three Reinach brothers and their relation to Jewish circles, see Pierre Birnbaum, *Les fous de la République. Histoire des Juifs d'Etat, de Gambetta à Vichy* (Paris: Le Seuil, Point, 1994), chap. 1. See also the Reinach colloquium.

25. For instance, Reinach cited the call number of Richard Simon's response at the Bibliothèque Nationale.

26. *L'Univers israélite*, April 22, 1921.

27. Letter from Joseph Reinach to A. Scheurer-Kestner, Oct. 8, 1897, *Correspondance d'A Scheurer-Kestner*. BNF n.a.f 23819, no. 135. See also the letters from Reinach to Scheurer-Kestner from August 1897, op. cit., nos. 29 and 30. Note that Voltaire never mentions the Lévy affair in either his *Siècle de Louis XIV* or his *Traité sur la Tolérance*, for example in his chap. 10, "On the Danger of False Legends and Wrongful Persecution," or in his *Commentaire sur Beccaria*, in which he also de-

scribes the reign of Louis XIV, or again in *L'Affaire du Chevalier de la Barre*. See *L'Affaire Calas et autres affaires* (Paris: Gallimard,1975). On the Calas affair, see Janine Garrison, *L'Affaire Calas. Miroir des passions françaises* (Paris: Fayard, 2004). Garrison wrote: "Was Voltaire for Calas what Zola was for Dreyfus? Both tried to win public opinion over to their side, and both succeeded" (p. 154). Here, Zola replaces Scheurer-Kestner in the role of Voltaire, and Zola was often compared to Masaryk in his defense of Hilsner. In view of his *Raphaël Lévy* and *Histoire de l'Affaire Dreyfus*, along with the courage he displayed throughout the Dreyfus Affair, Joseph Reinach might also have claimed the Voltaire role for himself. He thought of this himself in 1899, when he wrote: "The truth will always eventually triumph in France, by itself, in the clear light of day. Only one Calas has never been rehabilitated: mine. This is a national tradition that will not be broken. The second Calas is coming, accompanied by his champion." *Le Crépuscule des Traîtres* (Paris, 1899), p. 152. By contrast, note Millerand's violent attack on Reinach in the Chamber of Deputies in December 1897, at the exact moment that Reinach published his *Raphaël Lévy*. Millerand denounced "the person who in this very place is waging his campaign, although instead of trying to rehabilitate a new Calas, he might devote himself to other rehabilitations, perhaps within his own family." Quoted in Jean-Denis Bredin, *L'Affaire* (Paris: Julliard, 1983), p. 216.

28. Letter from Joseph Reinach to A. Scheurer-Kestner, Oct. 7, 1897, in *Correspondance d'A Scheurer-Kestner*, op. cit., no. 132. Note that around the same time, *Le Monde illustré* of Nov. 5, 1897, also compared Scheurer-Kestner to Voltaire, and in January 1898 *Le Siècle* published a series of articles on the "Calas Affair." See the introduction by André Roumieux to Auguste Scheurer-Kestner, *Mémoires d'un sénateur dreyfusard* (Strasbourg: Bueb et Reumaux, 1988), p. 41.

29. Schwarzbach, *Voltaire and Richard Simon*, pp. 47 and 52.

30. See Chapter 4.

31. *Archives israélites* 2 (1841), p. 376.

32. Note that Salomon Reinach, who had denounced the myth of ritual murder, reacted to the rising tide of anti-Semitism by joining the clandestine Committee of Defense Against Anti-Semitism organized by Grand Rabbi Zadoc Kahn. See Pierre Birnbaum, "La citoyenneté en péril: les juifs entre intégration et résistance," in P. Birnbaum, ed., *La France de l'Affaire Dreyfus* (Paris: Gallimard, 1994), p. 526.

33. Drumont, *La France juive*, pp. 771–776. Note that in 1882 Abbé Chabauty was already arguing that Raphaël Lévy was guilty: *Les Juifs, nos maîtres!* p. 186.

34. In this instance, Drumont referred explicitly to the *Archives israélites*. See *La France juive*, p. 775.

35. Drumont, preface to Henri Desportes, *Le mystère du sang juif chez les Juifs de tous les temps* (Paris: A. Savine, 1890), p. vi. In 1892, *Le Pèlerin*, taking its inspiration ostensibly from *La Croix* but also from Drumont and Desportes, devoted a ten-page story to ritual murder, including a number of frightening caricatures. The newspaper mentioned cases in Blois, Norwich, Lincoln, Prague, Regensburg, Trent, Damascus, and Corfu in addition to Metz. The story concluded as follows:

"Most Jews reject the crimes committed by some of their coreligionists. . . . In France, Jews bleed the resources of many groups by seizing control of public and private wealth." *Le Pèlerin*, Apr. 10, 1892.

36. These two quotes are taken from Desportes, *Le mystère du sang*, pp. 178–179. In the same year, Desportes published another, shorter pamphlet, also with a preface by Drumont: *Tué par les Juifs. Histoire d'un meurtre ritual* (Paris: Albert Savine, 1890). In the conclusion, he expressed regret that people had ceased to condemn "Talmudic murders" and added a threat: "This weakness will continue to grow worse until the Christian, tired of his slavery, at last rises up against the Jew, his master" (p. 59).

37. Jean de Pavly, *Le meurtre rituel des Juifs* (Orléans, 1897). Bibliothèque de l'AIU. U 1640 b.

38. Joseph Reinach, *Raphaël Lévy*, p. 7. Reinach reprinted his own text in *Essais de politique et d'histoire* (Paris: Stock, 1899).

39. Ibid., p. 66.

40. Reinach, *Histoire de l'Affaire Dreyfus*.

41. Reinach, *Raphaël Lévy*, p. 26.

42. Ibid., pp. 12, 30, 32.

43. Both quotes are from *La Libre Parole*, Dec. 13, 1897.

44. *Archives israélites*, Dec. 30, 1897.

45. *L'Univers israélite*, Dec. 27, 1897.

46. *Archives israélites*, Jan. 13, 1898. Prague made this judgment concerning the Hirtzel Lévy case, which was tried in Colmar in 1754.

47. Albert Monniot, *Le crime rituel chez les Juifs* (Paris: Pierre Téqui, 1914), p. 55.

48. Ibid., pp. 14, 22, 27, 119.

49. Ibid., p. 207. He also mentioned the *Abrégé du procès fait aux Juifs de Metz* along with another book, equally hostile to the Jews, by Emmanuel Michel, *Histoire du Parlement de Metz*.

50. Jean Drault, "Pourquoi fut brûlé vif le rabbin Raphaël Lévy," *La vieille France* 332 (1923), p. 29.

51. See, for example, Robert Launay, *Figures juives* (Paris: Nouvelle Librairie Nationale, 1921), p. 204.

Milton Keynes UK
Ingram Content Group UK Ltd.
UKHW010609081223
433911UK00004B/41/J

9 780804 774048